Traders, planters, and slaves

Traders, planters, and slaves
Market behavior in early English America

DAVID W. GALENSON
Department of Economics
University of Chicago

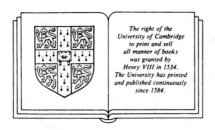

The right of the
University of Cambridge
to print and sell
all manner of books
was granted by
Henry VIII in 1534.
The University has printed
and published continuously
since 1584.

CAMBRIDGE UNIVERSITY PRESS
Cambridge
London   New York   New Rochelle
Melbourne   Sydney

PUBLISHED BY THE PRESS SYNDICATE OF THE UNIVERSITY OF CAMBRIDGE
The Pitt Building, Trumpington Street, Cambridge, United Kingdom

CAMBRIDGE UNIVERSITY PRESS
The Edinburgh Building, Cambridge CB2 2RU, UK
40 West 20th Street, New York NY 10011–4211, USA
477 Williamstown Road, Port Melbourne, VIC 3207, Australia
Ruiz de Alarcón 13, 28014 Madrid, Spain
Dock House, The Waterfront, Cape Town 8001, South Africa

http://www.cambridge.org

First published 1986
First paperback edition 2002

A catalogue record for this book is available from the British Library

Library of Congress Cataloguing in Publication data
Galenson, David W.
Traders, planters, and slaves.
        p.   cm.
Includes bibliographies.
1. Slave-trade – West Indies, British – History.
2. Slavery – Economic aspects – West Indies, British.
3. Royal African Company – History.   4. United States –
History – Colonial period, ca. 1600–1775.   I. Title.
HT1092.G35   1985   380.1′44′09729   85-14890

ISBN 0 521 30845 3 hardback
ISBN 0 521 89414 X paperback

To Stan

Contents

Contents

Tables

Tables

Preface

One of the richest fields of historical research in recent decades has been the economic and social analysis of slavery. This work has not only dealt with such economic issues as the efficiency, profitability, and viability of American slavery, but has also extended into the investigation of slave demography, the nature of slave culture, and the international political struggle to abolish slavery. This research has brought back into focus one of the classic questions about the history of economic development, concerning the role of the slave trade in the growth of modern capitalism. This issue was considered by Adam Smith, it was elevated into greater prominence by Karl Marx, and it was later examined by Alfred Marshall. Still later Eric Williams accorded the slave trade no less than the central role in explaining the origins of the industrial development of Western Europe.

At the heart of this concern with the historical relationship between slavery and modern economic growth has been an interest in the origins of modern market behavior. One of the most striking results of recent research on American slavery in the nineteenth century has been the discovery of the complexity and sophistication of the large competitive markets that characterized the slave economy in its mature form. This discovery in turn has raised new questions about the earlier history of American slavery. Did similar markets exist in the colonial period, when black slavery was introduced into the Americas? What was the economic structure of the transatlantic trade that provided African slaves to European settlers in the early colonies? Did the organization of early markets for slaves aid or hinder the development of the economy of colonial America? This book seeks to answer these questions by investigating the behavior of the traders and planters who participated in the early transatlantic slave trade. What emerges is a richly detailed picture of market behavior of a complexity and subtlety that far exceed what previously would have been expected in this early period. These results promise to have far-reaching implications for our understanding of market behavior and resource allocation in early English America.

Preface

This book examines a period in the history of the early Atlantic slave trade, the late seventeenth and early eighteenth centuries, that has largely eluded detailed quantitative investigation. There are compelling reasons for devoting special attention to this early period of the slave trade's operation. The seventeenth century was of crucial importance in the history of New World slavery, because it was the formative period during which slavery first appeared in English America, and in which the basic economic, social, and legal characteristics of systems of slavery in the West Indies and the North American mainland emerged. Changing supply conditions for slave labor have often been mentioned as a possible factor contributing to this introduction and growth of American slavery, but systematic evaluation of this possibility remains to be done. The late seventeenth century was also the period when an explosive growth of the transatlantic slave trade firmly established it as one of the major international trades, which it remained throughout the eighteenth century and into the nineteenth. Recent estimates suggest that more slaves were sold to Europeans on the Atlantic coast of Africa in the second half of the seventeenth century than in the previous 200 years combined.[1] Understanding how the slave trade operated in this period of dramatic expansion is clearly important in gaining historical perspective on the trade in the following centuries, as well as in assessing the trade's impact on early English America.

This study is based on the surviving records of the Royal African Company, which are held at the Public Record Office in London. This mass of records, which include the minutes of company committee meetings, lists of subscribers, correspondence with company employees, and accounts of trade, served as the basis for K. G. Davies's *The Royal African Company*, published in 1957, which provided a fascinating account of the history of the company and its operations in England, West Africa, and the West Indies. This study focuses primarily on a subset of the company's records of trade. Specifically, records of the Royal African Company's sales of more than 74,000 slaves in the West Indies between its first deliveries in 1673 and the effective cessation of its transatlantic slave trading in 1725 are contained in 24 volumes of invoice accounts. The coverage of these records over time and space, and the detail and care with which they were kept, make them an extraordinary source of evidence on the behavior of markets for slaves on both sides of the Atlantic.[2] Systematic analysis of the quantitative data in the accounts can provide important evidence on outcomes in these markets; qualitative evidence from the surviving collection of internal company memoranda and correspondence can also be used to add dimensions to, and gain perspective on, this quantitative analysis.

The computations in this study were supported by grants from the Sloan Foundation and the University of Chicago. A grant from the American Philosophical Association helped to support my research in England. Among the many archives and libraries that made this study possible, I owe a special debt to the staff of the Public Record Office, London, for their assistance in my work with the Royal African Company records.

Seminars at a number of universities allowed me to present preliminary versions of several chapters for criticism and discussion. Sections of the study were also presented at the annual meetings of the Social Science History Association at Bloomington, Indiana, in 1982, the Weingart/Social Science History Association Conference on "The Variety of Quantitative History" at the California Institute of Technology in 1983, and the annual meetings of the Economic History Association at Chicago in 1984.

Preliminary versions of parts of Chapters 3 and 6 have appeared in the *Economic History Review* and the *Journal of Economic History*.[3] I am grateful to the Economic History Society and the Economic History Association for permission to reproduce some of the material from those articles here. Photographs of records held in the Public Record Office (Figures A.1 and A.2) appear by permission of the Keeper of the Public Records.

My understanding of the operation of the slave trade in this period owes a particular debt to K. G. Davies's study of the Royal African Company. I am also grateful to Professor Davies for his encouragement of my work with the company's records, and for his comments on an early paper using that evidence.

Stanley Engerman, Robert Fogel, Richard Hellie, and Richard Sheridan read drafts of the entire manuscript of this book, and their detailed comments and discussions were extremely helpful to me in carrying out revisions.

For suggestions, advice, and comments on drafts of chapters, I am grateful to Andrew Abel, William Brock, Philip Curtin, Paul David, David Brion Davis, Lance Davis, Richard Dunn, Robert Forsythe, Robert Gallman, Barry Higman, Mark Hopkins, John James, Alice Hanson Jones, Roderick Kiewiet, Laurence Kotlikoff, Peter Lindert, Paul Lovejoy, Donald McCloskey, Russell Menard, Larry Neal, Colin Palmer, Clayne Pope, Jacob Price, Roger Ransom, Daniel Scott Smith, Richard Steckel, Peter Temin, Lorena Walsh, and Donghyu Yang. A number of my colleagues at the University of Chicago, including Gary Becker, Max Hartwell, John Huizinga, Charles Kahn, Frederic Mishkin, Melvin Reder, Sherwin Rosen, Theodore Schultz, Lester Telser, Robert Topel, and Arnold Zellner, read my work and generously gave advice and constructive criticism. I am also very grateful to Frank Smith of Cambridge University Press for encouragement and editorial assistance.

Daniel Levy performed invaluable research assistance at every stage of this project, including the programming of the bulk of the calculations, with unfailing energy and enthusiasm. I am also grateful to Thomas Dunn, Cebette Goldberg, Farley Grubb, Henry Otto, Jonathan Pritchett, and Sanghoon Shin for excellent assistance in preparing and analyzing the quantitative data sets. June Nason cheerfully and efficiently typed a succession of drafts of the manuscript.

D. W. G.

1

The Atlantic slave trade and the early development of the English West Indies

This book deals with one aspect of the Atlantic economy during the late seventeenth and early eighteenth centuries: the transatlantic slave trade to the early English West Indies. It uses an important body of quantitative evidence that has not previously been systematically analyzed in order to draw a series of conclusions about the conduct of the slave trade and the history of early English settlement in the Caribbean. Yet the book also addresses a set of issues that transcend the boundaries of both the West Indies and the early colonial era. These issues lie at the heart of current controversies concerning the origins of modern capitalism and the usefulness of modern economic theory in understanding long stretches of the past.

There is still much to be learned about how and when large-scale competitive markets first began to operate. Although a study of the early slave trade cannot solve that problem, it does reveal that such markets existed and functioned continuously and routinely more than 300 years ago. The participants in these markets were sophisticated traders who, though severely hampered by the lack of modern computers and methods of communication, sought to respond to changes in market prices by adjusting the composition of their cargoes to maximize their profits from trading. They also designed complicated auctions to increase their revenues, developed an extensive network of credit financing, and devised institutional arrangements that allowed risk sharing, not only among partners, but also with employees and purchasers.

This is not intended to suggest that the West Indies was the cradle of modern capitalism, nor is it intended to celebrate a particularly odious form of trade that ethical people later struggled long and hard to banish. It does demonstrate, however, that many of the complex trading arrangements and outcomes characteristic of large competitive markets today are not of such recent origin as is often presumed, but were actually worked out in considerable detail centuries ago. Economists such as Alfred Marshall have suspected that this was so, but the evidence needed to confirm their suspicions has been hard to acquire. The records of the Royal African Company, chartered in

1

1672 as the successor to the Company of Royal Adventurers Trading into Africa, provide a large piece of the elusive evidence.

The growth of the early English West Indies

English settlers first arrived in the West Indies in 1624, when Sir Thomas Warner occupied St. Christopher with a small group of followers. English influence in the region soon spread, as settlements appeared in Barbados in 1627, Nevis in 1628, and Antigua and Montserrat in 1632. The last major English settlement of the seventeenth century in the West Indies was established in 1655, when a military expedition seized Jamaica from the Spanish.

The islands of the English West Indies are small. Barbados, the wealthiest island in the seventeenth century, is at most a mere 21 miles long and 14 miles wide; its area of 166 square miles makes it less than one-seventh the size of the present-day state of Rhode Island, or just about two and a half times larger than the District of Columbia. The largest of the Leeward Islands, Antigua, has an area of 108 square miles; adding the 68 of St. Christopher, the 50 of Nevis, and the 33 of Montserrat gives a total of only 259 for the Leewards. Jamaica is of course much larger – 145 miles long and 50 miles wide, with an area of about 4,400 square miles, but even this is smaller than the state of Connecticut.

Yet during the colonial period these small islands had an economic importance far more than proportional to their size, and this was particularly true in the early colonial period that is the focus of this study. One indication of this appears in estimates of their populations; an overview for the relevant period is given in Table 1.1.

Two decades before the beginning of the period considered here, in 1650, Barbados had the largest population of any settlement in English America. Indeed only Virginia had more than half as many white residents.[1] Counting both whites and blacks, the total population of the English West Indies in 1650 was greater than that of all the British colonies in North America.

The white population of the English West Indies declined in the decades after 1650. By 1700 the white population of the West Indies as a whole was only one-third as large as that of New England, and less than half as large as the combined white population of the Chesapeake Bay colonies. The black population of the West Indies, however, had increased more than sevenfold in the second half of the seventeenth century. Whereas blacks had accounted for only one-quarter of the region's total population in 1650, in 1700 they made up four-fifths of the total. At the latter date there were nearly twice as many blacks in Barbados alone as in all the colonies of mainland British America combined. Barbados was still the largest colony in British America in total population, and the West Indies' total population continued to make it the largest region in British America.

2

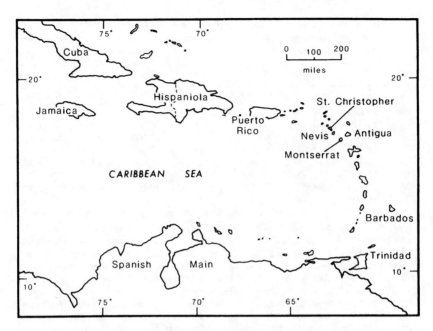

Map 1. The West Indies in the seventeenth century. *Source:* Adapted from Richard S. Dunn, *Sugar and Slaves: The Rise of the Planter Class in the English West Indies, 1624–1713* (Chapel Hill: University of North Carolina Press, 1972), p. xiv.

There was little change in the size of the West Indies' white population between 1700 and 1730. In 1730 the English West Indies as a whole had a white population only about as large as that of the colony of New Jersey. The West Indies' black population, which had doubled between 1700 and 1730, had risen to more than 85 percent of the region's total population. Jamaica now had by far the largest slave population of any British American colony.

Although the large population of the early English West Indies suggests the region's significance, even more striking evidence of its economic importance can be found in measures of its trade with England. Table 1.2 presents annual series derived from English customs records for the period 1697–1705 on the total value of imports into England from each of the West Indian colonies, as well as similar evidence on the value of English imports from the North American colonies for purposes of comparison.[2] The most remarkable fact revealed by these data is that the mean value of West Indian goods imported into England annually during this period (£608,000) was more than double the mean annual value of England's imports from all the North American mainland colonies combined (£283,000). Barbados alone nearly matched the latter figure, with mean annual exports to Britain valued at £250,000. West Indian goods accounted for fully 12.5 percent, or one-eighth, of the total value of

3

1. Atlantic slave trade and English West Indies

Table 1.1. *Population of the English West Indies, 1650–1730*

Year	Barbados			Jamaica			White
	White	Black	Total	White	Black	Total	
1650	30,000	12,800	42,800	—	—	—	13,700
1660	26,200	27,100	53,300	3,400	500	3,900	16,800
1670	22,400	40,400	62,800	8,000	7,200	15,200	11,000
1680	20,500	44,900	65,400	8,900	18,000	26,900	11,000
1690	17,900	47,800	65,700	8,600	32,000	40,600	9,800
1700	15,400	50,100	65,500	7,300	42,000	49,300	8,300
1710	13,000	52,300	65,300	7,200	59,200	66,400	9,000
1720	17,700	58,800	76,500	7,100	79,600	86,700	9,400
1730	18,200	65,300	83,500	7,600	100,900	108,500	10,000

Source: West Indies: John J. McCusker, "The Rum Trade and the Balance of Payments of the Thirteen Continental Colonies, 1650–1775" (unpublished Ph.D. dissertation, University of Pittsburgh, 1970), pp. 692–9; also see Richard S. Dunn, *Sugar and Slaves: The Rise of the Planter Class in the English West Indies, 1624–1713* (Chapel Hill: University of North Carolina Press, 1972), p. 312, and Robert V. Wells, *The Population of the British Colonies in America Before 1776* (Princeton, N.J.: Princeton University Press, 1975), pp. 196, 238.

North American mainland: Includes Maine, New Hampshire, Vermont, Plymouth, Massachusetts, Rhode Island, Connecticut, New York, New Jersey, Pennsylvania, Delaware, Maryland, Virginia, North Carolina, and South Carolina; U.S. Bureau of the Census, *Historical Statistics of the United States, Colonial Times to 1970* (Washington, D.C.: U.S. Government Printing Office, 1975), Part 2, p. 1168.

English imports from all sources in these years. The bulkiness of sugar as a commodity made the West Indian trade loom even larger as a source of employment for English ships: In 1686 the West Indies accounted for an estimated 21 percent of the total tonnage of English ships involved in overseas trade, and this share rose in later decades.[3]

Barbados was the leading West Indian exporter in this period; the annual average value of its shipments to England (£250,000) was greater than the annual mean value of those from Jamaica (£167,000), or the combined value of those from the Leewards (£191,000). The value of Barbados's exports placed it well ahead of the leading exporter among the mainland American regions, the Chesapeake Bay colonies of Virginia and Maryland, which together annually shipped goods to England worth an average of £217,000.

Although the West Indian colonies exported considerably more to England than they received in return, they were nonetheless an important market for British output. Table 1.3 shows the value of goods exported annually from England to the West Indian colonies during 1697–1705, as well as the corresponding figures for British exports to the North American mainland colonies. The average value of total annual English exports to the West Indies in this period (£286,000) was very close to the mean value of annual English exports to all the mainland colonies (£294,000). Shipments to the West Indies ac-

Table 1.1. (*cont.*)

Leewards		All West Indies			All North American mainland		
Black	Total	White	Black	Total	White	Black	Total
2,500	16,200	43,700	15,300	59,000	48,768	1,600	50,368
6,400	23,200	46,400	34,000	80,400	72,138	2,920	75,058
4,300	15,300	41,400	51,900	93,300	107,400	4,535	111,935
13,400	24,400	40,400	76,300	116,700	144,536	6,971	151,507
17,800	27,600	36,300	97,600	133,900	193,643	16,729	210,372
22,200	30,500	31,000	114,300	145,300	223,071	27,817	250,888
36,000	45,000	29,200	147,500	176,700	286,845	44,866	331,711
36,300	45,700	34,200	174,700	208,900	397,346	68,839	466,185
52,100	62,100	35,800	218,300	254,100	538,424	91,021	629,445

Table 1.2. *Value of English imports from the West Indies and North America, 1697–1705*

Year	Barbados	Jamaica	Leewards	Total West Indies	Total North America
1697	£196,533	£ 70,000	£ 60,006	£326,539	£281,850
1698	308,091	189,568	132,075	629,734	234,089
1699	273,948	174,845	207,462	656,255	259,636
1700	366,024	239,759	218,463	824,246	397,519
1701	280,678	235,215	222,707	738,600	309,140
1702	114,327	149,390	212,451	476,168	337,582
1703	223,591	182,552	220,345	626,488	257,252
1704	136,557	184,366	168,984	489,907	321,975
1705	353,579	75,388	277,608	706,575	150,964
Annual means, 1697–1705	250,370	166,787	191,122	608,279	283,334

Notes: Values are in £ sterling. The annual totals for the Leewards are based on entries for Antigua, Montserrat, and Nevis during 1697–9, and for those colonies and St. Christopher during 1700–5. The values for North America include entries for Carolina, Hudson's Bay, New England, New York, Pennsylvania, and Virginia–Maryland.
Source: Sir Charles Whitworth, *State of the Trade of Great Britain in Its Imports and Exports, Progressively from the Year 1697* (London: G. Robinson et al., 1776), pp. 1–9.

counted for 4.6 percent of the total value of English exports to all destinations during 1697–1705. Within the West Indies, Barbados was the largest importer of English goods, with an annual average value of £129,000, compared to £109,000 for Jamaica and £49,000 for the Leewards. The Chesapeake colonies, which were together by far the largest recipients of English goods on the mainland, accounted for an annual average of £161,000 in imports, somewhat more than any of the West Indian colonies.

1. Atlantic slave trade and English West Indies

Table 1.3. *Value of English exports to the West Indies and North America, 1697–1705*

Year	Barbados	Jamaica	Leewards	Total West Indies	Total North America
1697	£ 77,465	£ 40,726	£ 24,606	£142,797	£141,425
1698	146,851	120,778	38,683	306,312	460,953
1699	150,532	136,733	53,870	341,135	404,560
1700	167,609	100,848	64,596	333,053	344,345
1701	182,046	105,235	51,970	339,251	345,486
1702	104,405	95,658	54,803	254,866	187,786
1703	79,093	165,894	39,848	284,835	296,212
1704	121,519	89,952	55,770	267,241	176,091
1705	127,906	125,048	52,896	305,850	291,725
Annual means, 1697–1705	128,603	108,986	48,560	286,149	294,287

Notes: See Table 1.2.
Source: Same as for Table 1.2.

The economic importance of the colonial West Indies stemmed directly from the production of sugar. Sugar was introduced into the region in Barbados in the early 1640s. The climate and soil of the islands proved to be nearly ideal for sugar cultivation. The abundant yields of the newly planted cane fields combined with high prevailing European prices to make sugar an extraordinarily profitable crop, and it quickly became the dominant product of the English colonists in the West Indies. The rise of sugar production in the islands soon made England a major power in European sugar markets. In fact, it was during the period 1680–1720 that the English colonies probably reached their strongest competitive position in world sugar markets, for it has been estimated that during these four decades they were the single largest sugar producers in America, ahead of Brazil and the French West Indies. Indeed in 1700 the English West Indies produced nearly half of all the sugar consumed in Western Europe.[4]

West Indian production had a major impact on English sugar consumption. Falling sugar prices in England resulting from the enormous volume of imports from the West Indies transformed sugar from a luxury consumed primarily by the wealthy in the mid seventeenth century to a commodity consumed even by the poor in the eighteenth.[5] The increase in the use of sugar in England was dramatic: Estimates of per capita consumption suggest a fourfold increase between 1660 and 1700, and a further doubling between 1700 and 1725.[6] This increase was part of a major change in the diet of the English population in this period, because the greater use of sugar was closely tied to the rise of tea, and to a lesser extent coffee, during the eighteenth century.

Barbados dominated sugar production in the early English West Indies. Estimates for 1669 suggest that Barbados might have accounted for 80 percent of the islands' total sugar exports to England at that date.[7] This share fell over time as production increased in both the Leewards and Jamaica, yet at the close of the seventeenth century Barbados still accounted for roughly half the region's exports of sugar. The small size of the island, however, and perhaps also declining yields per acre owing to the intensive cultivation of past years, put a stop to further increases in Barbados's production, whereas total output in the Leewards and Jamaica continued to increase rapidly in the early eighteenth century. The Leewards began to export consistently larger quantities of sugar than Barbados during the 1710s and early 1720s, and Jamaica passed Barbados in this regard in the latter part of the 1720s. During the 1720s Barbados accounted for about one-quarter of the total sugar imported by Britain from the West Indies, with Jamaica sending about one-third of the total and the Leewards two-fifths.[8] Later, just after midcentury, Jamaica took advantage of its much larger area and became the largest sugar producer in the English West Indies.

Consequences of the sugar revolution

The introduction of sugar cultivation and its subsequent drive toward monoculture produced fundamental changes in the economy and society of the early English West Indies. Among the elements that together constituted the sugar revolution, no other had as great an impact on virtually all the conditions of life in the region at the time or implications as far-reaching for its future as the growth of slavery. This occurred first in Barbados. The process there has been somewhat better documented than for the Leewards and Jamaica. Available evidence from the other islands does suggest, however, that although there were differences in the timing of their experiences – both in the dates at which particular changes occurred and in their speed – the basic features of the process were similar in each case.

Slavery was present in the English West Indies almost from the time of the first settlement. When Captain Henry Powell brought the first shipload of English settlers to Barbados in 1627, among those who disembarked from the *William and John* were 10 Africans, who had apparently been captured from a Portuguese ship during the voyage out.[9] More blacks were brought into the colony during the next few years, but their numbers remained small. Any doubt about their status was eliminated by a declaration made in 1636 by the governor and council of Barbados that "Negroes . . . that came here to be sold, should serve for Life, unless a Contract was before made to the contrary."[10] Yet slavery remained a marginal institution in Barbados; in 1640 there were probably no more than a few hundred blacks among the island's total population of about 10,000.[11]

7

1. Atlantic slave trade and English West Indies

The economy of Barbados before 1640 was based on mixed farming on a relatively small scale. The settlers in the colony were forced to grow their own food while they searched, unsuccessfully, for a profitable staple crop. Initial hopes of making Barbados a thriving exporter of tobacco were disappointed when the tobacco grown there proved to be of a quality too poor to compete in European markets with the superior Virginian product. Subsequent experiments with cotton and indigo were even less successful. The inability of the early settlers to find a profitable staple crop meant that the demand for labor in Barbados grew relatively slowly in the 15 years after the colony's initial settlement.[12]

The colonists' demand for labor in these years was satisfied primarily by the importation of English indentured servants. Indentured servitude had been devised by the Virginia Company as a solution to the problem of how the major source of hired labor in England, service in husbandry, could be connected to the labor demands of New World planters. In seventeenth-century England, the majority of all hired labor was done by "servants in husbandry," young individuals of both sexes in the teen ages and early twenties who lived and worked in the households of their employers, usually on annual contracts.[13] The servants were provided with room and board and were often paid supplementary wages in cash or kind in return for their labor. English yeomen and husbandmen who had taken this source of labor for granted in England discovered that a problem arose of obtaining access to it when they transplanted their enterprises to America. The principal problem was that the £6 cost of transportation across the Atlantic was far beyond the savings of most young English servants. Consequently even those workers willing to accept the risks of migration in performing their life-cycle service in America were unable to travel there.

A solution to this problem was developed by the Virginia Company within little more than a decade after the first settlement at Jamestown. The company provided for English servants to be transported to Virginia in return for promises from the servants to work for the company for specified periods of years under conditions similar to those of servants in husbandry in England. The company was to provide all maintenance for the servants during their terms, and to give them freedom dues at the conclusion. These agreements were written into legal contracts of a standard English form, known as indentures. When these were made transferable, in order to enable the company to sell the workers' promises of service to planters for lump-sum payments, other English merchants entered this industry, effectively providing credit to prospective migrants.[14] Many English merchants who imported colonial tobacco recruited and indentured servants in England, sent them to Virginia on the ships bound there to collect the tobacco, and sold the servants' contracts to colonial planters upon the ships' arrival in port. Often these transactions were carried out as direct exchanges for tobacco. Indentured servants quickly became the principal source of hired labor in early Virginia, and white servitude became a central institution there and in other colonies of mainland North America. When the English began to settle in the West Indies, indentured servitude was readily extended to that region. As on the mainland, indentured servants drawn from England and Ireland became the major source of labor for the early planters in Barbados.[15]

The introduction of sugar cultivation in Barbados in the early 1640s radically changed this situation. The availability of a profitable export crop caused a sudden large increase in the demand for labor as planters scrambled to increase their output of the new crop. The existing flows of relatively small numbers of indentured servants were inadequate to provide the labor to produce sugar in the quantities desired by the colony's planters. Although firm quantitative evidence on the extent of the shortage is lacking, the urgent tone of planters' requests to their English merchants for new recruits in this period makes plain their dissatisfaction with the available supplies of bound white workers. In 1645, for example, William Hay wrote from Barbados to his uncle in Scotland:

Theise that are Upon the designe of Sugar here prosper well and make exceeding good Sugar . . . want of servants is my greatest bane and will much hinder my designe. The bilding of my house and setting Upp of my Ingenue [i.e., sugar mill] will cost above 50000 lib of Tobacco because I have not work men of my owen. In January next god willing I shall begin to make sugar. So pray if you come neare to any port where shiping comes hither indenture procure and send me [servants] . . . Agree for theire passages to be payed here . . . Lett them be of any sort men women or boys of 14 years of age, what I make not use off and are not serviceable for mee I can exchange with others especially any sort of tradesmen.[16]

Yet during this early period of sugar cultivation, changes in the attitudes of prospective migrants were apparently contributing to the scarcity of servants. As knowledge of the harsh working conditions involved in growing sugar under the tropical conditions of the West Indies spread in Britain, young Englishmen became increasingly reluctant to travel to the islands under indenture. The desperation of some planters to obtain workers may have led them further to aggravate the problem of the dwindling white labor supply with their response, as a number of English and Irish youths were apparently kidnapped to work in the sugar fields of Barbados. Although it cannot be determined how common this was, the reputation of the West Indies as a destination for kidnapped Englishmen – and even as a rumored site of white slavery – that was to haunt the efforts of merchants to recruit white workers for the islands for decades to come appears to have been established within a decade of the introduction of sugar cultivation in Barbados.[17]

It was in the face of this increasingly severe shortage of indentured white labor that Barbados's planters turned to the use of black slaves. Interestingly, there appears to have been a sharp contrast between the eagerness with which the colony's planters switched from servants to slaves and the reluctance with which the planters of the mainland's tobacco colonies made the same substitution four decades later.[18] The difference might have resulted in part from the low quality of the white workers in early Barbados. From the beginning the West Indies had seemed a dangerous place to Englishmen. Like many other frontier areas in history, it initially attracted those willing to gamble, some with their wealth, but all with their lives. Unlike in the mainland colonies, however, the society of the islands did not settle down as time went on, and the region's immigrants apparently continued to be drawn from the tougher elements of British society.[19] The planters' efforts to increase the numbers of white workers in the early years of sugar cultivation may have worsened this situation, by lowering the average quality of those recruited. One young English visitor to Barbados in 1654, who was struck by the natural beauty of the island, was equally impressed by the depravity of its population, remarking: "This Illand is the dunghill wharone England doth cast forth its rubidg. Rodgs and hors and such like peopel are thos which are gennerally Broght heare."[20] Unlike in the mainland colonies, a stable population of small planters and free white workers failed to grow in Barbados because of the shortage of land on the island, and the spread of sugar cultivation, with the economic superiority of large estates, made the prospects even worse for small planters and recently freed servants. Heavy migration out of Barbados began in the 1640s, and the overall white population of the island probably peaked and began to decline as early as the 1650s.[21] The transition to the use of slave labor by Barbados's planters therefore might have been speeded by the lack of a strong commitment to the use of white labor, perhaps because of the poor quality of many of the indentured servants they had relied on in earlier years.

Large numbers of black slaves began to arrive in Barbados early in the 1640s.[22] Initially the island's planters simply added the blacks to their field gangs, where they worked alongside white servants. In the course of two decades, however, the balance shifted, as slaves replaced the whites whose terms ended, and the numbers of new white recruits dwindled. By about 1660 it was probably unusual to see whites at work in the cane fields.

The substitution of slaves for servants in field work did not bring the use of white servants in Barbados to an end. It did produce a change in the role of indentured labor, however, for servants were now seen by planters primarily as a source of skilled labor. Consequently, in an intermediate phase there arose a racial division of labor by skill, as small numbers of indentured carpenters, coopers, potters, and a variety of other craftsmen were employed in constructing the buildings of the sugar plantations and refining and packing the sugar grown by the much larger numbers of slaves. This change in the role of indentured labor can be seen in descriptions of plantation labor forces and in the correspondence of West Indian planters. Unlike the earlier requests for any servants their English agents could send, specialized requests for those with particular skills appear in the later decades of the seventeenth century.[23]

This was not the final stage in the evolution of the West Indian labor force, however. Over time plantation owners increasingly had white servants teach their skills to slaves. In some cases they hired servants specifically for this purpose; for example in 1667 an estate manager in Jamaica reported to the absentee owner that he had indentured a white potter who would train slaves to refine sugar: "I have agreed with Thomas fforde Potter to serve you Three yeares . . . teaching two of your negroes to make potts and dripps and burne and Sett as well as himselfe."[24] In part, the lag of this replacement of skilled servants behind the initial transition from servants to slaves in field work might have been caused by the discovery by some planters that those blacks born in the West Indies were more easily trained than Africans.[25] It might also have been forced on planters by an increasing difficulty of obtaining even the smaller numbers of white craftsmen they needed in the late seventeenth century. In 1682 a group of West Indian planters complained to the king that

there is in a manner a totall stop of sending any more Servants into yor. Maties said Plantations, which will in a short time disable the Inhabitants of them from carrying on their Trade by leaving them without any persons to governe and direct their Negros and utterly disable them from furnishing the proportion of men to the Militia, which yor. Maties Laws there require.[26]

Two years earlier the governor of Barbados had written to the Lords of Trade and Plantations on the same issue. In his letter he detailed the causes of the shortage of servants:

First my Lords by reason of the great numbers of people gon off from this place to Carolina Jamaica Antega and the rest of the Leeward Islands where they hope to gett land which this Island having none to give; Supplies will not come at us and those that doe come wch are not many are bound to serve only for foure or att most five yeares; their time expired they are ready for to seeke a new fortune as they hope to obteyne else where besides my Lords Since they [i.e., the planters] have found the conveniency by the Labor & cheape keeping of Slaves they have neglected the keeping of white men with whom alone they formerly carried out their Plantations neither for the former reasons and for the strict acts in England for Trade can they have any white servants to come to this place though for their owne safety they would willingly embrace him thus farr for some of ye reasons of the Diminution of the Militia.[27]

By the close of the seventeenth century there were few white servants in the West Indies; indentured servitude survived into the eighteenth century only as a marginal supplier of skilled craftsmen. After 1700 most of the indentured workers in the West Indies served in managerial positions on large plantations, under conditions very different from those earlier bound white laborers who had arrived in the region in the early years of the sugar revolution.[28]

The displacement of white servants by black slaves, and the rise of a black majority among the populations of all the islands in the English West Indies by the close of the seventeenth century were closely related to another important consequence of the sugar revolution: the growth of a wealthy group of large plantation owners who dominated the economic and political life of the region. The technology of sugar production, with high fixed capital requirements for the mill, the boiling and curing houses, and the distillery, resulted in considerable economies of scale, with declining average costs of production on plantations over a greater range of capital and labor utilization than perhaps any other industry of the seventeenth century. With an initial expenditure of several thousand pounds sterling required to start up a sugar plantation of even moderate size, West Indian planters quickly realized "that the business of sugar planting is a sort of adventure in which the man that engages, must engage deeply," and throughout the islands the consolidation of many small farms into large plantations followed the adoption of sugar as the staple crop.[29]

A census of property taken by the governor of Barbados in 1680 clearly reflects the impact of the economies of scale in sugar production on land-ownership in the colony. Even at this date, well after the establishment of sugar as the colony's dominant product, there remained many small land-owners on the island, as its 90,000 acres were divided among more than 3,000 property holders, with a mean holding of about 30 acres, and a median holding of only 10.[30] Yet more than half the island's total acreage was owned by 175 great planters, who made up less than 6 percent of all property holders; the mean size of their estates was 270 acres. These same great planters owned more than half of all the slaves in Barbados, with average holdings of 115 per estate. Although the planting elites of the Leewards and Jamaica were smaller and somewhat less wealthy than that of Barbados in this period, the same underlying economic forces appear to have been at work, producing similarly high concentrations of wealth holding in the hands of relatively few great planters.[31] In comparison, planters on the North American mainland were much less wealthy. In the second half of the seventeenth century, the wealthiest 5 percent of property holders in the most prosperous section of Maryland owned an average of only 30 slaves each, little more than a quarter of the average number owned by their counterparts in Barbados.[32] Nearly a century later Adam Smith would remark that "our tobacco colonies send us home no such wealthy planters as we see frequently arrive from our sugar islands"; it is clear that this was equally true in the seventeenth century, as already in this earlier period the West Indian sugar planters were by far the wealthiest men in English America.[33] The inequality of wealth holding also appears to have been substantially greater in the West Indies than in the mainland American colonies.[34]

The distribution of wealth was in turn closely related to that of political power in the early West Indies. The 175 wealthiest planters in Barbados in

1680 included not only 10 of the 12 members appointed to the colony's council by the governor, but also 20 of the 22 members elected by the island's freeholders to its assembly.[35] They furthermore accounted for four-fifths of the colony's judges and three-quarters of its justices of the peace. The same dominant position carried over to the highest levels of the colony's militia, for by Barbados law a planter had to own at least 100 acres to qualify as a field officer. The sugar revolution in the West Indies therefore created a society in which great wealth was concentrated in the hands of relatively few, and in which political power and social status accrued to the same small elite.

The slave trade and the role of the Royal African Company

The availability of a steady supply of slaves was critical to the success of the sugar revolution. Initially the planters of Barbados and the Leewards appear to have depended on Dutch traders for their slave cargoes. Although some shipments were brought by private English traders, the transatlantic slave trade was dominated during the 1640s and 1650s by the Dutch West India Company.[36]

English interest in West African trade was growing in this period, and in 1660 Charles II granted a charter to the Company of Royal Adventurers into Africa.[37] This company was ill conceived, for its principal objective was to be the search for gold in West Africa. It was also poorly subscribed and poorly managed, and after several years of desultory trading it surrendered its charter. A new charter was granted in 1663 to a reorganized company, to be known as the Company of Royal Adventurers Trading into Africa. The new charter contained the same provisions concerning gold as that of 1660, but now the investors had added another prospective source of profit: The new charter explicitly mentioned the slave trade, granting the company the exclusive right among English traders to buy slaves on the West African coast.

During the next seven years the Royal Adventurers made some progress in setting up forts and trading outposts on the African coast. The company also established a significant English presence in the transatlantic slave trade; for example, between August 1663 and March 1664, it delivered more than 3,000 slaves to Barbados.[38] By 1665, however, the company had already run into serious financial difficulties, owing chiefly to the failure of colonial planters to pay for the slaves they had purchased on credit. When war broke out between the English and the Dutch on the West African coast in 1665, the company's trade was interrupted, and it could not be renewed until peace was restored by the Treaty of Breda in 1667. The settlement clearly established the right of the English to compete with the Dutch in the slave trade. By this time, however, the outstanding debts of the Company of Royal Adventurers appear to have crippled it, and it never successfully regained a firm position in the slave trade.

1. Atlantic slave trade and English West Indies

In spite of its weak financial position, the company vigorously defended its right to a monopoly of the English share of the transatlantic slave trade. An appeal by Barbados's planters to the House of Commons in late 1667 for "an open trade" in slaves drew a prompt and scathing reply from the company's secretary, Sir Ellis Leighton, who sneered "that open Marketts and free Trade are best for those that Desire Them is Certaine, and so is it . . . to Buy Cheape, and sell Deare, and most of all to have their Commoditys for Nothing." Yet Leighton went on to argue that free trade would soon leave the English West Indies dependent for slaves on Dutch traders, whose high prices not only would hurt the planters of the other islands and English trade in general, but would also eventually harm the shortsighted planters of Barbados.[39] The company began selling licenses to private individuals to trade within the limits of its monopoly, and the bulk of English trade in West Africa at the close of the 1660s was consequently in the hands of private traders. But the revenue generated by these sales proved insufficient to save the company. An attempt to revive the company through a financial reorganization began in 1670, but in the course of these discussions it was decided to replace the Royal Adventurers with a new company. As a result, in 1671 the Company of Royal Adventurers was effectively put into bankruptcy.[40]

A charter was granted to the Royal African Company by Charles II in September 1672.[41] A clause of the charter stated that no English subject other than those thereby incorporated was to visit West Africa except by permission of the company, and empowered the company to seize the ships and goods of all who infringed its monopoly. This charter is the basis from which many historians have concluded that the Royal African Company held an effective economic monopoly of the transatlantic slave trade to the English West Indies from 1672.[42] Yet at least five potential sources of competition existed in part or all of this trade, some legal and others illegal, and these must be considered before any conclusions can be drawn concerning the effectiveness of the company's monopoly of the English slave trade.

One source arose from the terms of the charter. Although West Africa was by far the largest source of black slaves in the seventeenth century, others also existed. Between 1675 and 1690 shipments of slaves are known to have been made from Madagascar to the English West Indies, and under its charter the Royal African Company had no legal power to prevent these shipments. Madagascar lay within the territorial trading monopoly of the East India Company, but the latter was not actively engaged in trade there, and paid no attention to appeals from the Royal African Company asking its cooperation in preventing these independent traders from obtaining slave cargoes.[43]

A second source of competition was international. Throughout its existence the Royal African Company faced powerful competition for slaves in West African markets from Portuguese, French, and Dutch traders. As shown in Table 1.4, the colonies of British America received less than one-fifth of the

Table 1.4. *Shares of the Atlantic slave trade by imports of major regions, 1650–1700*

Importing region	1651–75		1676–1700	
	n	*%*	*n*	*%*
Old World	3,000	0.8	2,700	0.4
Spanish America	62,500	17.0	102,500	17.0
Brazil	185,000	50.2	175,000	29.0
British Caribbean	69,200	18.8	173,800	28.8
French Caribbean	28,800	7.8	124,500	20.7
Dutch Caribbean	20,000	5.4	20,000	3.3
Danish Caribbean	—	—	4,000	0.7
Total	368,500	100.0	602,500	99.9

Source: Philip D. Curtin, *The Atlantic Slave Trade: A Census* (Madison: University of Wisconsin Press, 1969), p. 119.

total slaves carried from Africa across the Atlantic in the third quarter of the seventeenth century, and less than 30 percent of those traded in the final quarter of the century. Not surprisingly, the correspondence of the Royal African Company's agents in Africa shows a constant awareness of the struggle against foreign traders for the West African trade. The presence of this substantial foreign competition in Africa suggests that whatever economic monopoly power the company's charter conferred must have stemmed from its position in markets at the other end of the Middle Passage, in the West Indies.[44]

Competition from three other sources affected the company's market position in the West Indies. One of these was authorized by the company, and arose from its practice of making partial payment for freight charges and commissions to the owners of hired ships and to ships' captains in the form of slaves. These consignments of slaves, which were turned over by company agents to a ship's captain upon arrival of a cargo at its West Indian destination, were sold by the captains independently of the sales held by the company agents. This created direct competition for the company's agents, a fact they recognized clearly. In 1684, for example, the company's agents in Barbados complained of this practice:

It is a most undoubted Truth & by experience wee soe find it that the Liberty the Company are pleased to give their Commanders [ship captains] to sell theire Freight & Commission Negroes when & where they please after they are divided & delivered to them is a great hinderance to the sale of both [i.e., sales of both the captains and the company agents]; both using all possible endeavours to sell theire Negroes as well as they can & the Customers take advantage to beat down the Markett by holding off till they can by that meanes get better pennyworths' from either then otherwise they could hope for if all were to be disposed off by one Interest. Nor is it a small Detriment to the Company that by this Liberty the Masters of these shipps forstall the Company's Market.[45]

The numbers of slaves involved in payments for freight charges were substantial, for the company insisted that owners for hired ships take a minimum of one-quarter of their earnings, and often as much as two-thirds, in the form of slaves; in all, it has been estimated that this arrangement resulted in the transfer to shipowners of the disposal of nearly 20 percent of all slaves delivered by the Royal African Company to the West Indies.[46] The company obviously had it within its power to eliminate this form of competition, but it chose not to because of severe problems of debt collection and cash flow, which will be discussed later in this chapter.

Unauthorized competition for the company's trade resulted from common illicit practices. Ships' captains and crews frequently sold slaves in the West Indies that they had carried from Africa on their own account, in violation of company regulations. Even worse, captains stole some of the company's slaves for their own profit, selling slaves privately in the islands who they subsequently reported to company agents as having died in the passage. The Royal African Company's attempts to set up monitoring systems to prevent these illegal activities do not appear to have been very effective. Although the scale of these abuses cannot be determined, that such violations repeatedly came to light suggests that this practice of illegal trade was common.[47] The company itself certainly believed this to be the case. After a series of investigations of captains believed to be stealing and smuggling the company's slaves, in 1687 the company wrote to its agents in Antigua in frustration:

Itt is not more than needfull that you watch the shipps narrowly att their arrivall for we have made such discoverys of frauds used by their Masters wee imploy that we have good grounds to beeleeve that there are few or none of them but doe or attempt to run negroes.[48]

The final source of competition faced by the company, which received the most public attention at the time, was from the activities of independent English slave traders, referred to by the Royal African Company as "interlopers." Although this trade was illegal in the early period of the company's activity, these "separate traders" were present from the beginning. During the four years from 1679 to 1682, for example, 32 interlopers were sighted and reported to the company by its agents in Barbados, Jamaica, Antigua, and Nevis; of these only 4 were seized by the agents. The actual number of these illegal cargoes was probably higher, for the records from which this count is drawn may be incomplete, and other voyages probably went undetected by company agents. In comparison, in the same four years the company delivered about 70 cargoes to the West Indies. K. G. Davies concluded that "it seems likely . . . that while the interlopers were delivering

Table 1.5. *Royal African Company slave deliveries to the English West Indies as a share of total black net migration, 1670–1710*

Decade	Barbados	Jamaica	Leewards	Total
1670s	39%	32%	27%	33%
1680s	80	67	47	68
1690s	22	13	4	14
1700s	33	17	16	21

Sources: K. G. Davies, *The Royal African Company* (London: Longmans, 1957), p. 363; David W. Galenson, *White Servitude in Colonial America: An Economic Analysis* (Cambridge: Cambridge University Press, 1981), p. 218.

fewer slaves to the Plantations than the company the margin between them at this time was not as great as might be supposed."[49]

An indication of what this margin might have been over time is given in Table 1.5, which compares Davies's estimates of total company deliveries of slaves to the islands by decade with independent estimates of the total net migration of blacks to the islands. This evidence clearly reveals that the 1680s were the period in which the company accounted for the largest proportion of total slave deliveries to the English West Indies; whereas in each of the other decades the company's share of total slave deliveries to the region was one-third or less, during the 1680s it accounted for more than two-thirds of total deliveries, including fully four-fifths of those delivered to Barbados. It might appear tempting to infer that the company could have exercised significant monopoly power in the islands at least during the 1680s, because of its quantitatively dominant role in the trade to the region during that decade. Yet a consideration of the circumstances under which the company operated in that decade suggests that this inference would probably be incorrect.

The standard economic analysis of monopoly attributes the source of monopoly power to the ability of the seller to restrict the volume of output in an industry. The consequence is that the monopolist can sell his goods at a higher price than the market would sustain at higher levels of sales. The seller's ability to restrict the level of total output in the market is of course a consequence of his dominant position in the market, which normally results from his control of a large share of overall production. Yet the contention that its control of a large share of the slave trade to the English colonies gave the Royal African Company the ability to exercise monopoly power over West Indian slave prices during the 1680s by restricting the levels of their deliveries appears invalid, for the company's control of that large share was due in significant part precisely to the ability of West Indian purchasers to force the company to bring them larger supplies of slaves than it wished to deliver.

1. Atlantic slave trade and English West Indies

Jamaica offers an illustration of the company's problem. During 1675–9 the company delivered an average of 1,000 slaves to Jamaica annually. In 1680 Jamaica's planters complained to the British Lords of Trade and Plantations that the company was not bringing them adequate supplies of slaves. They demanded that they be brought at least 3,000–4,000 annually, at lower prices than they had been paying. The Royal African Company replied by pointing out that the planters had not even been willing to pay for those slaves they had received to date, claiming that Jamaica's current debt to the company was £60,000 (roughly the value of 4,000 slaves). The settlement suggested by the Lords of Trade was that the company should deliver 3,000 slaves to Jamaica annually, to be sold at six months' credit for a maximum of £18 each. The company found this proposal unacceptable, and after several years of discussions a compromise was reached, under which the company was to deliver 3,000 slaves to the island annually without price controls.[50] In the event the company appears to have provided slaves to Jamaica at roughly this rate during only 1685–7. Yet during the eight years from 1680 through 1687, the company delivered an average of 2,000 slaves to Jamaica annually, double the rate it had during 1675–9, and probably substantially more than it would have supplied in the absence of effective political pressure from the planters through the mechanism of the scrutiny of the Lords of Trade; the company's annual average deliveries to the island during the four years of negotiations mediated by the Lords of Trade, 1680–3, were more than 50 percent higher than those of the previous five years. This political pressure was apparently equally present from planters in Barbados and the Leewards. The Royal African Company's large market share during the 1680s might therefore have been more a symptom of its inability to exercise monopoly power in the West Indies than a signal of the dominance that would have allowed it to raise slave prices above a competitive level through the restriction of deliveries.

The economic threat posed to the Royal African Company by the independent separate traders throughout its career resulted from the interlopers' lower overhead costs. Because they did not bear the cost of maintaining forts and factories in West Africa, the interlopers could prosper on smaller profit margins in the slave trade than the company. As a consequence, convincing complaints were voiced by company agents that interlopers were able both to outbid the company for slaves in Africa and to undersell the company in the West Indies. This advantage of the interlopers was apparently not offset by the risks they ran of seizure. The interlopers were popular among planters in the West Indies, and even when Royal African Company agents were able to seize the ships of interlopers the company was unlikely to receive legal judgments against them in colonial courts dominated by planters who favored free trade in slaves. Indeed interlopers were sometimes awarded damages by colonial courts when they were seized by company agents.[51] The indifference of many colonial governors, and the hostility of others, hampered the defense of the company's monopoly by its agents in the West Indies, for the agents rarely received official assistance in their efforts. The company was somewhat more successful in seizing and prosecuting interlopers in Africa, but the long coastline and many possible trading posts made the task too difficult to produce a high rate of success. Many company employees in Africa themselves served to undermine the company's efforts by trading directly with the interlopers.

A survey of the surviving evidence led K. G. Davies to conclude that in spite of the company's apparent advantages, which included the strong support of Charles II for its monopoly, its large capital, and the permanent African settlements and staff it commanded, even in the first two decades of its operation the company did not compete successfully with the interlopers.[52] Davies judged that any disadvantages forced on the private traders were outweighed by the costs incurred by the company in maintaining its settlements on the African coast and paying the hundreds of employees who lived in them, because of the small economic value of the forts to the company's slave trading. Yet this lack of success could alternatively have been the result of structural inefficiencies that plagued the company's operations, which will be discussed later in this chapter, and so the question can still be raised of what the value of the legal monopoly granted by the king to the company was.

If a significant value of the monopoly were to be found, it would have had to derive from the company's position in the West Indies, for the international competition described earlier probably meant that even an effective monopoly of British trade in Africa would have carried little economic benefit for the company's activity in trading and purchasing slaves there. Yet for reasons discussed earlier, it does not appear that the company did derive any significant benefits from its legal monopoly in the West Indies, even during the 1680s when it established a position as the primary supplier of slaves to the region's planters. For the Royal African Company was constrained in exercising monopoly power by raising slave prices not only by the competition of interlopers, but also by the political pressures exerted by the planters. Ironically, it was the actions forced on the company in order to defend its legal monopoly that robbed the monopoly of its economic value: The quantities delivered and prices charged by the company for slaves were the key evidence cited by opponents of the legal monopoly in their appeals to the British government for free trade, and the company's desire to keep the legal monopoly appears to have prevented it from attempting to exercise monopoly power, by reducing slave deliveries and raising prices, for fear of providing ammunition to its opponents. The question of why the company believed the legal monopoly was worth maintaining becomes an intriguing one in this light. The company's sustained lobbying efforts to regain its legal status after 1688 suggest that it did believe the monopoly to be potentially valuable. Yet that the economic value of the legal monopoly could probably never realistically have been expected to be large is suggested by K. G. Davies's telling observation that the British government wanted the company not only to supply its colonies with slaves, but also to supply them at a price low enough to allow the English colonies to compete on favorable terms in world sugar markets.[53] In consequence, the company would at best have been in the position of a regulated public utility, whose behavior in determining output levels and prices was subject to constant public scrutiny and political pressure. In the event, the legal monopoly was unenforceable, and the company also had to contend with the direct competition of independent slave traders operating illegally. Under the circumstances, company officials can probably be forgiven for feeling they were caught between the two jaws of a powerful vise; their continued struggle against these forces is probably evidence of a triumph of hope over experience.

The English political setting for the company's operations changed dramatically with the Glorious Revolution. Through 1688 the company had consistently enjoyed the support of the king, in negotiating both with colonial governors over the restraint of interlopers and with colonial planters over the terms on which slaves were to be supplied to the colonies. Even if, as suggested earlier, this support was not sufficient to produce outright victories for the company in either case, it was a significant element in the company's favor. In December 1688, however, the company recognized that the flight of James II from Whitehall effectively marked the end of royal monopolies. Although the company continued to claim publicly that its charter was still in force during the 1690s, it understood that this was not true, and that it could take no actions to defend its monopoly. In 1691 the company wrote to its agents in the West Indies, who for many years had been under orders to seize interlopers, instructing them that they no longer had any powers derived from the charter to do so.[54]

The possibility remained of securing a new authorization for monopoly based on an act of Parliament, and the company initiated an attempt to do this in 1690. This effort faced the opposition of lobbies organized by West Indian planters seeking cheap slaves, English merchants seeking access to West African markets, and shipowners seeking higher rental prices for their ships. The company's attempt to obtain a new legal monopoly was not successful, but the process began a series of inquiries and debates, in the public press as well as in Parliament, that was to stretch over the next two decades. In the meantime, litigation in England forced the company to pay damages to many interlopers for seizures that had occurred before the Revolution of 1688.[55]

A new phase in the legal basis of the English slave trade began in 1698, with an act of Parliament that put into effect a compromise between the Royal African Company and its opponents. The act stemmed from a continuing concern by the English Parliament with the strategic importance of the company's forts in Africa. Although the act officially threw open the West African trade to all Englishmen, independent traders were to pay a duty of 10 percent *ad valorem* on all their exports to West Africa, and the proceeds were to accrue to the Royal African Company for the maintenance of its African forts. The act further specified that the separate traders were to enjoy the same protection and privileges at the forts as the company's servants.

The act of 1698 remained in effect for 14 years. The Royal African Company's slave-trading activity, which had declined during the 1690s, revived during the 10 years following passage of the new act, but the company's efforts died away as it increasingly found itself unable to compete with the separate traders even on these somewhat improved terms. The decline of the company's trade that occurred after 1709 was never fully reversed thereafter for more than brief surges of one or two years. K. G. Davies argues that the separate traders had four advantages over the company in the era of the 10 percent act. First, their small scale enabled the owners carefully to supervise their businesses. Second, they were more flexible in adapting to changing conditions in the trade. Third, because they were not committed to remaining in the slave trade, they could readily leave if they failed to realize profits, rather than continuing to trade in the face of mounting losses, as did the company. And fourth, they were practically exempt from interference or direction by public authority.[56]

When the act of 1698 expired in 1712, the Royal African Company made a final, unsuccessful attempt to secure a new monopoly, and an official era of free trade began. The company made several brief attempts to win back its position in the slave trade, one in 1713–14, another in the early 1720s, and a third in 1730, but these were ill-fated. After 1730 the company's involvement in the transatlantic slave trade was practically at an end. The company continued to run its forts in Africa, but the costs of operation were increasingly met by government subsidies. The company's last functions were taken from it by an act of Parliament in 1750, and the company itself was formally terminated by another act in 1752.

The Royal African Company and the organization
of the slave trade

The organization of the slave trade posed many difficulties in the late seventeenth century, for the trade was a complex one, involving many different kinds of transactions in locations separated by great distances and poor communications. In addition to the hazards posed to shipping by such external forces as disease, storms, and pirates, and to commercial relations by the complicated and delicate diplomacy involved in dealing with African nations and rival European traders, the Royal African Company was faced with numerous internal problems, the severity of many of which resulted from the difficulty of supervising employees stationed in Africa or the West Indies. The contexts in which some of these problems arose, and the attempts made by the company to solve them, can be seen from a description of how slaving voyages typically proceeded.

A voyage began by obtaining and outfitting a ship in England. The company might either own the ship or hire it. In the early years of the company's operation, it relied primarily on hired ships; three-quarters of the ships the company sent out from England to Africa during 1680–5 were hired. In later years the company came to own a larger number of ships; about three-fifths of the ships dispatched on slaving voyages for the company during both 1700–9 and 1719–25 were its own.[57]

The agreements by which the company hired ships provided for a very unusual method of payment.[58] The typical engagement was for a voyage from England to the West Indies by way of West Africa. The hire contracts, or "charterparties," contained many clauses, and included agreements between the Royal African Company and the ship's owners specifying the size of the crew, the number of passengers, the places of loading and discharge and the time to be spent at each, the composition and value of the cargo to be carried to Africa, and the number of slaves the company intended to ship to the West Indies. Yet the rental payment for the whole voyage was calculated solely as a flat sum per slave delivered alive by the ship in the West Indies, with no separate payment for the voyage out from England to Africa. That no payment was made for slaves who died in passage obviously gave the ship's captain, who was normally a part owner of the ship, a strong incentive to minimize the mortality of the slaves loaded on board in Africa, and thus to protect the company's investment in these slaves.[59] Another unusual feature of the agreements was the requirement that shipowners take a substantial part of their earnings – between one-quarter and two-thirds – upon the ship's arrival in the West Indies in the form of slaves. These slaves would then be sold by the ship's captain. Although this arrangement created competition between ships' captains and company agents in the sale of slaves, it allowed the Royal African Company to improve its cash flow, and it shifted some of the costs of selling the slave cargoes and collecting the resulting planters' debts to the shipowners. The rental agreements terminated in the West Indies, and the captain was then on his own in finding a cargo of sugar to carry back to England. Because slaves could rarely be sold to West Indian planters for immediate payment in sugar, and they might be sold for bills of exchange that could be sent to London in an envelope, the company did not wish to be committed to filling the ship on this final leg of its voyage.

The journey from England to West Africa normally took one to three months.[60] The specific African destination might be any one of a large number of ports stretched over 2,000 miles of the West African coast, from the Senegal River at the north to Angola at the south. For commercial pur-

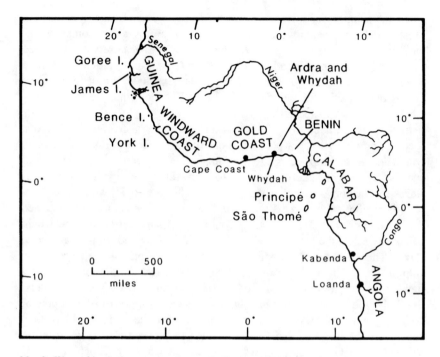

Map 2. West Africa in the seventeenth century. *Source:* Adapted from K. G. Davies, *The Royal African Company* (London: Longmans, 1957), p. 8.

poses, the Royal African Company divided West Africa into six regions; from north to south, these were "Northern Guinea" – primarily the region around the Gambia River – the Windward Coast, the Gold Coast, Ardra and Whydah, Benin and Calabar, and Angola.[61] Although there were some fluctuations over time in the relative importance of these regions for the company's trade, all remained significant suppliers of slaves throughout the company's principal period of involvement in the slave trade. There were a number of important differences among these regions in the way the Royal African Company conducted its activities, however. The kinds of products the company traded for slaves, and purchased in addition to slaves, varied by region. Even more basically, there were regional differences in the format of the company's trade. The major distinction was between what K. G. Davies has called "castle-trade" (or "factory-trade") and "ship-trade." Castle-trade was practiced where the company maintained settlements, whether permanent, fortified garrisons, called "forts," or small, unfortified, often temporary trading posts with perhaps no more than one or two men, called "factories." At any time, the company normally maintained two dozen or more settlements in West Africa, with the largest number on the Gold Coast,

23

where the company's largest permanent fort, Cape Coast Castle, was located. Most of the settlements were small factories with only a few company employees. At its peak level, in 1689, the company's African service numbered about 330 Englishmen, of whom 130 were at Cape Coast; a total of 48 more were at Accra, Ft. Royal, and Anomabu, its next three largest forts on the Gold Coast, leaving about 150 men scattered at more than 20 other settlements, mostly small factories.[62]

In the castle-trade, the ship's captain would be instructed to sail to a specified company fort, or perhaps to one of the larger factories. The captain would deliver his ship's cargo to the company factor who was resident there, and the factor would be responsible for furnishing a designated number of slaves for the ship's cargo. Alternatively, in the ship-trade, which was practiced in regions such as the Windward Coast where the company maintained no settlements, the ship's captain would act as supercargo, and he would personally select the places where he would trade his goods to the natives for slaves. These two types of trade were often both used on a single voyage, as a ship unable to fill its quota of slaves at a fort might travel along the coast looking for opportunities to buy additional slaves directly from native traders. Similarly, many voyages ultimately visited several regions in the course of collecting a cargo of slaves. It was common for the company to instruct captains to go first to Cape Coast and then to proceed elsewhere, often to Whydah, if the Gold Coast failed to provide a full cargo. In recognition of the greater responsibilities of the ship-trade, captains who purchased their own cargoes normally earned commissions of 4 slaves in 100 delivered alive in the West Indies, compared to 2 in 100 on those put on board by company factors.[63]

The economic rationale for maintaining Royal African Company settlements in West Africa was that factors who specialized in trading with the natives could hold supplies of slaves on hand and thereby expedite the departure of company ships for the West Indies. In fact the factories and forts probably imposed net costs rather than savings on the company; the company itself was convinced that this was the case. Yet the company could not abandon its forts because of political considerations. The forts were a principal justification for the legal privileges granted to the Royal African Company. Both the original royal monopoly of the African trade and later subsidies given to the company by Parliament were intended to compensate the company for maintaining its forts in order to sustain an English presence in West Africa and protect English political and economic interests in the region. K. G. Davies has argued that the company's forts probably did serve this purpose, for although their military strength was not great, the very existence of permanent English forts garrisoned with troops might have been sufficient to deter France or other European powers from attempting to dominate the region and exclude other nations from its trade. The balance of power that the company helped to preserve, however, also made it possible for small independent English slave traders to deal freely on the West African coast, thereby destroying the value of the Royal African Company's legal monopoly of English trade on that coast, and making the forts an economic liability to the company.[64]

The failure of the company to derive economic gains from its African forts and factories could also have been the result of the poor service given to the company by its employees in Africa, and of the inability of the company to monitor their performance effectively. Considerable care was called for on the part of factors in purchasing and holding slaves. Supplies of slaves held in reserve under poor conditions at company factories could quickly become costly losses owing to mortality if factors carelessly purchased slaves infected with contagious diseases, or were not quick to isolate slaves who exhibited symptoms. Similarly, poorly chosen slaves could result in the failure to recover freight charges when sent to the West Indies; company records contain many complaints from West Indian agents that the cargoes they received contained too many very young and very old slaves, and these complaints persisted over time in spite of reprimands sent from London to the factors in West Africa. In order to prevent the shipment of slaves who would not yield profits in the West Indies, ships' captains were sometimes required to sign declarations that the cargoes they received from factors were made up of slaves between stated minimum and maximum ages. Yet this check was not always effective, as for example on several occasions, when taken to task by angry agents in the West Indies for signing false declarations, the captains replied that "ye Agents upon ye [African] Coast foarst them to Signe to it."[65]

Factors employed by the company in West Africa appear commonly to have violated its regulations in a number of ways. Many carried on trade privately with the natives, to the detriment of company trade. Even more treacherously, many factors sold slaves to the independent slave traders, or interlopers, who violated the company's legal monopoly prior to 1698. The factors thereby directly helped the company's competitors to undercut its profits by affording them the economic benefits of convenient supplies of slaves that resulted from the company's expenditures to maintain its forts. In 1680 the company's agents in Barbados reported that "Some of the Masters of the Companys Shipps tell us, Some of the factors on the Coast [of West Africa] keep the best of the Negroes to sell to the Interlopers," and they added piously: "which if true, wee know not what to expect, If the company be betrayed by such as they trust there."[66]

The accounts kept at the African factories were poor, not only because of the dishonesty of the factors, but also because of their incompetence. The Royal African Company recognized that the accounts were unreliable, but was frustrated by its inability to require them to be kept more accurately. The company attempted to prevent abuses by requiring its employees in Africa to post substantial bonds for their good behavior and performance, but the company does not appear to have recovered any significant damages from this source, perhaps because conclusive proof of misconduct was so difficult to obtain.[67] K. G. Davies has convincingly attributed the low standards of performance of company employees in West Africa to a combination of the extraordinarily unpleasant and dangerous conditions faced by Englishmen in the region in the seventeenth century and the failure of the company to provide adequate economic incentives for them.[68] The latter can in turn probably be attributed in large part to the difficulty of determining whether an employee had performed well or not, for although the company was well aware of the monitoring problem its efforts to solve it were ineffective.

The slaving ship would leave Africa when it had loaded its intended complement of slaves. If this had not been done by the end of the period specified in the charterparty, the company would have to pay demurrage charges to prolong the ship's stay. The time elapsed between a ship's first arrival and final departure from Africa could vary enormously, for whereas one ship might obtain a full cargo from the stock of slaves held at a single factory, another might have to make many stops to obtain a cargo, or wait at a location in the hope of attracting fresh supplies. An African stay of four months was usually considered necessary to obtain a cargo of slaves; among 36 voyages made on behalf of the Royal African Company during 1719–25, the shortest stay in Africa was 33 days, the longest was 9.5 months, and the median stay was just under 3.5 months.[69] The company's correspondence with its factors in Africa suggests that the availability of slaves on the coast was unpredictable, and fluctuated sharply over short periods. Evidence on the company's slaving voyages of the early 1720s is consistent with this, for not only did many ships have to leave Africa without their full intended complements of slaves – 14 of the 32 for which this information is available sailed from Africa with less than 90 percent of their intended cargoes – but they did so in spite of having waited substantial periods on the coast. A strong negative relationship appears across ships between the proportion of a ship's intended cargo it had succeeded in loading upon departure and the duration of its stay on the coast; that this was the result of an erratic and fluctuating supply is suggested by the absence of any statistically significant relationship between the size of a ship and the length of its stay in Africa. What these results appear to imply is that ships that arrived at times when slave supplies were abundant were able to load full cargoes and leave Africa quickly, regardless of their size, whereas ships that arrived at times of scarcity could expect long waits on the coast, even if they were small.[70]

The Royal African Company's organizational problems were not restricted to Africa; other difficulties appeared after the slave cargoes had been loaded. Ships' captains were sometimes accused of taking the slaves consigned to them by factors and exchanging them elsewhere in Africa for equal numbers of less valuable slaves, keeping the profit for themselves at the expense of company revenues in the West Indies. Factors who suspected particular captains to be dishonest might mark or brand the slaves they gave to the captains in order to prevent this, but since this procedure was not routine, the factors apparently had to be prepared for considerable acrimony, and even resistance, in their dealings with these captains.[71] Captains were also sometimes believed to have concealed some slaves upon arrival in the West Indies, reporting them to have died in transit, in order to sell them on their own account. One measure taken to prevent this was to require a ship's surgeon to certify all slave deaths that occurred in passage, but it cannot be determined how frequently the Royal African Company did this.[72]

The voyage from Africa to the West Indies normally lasted between six weeks and three months.[73] When a ship arrived in the colony designated by its charterparty, the resident Royal African Company agents would come on board to inspect its slaves. They determined which were healthy enough to "go over the side" (i.e., to be taken ashore) and consequently for which freight charges were to be paid, and they immediately turned over an appropriate number of the slaves to the captain in partial payment of the freight charges and of his commission. The company's agents would not take delivery of very unhealthy slaves, who would be left on the ship until they had died or recovered, at which time a further accounting of freight charges would be made. Once delivery of a cargo had been taken by the agents, they might take the slaves ashore for sale; alternatively, sales were sometimes held on board ship.

The agents were responsible for selling the slaves. When the sale of a cargo of slaves was completed, the agents would send a full accounting of the sale to the company in London. Because virtually all sales were negotiated for future payment, the accounts indicated which planters owed money to the company, and in each case how much. The agents were furthermore responsible for collecting these debts at the agreed future dates, and for transmitting the proceeds to London. Payment might be in the form of bills of exchange, but was more commonly made in sugar. In the latter case the agents would hire ships to transport the sugar to England, and negotiate the freight costs.[74] Only when the proceeds of the slave sales were sent to London did the agents receive their payment, in the form of a commission equal to a fixed percentage of the amounts transmitted, normally within a range of 7 to 10 percent of the total.[75]

The difficulties the Royal African Company faced in monitoring the performance of their West Indian agents provided considerable opportunities for economic abuse. Agents were sometimes accused of recording lower prices in the accounts they sent to London than they actually received for slave sales, and then pocketing the difference. The company frequently quarreled with its agents over questions arising from tangles in their bookkeeping. Yet again the company was frustrated by the difficulty of measuring the true quality of the agents' work, for skillful cheating was unlikely to be detected, and discrepancies in accounts were common under the best of circumstances in the seventeenth century. The division of West Indian agencies between two individuals, and occasionally among three, appears to have been an attempt by the company to make abuses more difficult by providing some local monitoring of the agents' performance.

The company might also have hoped that this division of the agency would provide some competitive stimulus for the agents to be more energetic in attacking the problem that ultimately ruined the company. This was the job of forcing purchasers of slaves to make the payments that would reduce the enormous floating debt that grew steadily over time, effectively making the Royal African Company the banker of the English West Indies, much against its will. Collecting planters' debts was of course expected to be difficult in societies whose legal systems were in great part designed and controlled by planters who were themselves debtors. As early as 1664 Thomas Modyford, then the Barbados agent of the Company of Royal Adventurers and soon to become governor of Jamaica, explained that the existing laws of Barbados made debt collection by the company there nearly impossible. Furthermore, he noted that in spite of the willingness of the governor of Barbados to change the legal procedures in favor of the company, no such change was likely, for this would require the consent of the colony's council, and in Modyford's words "ye old planters in ye councill, carry it in favour of their brethren."[76] Surviving Royal African Company correspondence contains abundant evidence of the company's repeated attempts to use both moral and economic incentives to motivate their agents in the West Indies to put more effort into debt collection, but the collection problem was never adequately solved.[77] Whether this was caused in significant part by a lack of diligence by the agents, or resulted almost exclusively from the formidable nature of their task, the company never knew, nor do we today.

2

Shipping and mortality

This chapter considers some basic quantitative characteristics of the Middle Passage from evidence generated in the course of the Royal African Company's trading between 1673 and 1725. The evidence presented here, on the sizes of slave cargoes and the ships that carried them, the seasonality of the trade, and the correlates of mortality on the slaving voyages, will perform two general functions, both of which will serve as a prelude to the chapters that follow. One is to provide a quantitative picture of what constituted typical patterns and outcomes in the slave trade of the late seventeenth and early eighteenth centuries. The other, which emerges from an investigation of the factors that gave rise to these patterns and outcomes, is to give an indication of the extent to which the early transatlantic slave trade was a business that responded in systematic and rational fashion to a variety of underlying forces.

The size of slave cargoes

Some summary information on the size of slave cargoes shipped by the Royal African Company is presented in Table 2.1, which shows the mean number of slaves delivered per shipload. Over the entire period of the company's trading, the mean size of cargoes delivered by ships in the sample analyzed here was 231 slaves. The decennial breakdowns do not reveal any significant secular trends in this mean cargo size.[1]

The typical size of the company's slave cargoes varied according to their destination. Whereas the mean cargo of 235 slaves delivered to Barbados did not differ greatly from the mean number of 270 delivered to Jamaica, the mean size of cargoes delivered to the Leeward Islands, of 163 slaves, was considerably smaller.[2] One possible reason for this difference is that some cargoes bound for the Leewards could have been divided prior to sale, so that the slaves from a single shipload might have been sold in more than one of the islands. Such cases could not be identified in the invoices analyzed here if some slaves had been taken from their original ship of passage and transferred to another ship to be carried between the islands. A related possible cause of

2. Shipping and mortality

Table 2.1. *Mean sizes of Royal African Company slave cargoes, by decade*

Decade	Mean slaves per cargo	Standard deviation	Number of cargoes
1670s	232	112	72
1680s	217	122	121
1690s	296	148	39
1700s	222	136	75
1710s	187	74	7
1720s	227	124	18
All	231	128	332

Source: Public Record Office, Treasury 70/936–59.

the smaller shipments delivered to the Leewards, which will be discussed later in this chapter, is that some ships bound for those islands appear to have sold portions of their cargoes in Barbados before sailing on to the Leewards. Although available evidence does not make it possible to determine how common this practice was, it could have contributed to the result observed here. A different cause of the smaller cargoes of slaves delivered to the Leewards is suggested by an instruction sent by the Royal African Company to one of its factors in West Africa in 1700:

so often as you have any Small Ships of ours return to you from the Islands, and that they have no particular direccons where to go with their Negroes, in such case give them quick dispatches for the Leewd. Islands sometimes to Antego & at others to Montserrat & Nevis to our ffactors there.[3]

Although no explanation is offered by the company, the use of smaller ships could have been a reasonable response to the relatively small size of the markets of the individual islands of the Leewards in comparison to those of Barbados and Jamaica. It is not known how long orders like this one were in effect or how great an impact they had, but this policy could have contributed to the smaller mean cargoes delivered to the Leewards.[4]

An important influence on the size of slave cargoes in this era was the periodic outbreak of war between England and France. In wartime French privateers posed a threat to company ships everywhere, beginning with their departure from England and continuing throughout their voyages to Africa and on to the West Indies. From his study of the company's shipping, K. G. Davies concluded that the effect of war on the Royal African Company's trade was not simply to increase the use of larger, heavily armed ships. He argued rather that the most significant effect of war was to reduce the number of medium-sized ships, those too large to escape the attention of hostile ships but

Table 2.2. *Mean sizes of Royal African Company slave cargoes in periods of peace and war*

Period	Status	Mean slaves per cargo	Standard deviation	Number of cargoes
1673–88	Peace	221	119	183
1689–97	King William's War	290	145	42
1698–1701	Peace	233	109	24
1702–13	Queen Anne's War	222	143	61
1714–25	Peace	217	116	22
All		231	128	332

Source: PRO T70/936–59.

not large enough to mount heavy armaments, whereas smaller ships, which were less conspicuous, continued in use by the company during war as in peace.[5]

Davies's analysis implies that the mean size of slave cargoes might have either increased or decreased during war, depending on the relative numbers of large and small ships in use. Yet it would also imply unambiguously that in wartime the dispersion of cargo sizes should have been greater than in times of peace.[6] Table 2.2 confirms this implication. Whereas the mean size of Royal African Company slave cargoes was larger during King William's War (1689–97) than during the preceding and following periods of peace, and Queen Anne's War (1702–13) produced mean cargo sizes little different from peacetime levels, the standard deviation of cargo sizes rose sharply during both these periods of war and fell again as sharply at their conclusions.

The Royal African Company's invoices of slave sales that are the principal source of quantitative evidence for this book do not contain information on the sizes of the ships employed in the transatlantic trade. Some separate registers of the company's shipping, however, do provide information on the tonnage of slaving ships used by the company.[7] The distribution of the tonnage of ships used during 1720–5, obtained from one of these registers, is presented in Table 2.3, together with similar distributions for company ships for two earlier periods, tabulated by K. G. Davies from several volumes of correspondence. The mean size of ships used in 1720–5, of 179 tons, was similar to that found by Davies for 1691–1713, of 186 tons, and was about 20 percent greater than the mean of 147 tons obtained by Davies for 1680–8. A distinct change in the distribution of ships' sizes appears between the two earlier periods and the later one, however. Half the ships used by the company during 1720–5 were between 100 and 200 tons, as were 48 percent of those used in 1680–8 and 41 percent in 1691–1713. Nearly one-third, however, of the ships used in the 1720s (0.32) were between 200 and 300 tons, compared

2. Shipping and mortality

Table 2.3. *Tonnage of ships dispatched by the Royal African Company*

Tonnage	1680–8		1691–1713		1720–5	
	n	%	*n*	%	*n*	%
Under 50	11	4.4	9	4.9	0	0
50–99	58	23.3	28	15.2	4	10.5
100–49	85	34.1	60	32.6	8	21.1
150–99	34	13.7	16	8.7	11	28.9
200–49	31	12.4	17	9.2	8	21.1
250–99	11	4.4	12	6.5	4	10.5
300–49	6	2.4	22	12.0	3	7.9
350–99	3	1.2	8	4.3	0	0
400 and over	10	4.0	12	6.5	0	0
Total	249	99.9	184	99.9	38	100.0

Sources: 1680–8 and 1691–1713: K. G. Davies, *The Royal African Company* (London: Longmans, 1957), p. 192. 1720–5: PRO T70/1225.

with only about one-sixth of those in each of the earlier periods (0.17 and 0.16, respectively). The earlier periods had larger shares of very small ships (0.28 and 0.20 under 100 tons, respectively) than did the 1720s (0.11), and very large ships were also used more frequently in the earlier periods (0.08 and 0.23, respectively, of 300 tons and over, including 0.04 and 0.07 of 400 tons and over) than during the 1720s (0.08 of 300 tons and over, and none over 400 tons). Therefore, although the central tendency of the distribution of ships' sizes does not appear to have changed greatly during the course of the Royal African Company's trading, there was a tendency for the ships the company used to become increasingly concentrated over time in the middle range of sizes, between 150 and 250 or 300 tons.[8] With respect to size, the company's shipping was typical of the English trade to the West Indies in this period. Ralph Davis found that between the mid seventeenth and mid eighteenth centuries, the typical London ship sent to the West Indies was of 150–200 tons.[9]

Combining the evidence on ships' tonnage from the period 1720–5 with information on the sizes of their slave cargoes loaded in Africa yields a mean ratio across ships of 1.66 slaves per ton.[10] This figure was somewhat lower than the company desired it to be: A separate entry in the shipping register for 1720–5 indicates the number of slaves each ship was intended to carry on its voyage. Although the number loaded was occasionally slightly higher than that stated as intended, many ships were unable to obtain a full complement of slaves, and their actual cargoes upon departure fell short of the desired number: 14 of 32 ships left Africa with less than 90 percent of their desired cargoes, and 6 of these carried less than 80 percent of their intended complements.[11] The mean across ships of the ratio of intended slaves to the ship's tonnage was 1.87 slaves per ton. A negative though relatively low correlation of −0.275 appears in the sample from 1720–5 between ship size and the number of slaves loaded per ton, indicating that larger ships tended to carry fewer slaves per ton.[12]

The seasonality of the slave trade

Tables 2.4 and 2.5 present an overview of the seasonality of the Royal African Company's slaving voyages to the West Indies during 1673–1725. Table 2.4 shows the monthly distributions of the total numbers of cargoes delivered to Barbados, the Leeward Islands, and Jamaica during the period, and Table 2.5 presents the monthly distributions of the total numbers of slaves delivered to each of these destinations.

The dates used for these tabulations are those entered on the accounts of the sales of slave cargoes in the Royal African Company's invoice accounts. They appear to represent the date on which the account of the sale was completed by the agents, to be sent off to the company offices in London. The accounts of cargoes were not sent off until the agents had a complete record of the disposition of all slaves delivered to them in the shipment, and they were normally dispatched promptly once this accounting could be done; the dates tabulated here therefore indicate the closing dates of sales. Although the length of sales is not known in most cases, the typical time elapsed between the initial sales from a cargo and the final sales might have been between one and three weeks. The company's sale of a cargo furthermore typically did not begin until three or four days after the arrival of a ship in port. The tabulations are consequently based on dates an average of about two to four weeks after the actual dates of arrival of the slave cargoes in port.[13]

Both Tables 2.4 and 2.5 indicate the existence of a marked, though not extreme, seasonality in the delivery of slaves to to the West Indies. The figures on shiploads delivered to all destinations show that a relatively large number of shipments arrived in late winter, spring, and early summer, with a peak in May and June. The number of cargoes arriving was relatively low from August through the fall and early winter.

The monthly distribution of total slaves delivered naturally follows the same basic pattern as that of cargoes. An additional tendency for cargo sizes to vary positively with the level of shipping activity produced a slightly greater variation in total slaves delivered than in cargoes arriving from season to season. July had the largest mean cargo sizes of any month, and the three months from May through July together accounted for nearly one-third of total slave deliveries (32.1 percent), whereas August through September, three of the lowest months in average cargo size, accounted for less than one-fifth (19.5 percent) of the total deliveries.

33

Table 2.4. *Monthly distributions of cargoes delivered to Barbados, Leeward Islands, and Jamaica, 1673–1725*

Month	Barbados		Leeward Islands		Jamaica		All	
	n	%	n	%	n	%	n	%
January	11	8.5	3	3.6	8	6.7	22	6.6
February	8	6.2	6	7.2	17	14.3	31	9.4
March	14	10.9	6	7.2	7	5.9	27	8.2
April	16	12.4	8	9.6	5	4.2	29	8.8
May	11	8.5	12	14.5	12	10.1	35	10.6
June	12	9.3	11	13.3	12	10.1	35	10.6
July	7	5.4	7	8.4	15	12.6	29	8.8
August	8	6.2	5	6.0	9	7.6	22	6.6
September	10	7.8	9	10.8	8	6.7	27	8.2
October	9	7.0	4	4.8	13	10.9	26	7.9
November	9	7.0	6	7.2	7	5.9	22	6.6
December	14	10.9	6	7.2	6	5.0	26	7.9
Total	129	100.1	83	99.8	119	100.0	331	100.2

Source: PRO T70/936–59.

Table 2.5. *Monthly distributions of slaves delivered to Barbados, Leeward Islands, and Jamaica, 1673–1725*

Month	Barbados		Leeward Islands		Jamaica		All	
	n	%	n	%	n	%	n	%
January	2,951	9.7	306	2.3	2,296	7.2	5,553	7.3
February	2,142	7.1	1,384	10.2	3,478	10.8	7,004	9.2
March	3,325	11.0	973	7.2	1,704	5.3	6,002	7.9
April	4,062	13.4	1,311	9.7	906	2.8	6,279	8.3
May	2,115	7.0	2,722	20.1	3,700	11.5	8,537	11.2
June	2,496	8.2	991	7.3	3,808	11.9	7,295	9.6
July	2,286	7.5	1,263	9.3	5,004	15.6	8,553	11.3
August	1,816	6.0	518	3.8	2,233	7.0	4,567	6.0
September	1,444	4.8	1,132	8.4	2,110	6.6	4,686	6.2
October	1,783	5.9	671	5.0	3,081	9.6	5,535	7.3
November	2,292	7.6	802	5.9	2,509	7.8	5,603	7.4
December	3,594	11.9	1,454	10.7	1,282	4.0	6,330	8.3
Total	30,306	100.1	13,527	99.9	32,111	100.1	75,944	100.0

Source: PRO T70/936–59.

This observed seasonality of the arrival of slave cargoes in the West Indies is consistent with influences on the trade in both Africa and the Caribbean. There is some evidence that slave traders attempted to avoid picking up slaves during the West African rainy season. During this period, which normally ran from June through August, disease levels were higher among the African population, and the mortality rates of slaves would consequently have tended to be higher during the passage to America.[14] With voyages lasting about two months from Africa to the West Indies, a reduction in shipping during the rainy season would have produced a decline in arrivals in the West Indies from August through October. Ships' captains also preferred not to arrive in the West Indies during these latter months in order to avoid the risk to their ships during hurricane season. The best time to arrive in the islands was generally considered to be February through May, when captains could hope to sell their slave cargoes and make a quick departure from the islands with a cargo of sugar from the season's harvest.[15] A Royal African Company agent in Barbados raised additional considerations involving conditions in the islands when he advised the company that "the best time for Negroes to arrive is between December & June, being a healthy time & affording plenty of provisions, and ye rest of ye Year being ye reverse."[16]

The same basic seasonal patterns apply to each of the three destinations shown in the tables, but the precise timing appears to differ among the destinations. The seasonal distribution of cargoes arriving in both Jamaica and the Leewards appears to have lagged several months behind that of Barbados. Although the distributions are somewhat erratic, and the differences do not appear to have been great, Table 2.4 indicates, for example, that the two consecutive months that together accounted for the greatest share of total cargoes delivered to Barbados were March and April. The analogous months for the Leewards were May and June, whereas for Jamaica they were June and July. When the full percentage distributions for cargoes delivered by months are compared in pairs across colonies, the strongest correlations between that for Barbados and the others appear when the Barbados distribution is compared with those of Jamaica and the Leewards after each of the latter two is lagged two months.[17]

Differences in the seasonality of the sugar harvest among the islands could have contributed to the observed differences in the seasonality of slave deliveries. Although slaves were normally sold for credit, and it was therefore not necessary for buyers to have sugar on hand to exchange for the slave cargoes, shipowners and captains preferred to have their ships arrive in the islands at times when cargoes of sugar could be obtained quickly for their return trips to England. That the sugar harvest began in January in Barbados and the Leewards, but not until March in parts of Jamaica, might explain in part why the peak season for slave deliveries in Jamaica was later than elsewhere in the English West Indies.[18]

2. Shipping and mortality

Other considerations also influenced the timing of slave deliveries. Barbados was the closest of the English islands to Africa, and normally the first reached by slavers on their transatlantic voyages. The relative distances to the three destinations could therefore have produced some difference in the timing of arrivals. Any effect from this source would normally have been minor, however, for the voyage from Barbados to the Leewards typically took less than a week, with Jamaica in turn less than a week's sail beyond.

The location of Barbados, however, made it a potentially attractive place for slave traders to stop even if their final destinations lay elsewhere in the English West Indies. Some captains bound for Jamaica or the Leewards would put into Barbados to replenish their supplies of food or medicine after a particularly long or arduous voyage. They might then delay some time in port in an attempt to allow the slaves to recover their health before again setting sail. In other cases, regardless of the difficulty of the transatlantic crossing, some captains stopped in Barbados in order to sell portions of their slave cargoes before proceeding to Jamaica or the Leewards. This procedure had the advantage that the captain could try the market in Barbados, and sell some of his slaves if the planters' bids were to his taste, or alternatively continue on to the more distant markets if the bids were not high.[19] In 1708 the Royal African Company's agents in Barbados specifically urged the company to instruct its captains routinely to follow this practice of stopping to make their initial sales in that island, as a company memorandum noted that the agents

Think that it would be in ye Company's Interest to order their ships bound to Jamaica or Leeward Islands to touch at Barbadoes in their way thither & make tryall of ye Markett, people being fonder of buying ye first day than afterwards, the Ship need not stay there above four days.[20]

The implication that this advice was solely for the company's interest was of course a bit disingenuous. The self-seeking nature of the recommendation would have been immediately apparent to the company, for the agents in Barbados would receive commissions on any slaves sold in their colony. Furthermore, both the agents' comment that the ship need make only a brief stop of four days – three to allow the agents to publicize a sale throughout the island and allow planters to travel to the port of Bridgetown, and one day to conduct a sale – and their bland explanation that people were fonder of buying the first day than afterward were based on their knowledge that a cargo's most valuable slaves, which afforded the largest commissions, would sell quickly on the first day. After this the ship's departure for the Leewards or Jamaica would spare the agents the trouble of selling off the remaining, lower-priced slaves, who yielded them smaller commissions for typically more prolonged efforts.[21]

The frequency with which slaving ships stopped at Barbados, either to replenish supplies or to sell off some of their slaves, before proceeding to other destinations in the English West Indies cannot be determined. Some specific cases of ships that stopped in Barbados for each of these reasons can be found in a variety of scattered references, but no evidence is available with which to assess their typicality.[22] Complaints from planters in the Leewards about the quality of the slaves delivered to them by the Royal African Company clearly indicate that they believed that the partial sale of cargoes in Barbados was a common practice, so that they were left to buy only those slaves unwanted by purchasers in Barbados. These planters appear to have been consistently frustrated by the company's disregard of their requests that it send shipments to them directly from Africa.[23] The company's agents in the Leewards also complained about receiving slave cargoes by way of Barbados, for the commissions gained by the agents in Barbados from the sale of the best slaves there were of course lost by the agents in the Leewards.[24]

Although it is not possible to determine whether this was responsible for the differences observed in the seasonality of slave deliveries to the various colonies served by the Royal African Company, the practice of some captains of stopping in Barbados in the course of voyages intended to deliver cargoes to the Leewards Islands and Jamaica could certainly have contributed to the apparent lag in the seasonality of deliveries to the latter two destinations compared with that of Barbados. It should be emphasized, however, that this did not change the basic seasonality of the trade, which appears to have been produced primarily by factors that influenced the safety of shipping and the health of the valuable slave cargoes.

Mortality in the Middle Passage

Mortality has long been one of the most intensively studied aspects of the transatlantic slave trade. The horror of the Middle Passage was among the earliest themes of the abolitionists, who stressed the enormous loss of life that occurred on slave ships. Because of this, the measurement of mortality in the slave trade became one of the focal points of the British parliamentary debates of the late eighteenth century over the abolition of the trade, and since then it has remained a primary concern of research on the slave trade. An interest in determining the causes of the observed mortality experience has been closely linked to these efforts at measurement throughout their history, although the focus has shifted over time, from the emphasis of the abolitionists on the crowding of the slaves as the major cause to modern epidemiological explanations.

Studies of mortality in the transatlantic trade have generally focused on those deaths that occurred between the time of a ship's departure from the African coast and its arrival in an American port. The authors of these studies have recognized that this interval of transatlantic passage was only part of the longer period that is of interest, which began with the capture or enslavement

37

of members of an African population, their journey to the African coast, and their imprisonment there awaiting sale to a European trader, then continued during their transatlantic voyage and arrival in America, and concluded with their sale, journey to the farm or plantation of a purchaser, and their adjustment to a new environment.[25] Yet the difficulty of obtaining information on the demographic experiences of slaves during this longer period has generally forced investigators to restrict their studies to parts of this voyage taken separately, and in spite of this some basic quantitative facts about parts of the journey have remained elusive. Even the study of slave mortality during the transatlantic crossing has been severely hampered by a scarcity of reliable and detailed quantitative evidence, although this may be the portion of the longer journey that received the most attention from contemporaries, and that has since been most intensively studied by historians.

There are few collections of evidence on significant numbers of slaving voyages that contain information on both the passage times of the ships and the numbers of deaths they suffered in transit.[26] This treatment will utilize one such collection, drawn from Royal African Company records, that has not previously been systematically analyzed. The evidence is contained in a volume that provides summary records of all voyages made on behalf of the company from 1719 through 1733.[27] Many of the voyages recorded in the book did not involve the transport of slaves, for during these years the company's trade became increasingly concentrated in shuttle shipments of goods between England and the West African coast. The volume does contain summaries, however, of a total of 38 transatlantic slaving voyages that were made on the company's account between 1720 and 1725. Information on some significant aspects of these voyages is given in Appendix B. Although the sample is small, it is rich in detail in comparison with other data sets that have been used to study mortality in the slave trade. Information on some variables is missing in some cases, but for most of the voyages the register not only includes the dates of departure from an African port and arrival in the West Indies, and the number of slaves loaded and delivered, but also provides information on a number of other characteristics of both the ship and its voyage that have been considered of possible relevance to the determination of levels of mortality in the slave trade. The limited sample size imposes some constraints on the empirical analysis and necessitates caution in the interpretation of some results, but the detail of the information available on these voyages begins to make possible a genuinely multivariate approach to the analysis of the causes of mortality in the Middle Passage.

The sample analyzed here contains information on the mortality experience of the slaves carried on a total of 35 voyages.[28] These ships left Africa with a total of 10,331 slaves. Of these 1,342, or 13 percent, died before the ships arrived at their American destinations. This figure is substantially lower than the level of losses experienced by the Royal African Company three decades earlier; figures reported by the company to a parliamentary investigation indicated that 23.7 percent of the slaves shipped by the company during 1680–8 died in the passage to the West Indies.[29] The company's aggregate mortality experience during 1720–5 appears to have been typical of the transatlantic slave trade during most of the eighteenth century, however, as studies of the Danish, Dutch, and French trades in the period have found losses in the range of 12–17 percent of the slaves carried.[30] These rates of passage mortality for slaves appear to have been substantially higher than the mortality rates encountered by the participants in free migrations of comparable distance and duration in the eighteenth century; one recent investigation has estimated that 3.8 percent of a sample of Germans who migrated to Pennsylvania during the eighteenth century died in the course of the transatlantic voyage.[31]

The proportion of slaves who died in the Middle Passage varied considerably among individual voyages. Losses could be quite low; one of the ships in the sample considered here lost less than 1.5 percent of its slaves during the voyage, and six had losses of less than 5 percent of their initial cargoes. In stark contrast to these, one of the ships in the sample lost 26 percent of its slaves in its passage to Barbados, and seven suffered the loss of 20 percent or more of their initial cargoes. The mean proportion of slaves dead in passage for the 35 ships in the sample was 12 percent.[32]

The existence of significant variation in the mortality experiences of different voyages serves as the point of departure for an investigation of the causes of mortality in the Middle Passage. As mentioned earlier, the Royal African Company shipping register from which this information on mortality is drawn also contains information on a number of characteristics of the individual ships and the circumstances of their voyages. Many of these, such as the length of the voyage, the size of the ship, the number of slaves carried, the places the ship visited in Africa, and the season of the voyage, have been considered in other investigations as possible influences on passage mortality rates. The availability of information on these variables for particular voyages allows us to test for the existence of consistent relationships between each of them and the level of mortality on a voyage. The approach taken here will be to employ a ship's mortality rate for a specific voyage as the dependent variable, and to investigate the effects of a series of independent variables on it through the use of regression analysis. The estimation of multiple regression equations, in which mortality rates are taken to be a function of a number of other variables, can help to isolate the specific effect on mortality rates of each of a number of independent variables, by measuring the magnitude and statistical significance of the relationship between each of the independent variables and mortality rates.

The primary dependent variable that will be used in this analysis is the average daily mortality rate per thousand slaves experienced on a voyage.[33]

2. Shipping and mortality

Table 2.6. *Effect of voyage duration on mortality rates*

Independent variable	Estimated coefficient	Standard error	Significance level
Intercept	2.518	0.597	0.0002
Duration of voyage (days)	−0.0076	0.0083	0.37
$R^2 = 0.026$, $F = 0.826$, $n = 33$			

Note: The dependent variable is average daily mortality rate per thousand slaves per voyages.
Source: Data are drawn from PRO T70/1225. See text and Appendix B.

Although other variants of the mortality rate could be used, perhaps most obviously the simple percentage of a ship's cargo lost in passage, use of the average daily mortality rate appears preferable for several reasons. Chief among these is that many of the independent variables to be considered seem likely to have affected the rate at which slaves died in passage, rather than simply the total proportion that died on a voyage, and consequently their total impact on mortality would be expected to have depended on the duration of a voyage. Although allowance could be made for this in analyzing the simple percentage lost, the required procedure would be relatively cumbersome, and it is more convenient to use a dependent variable that is already a rate standardized for time.[34] The mean value across ships of the average daily mortality rate was 0.002009, or an average of just over two deaths per day per thousand slaves.

The results shown in Table 2.6 are for a regression equation in which the average daily mortality rate per thousand slaves for a voyage is expressed as a function of the length of the voyage. The estimated coefficient of voyage length is small in absolute value and statistically insignificant at conventional levels. This suggests that the length of a ship's voyage had no effect on the average daily mortality rate experienced by the slaves on the ship.[35] It might be emphasized that this does not imply that the total number of deaths that occurred on longer voyages was not normally higher than on shorter voyages; indeed it implies the contrary. What it indicates is that the average rate at which slaves died per day, or per month, was no higher on long voyages than on shorter ones.[36]

This result is perhaps less surprising than it might initially appear. A number of authors have suggested that the rate at which slaves died on the transatlantic voyage might be expected to increase on very long voyages. Thus it was suggested that as the length of a voyage increased past some point, the provisions on the ship might run out or begin to spoil, and mortality rates would increase, whether owing directly to starvation or to lowered resistance to disease as a result of poor nutrition.[37] Some statistical support

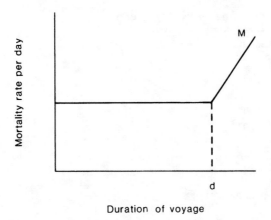

Figure 2.1. Relationship between slave mortality and duration of voyage.

has been provided for the proposition that average daily mortality rates were higher on very long slaving voyages than on shorter ones.[38] It should be noted, however, that this effect has no obvious implications for mortality rates on voyages of less than the length at which provisions become scarce. It might be suggested a priori that there are reasonable grounds for believing that the normal relationship between mortality rates and voyage duration would be of the shape shown schematically in Figure 2.1.

The figure shows an initial period in which the daily mortality rate M on a voyage is independent of the voyage's length, followed by a subsequent period in which daily mortality rates rise with further increases in voyage length. The transition between the portions of the relationship occurs at a duration d equal to the maximum length of the voyage expected by slave shippers. The logic of this is simple. A ship's captain could provision his ship with knowledge of the number of slaves he would carry from Africa, but with uncertainty about the length of his voyage. From both his own experience and the advice of other traders, however, he would have some expectations about the probable length of the voyage he faced on a particular route. On the basis of these expectations, he would determine the maximum duration he anticipated for his voyage, and provision his ship accordingly, in order to have sufficient food and other provisions for his slave cargo for a voyage of that length. Beyond this maximum anticipated duration – which could vary from one captain to another – shortages of provisions would begin to cause higher mortality rates, as noted earlier.[39] For journeys shorter than d, however, food supplies would be adequate, and there are no obvious grounds for predicting either a positive or a negative relationship between daily mortality rates and time.[40] The finding here of independence between average daily mortality rates and voyage duration in the slave trade might therefore simply imply that

2. Shipping and mortality

Table 2.7. *Effect of crowding on mortality rates*

Independent variable	Estimated coefficient	Standard error	Significance level
Intercept	3.195	1.026	0.004
Duration of voyage (days)	−0.0051	0.0089	0.57
Slaves per ton	−0.507	0.623	0.42
$R^2 = 0.047$, $F = 0.740$, $n = 33$			

Note: The dependent variable is average daily mortality rate per thousand slaves per voyage.
Source: Data are drawn from PRO T70/1225. See text and Appendix B.

captains who carried slaves for the Royal African Company were normally sufficiently well informed and careful in anticipating the lengths of their voyages to avoid running short of provisions; that is, that most voyages would fall on the segment of the mortality schedule of Figure 2.1 to the left of *d,* and that as a result average daily mortality rates did not vary with the length of a voyage.

One of the earliest issues to be raised in relation to mortality on the Middle Passage was that of the crowding of the slaves. This was a principal concern of early British parliamentary hearings on the slave trade, and British legislation of 1788 aimed at regulating the trade's operation set limits on the maximum numbers of slaves that could be carried on ships of different sizes. Recent studies have found that within the ranges observed in practice, differences in the degree of "tight-packing" of the slaves were apparently not related to variations in mortality.[41] This same result appears in the data analyzed here. Table 2.7 shows that when the ratio of slaves carried to the ship's recorded tonnage is added as an independent variable while controlling the duration of the voyage, the number of slaves per ton has no statistically significant effect on ships' average daily mortality rates.[42] This result has been regarded as a reasonable one by recent investigators, for slave traders could control the degree of crowding on their ships, and would not wish to crowd the slaves to an extent that would raise mortality rates, thereby resulting in the loss of their investments in the slaves.[43] The result therefore again appears consistent with rational behavior, in the form of careful planning of slaving voyages, on the part of slave traders.

The Royal African Company was well aware of the dangers of overcrowding in raising mortality among their slave cargoes, and was at pains to prevent the practice. In particular, the company was concerned to head off attempts by its ships' captains and West Indian agents to register ships for more slaves than they could safely carry. The captains and agents, who were paid commis-

42

sions on the slaves they delivered and sold in the West Indies, respectively, wished to obtain large cargoes, and were less worried about gambling with the safety of the slaves than was the company, which paid for the slaves loaded in Africa and therefore bore the cost of any deaths that occurred in transit. The company enlisted the aid of its factors in West Africa to override the requests of ships' captains and West Indian agents in order to prevent overcrowding on its ships. In one instance the company wrote to an agent in Africa to advise him in loading a ship:

Wee judge this ship will conveniently take in 500 Negroes, she had more last Voyage, but wee fear the crouding too many into her might be the Occasion of a greater Mortality, which wee would study all wayes possible to prevent.[44]

On a number of occasions Sir Dalby Thomas, the company's agent-general at Cape Coast Castle, advised the company on the sizes of slave cargoes ships could carry without causing "a great mortality," and in 1708 the company used Thomas's advice as the basis for a reproach to its agent in Antigua for sending a ship to Africa with orders to carry too large a cargo:

We take notice you are fitting out the sloope Flying Flame for the coast for 140 negroes, Sir Dalby affirmes you are very much in the wrong to crowd your sloopes so very full of negroes – this very sloope you designed last time should take in 150, Sir Dalby put aboard but 120 which was as many as she was fit to take in and she lost but six.

The company furthermore recalled an earlier case in which the agent had sent the *Mary* to carry 200 slaves, noting that the latter "is not so big as our ship the Dorothy which was at the same time on the coast and the captain would not take in more than 140 slaves."[45] In a general attempt to prevent over-crowding of its ships, in 1712 the company instructed its factors at Cape Coast Castle to furnish the ships with slave cargoes and dispatch them quickly,

though not with their full complement of negroes if upon a survey you find the ship is appointed to take in more negroes than she can conveniently stow. Pray lade no more then are necessary to prevent mortality which has often happen'd by crowding the ship with too many negroes.[46]

Perhaps as a result of disputes between captains and factors over the proper sizes of slave cargoes, by 1713 the company had apparently supplied guide-lines to its employees concerning the minimum space to be allowed per slave in determining the number of slaves a ship could carry. In that year an agent in Antigua complained that the company's factors in West Africa had sent a ship with a cargo of only 110 slaves, even though according to "the Dimensions given by your Honours," which were to allow each slave "five foot in length, Eleven Inches in Breadth, and twenty three Inches in height," the ship could carry more than 160.[47]

What may appear to be a surprising result appears in equation 1 of Table

2. Shipping and mortality

Table 2.8. *Effect of ship, cargo, and crew size on mortality rates*

Equation	Independent variable	Estimated coefficient	Standard error	Significance level
1	Intercept	0.834	0.768	0.29
	Duration of voyage (days)	−0.0053	0.0074	0.48
	Ship tonnage	0.0085	0.0028	0.005
	$R^2 = 0.254, F = 5.113, n = 33$			
2	Intercept	0.832	0.783	0.30
	Duration of voyage (days)	−0.0052	0.0079	0.52
	Ship tonnage	0.0087	0.0051	0.10
	No. of slaves	−0.00017	0.0030	0.96
	$R^2 = 0.254, F = 3.296, n = 33$			
3	Intercept	0.660	0.801	0.42
	Duration of voyage (days)	−0.0074	0.0074	0.32
	Size of crew	0.064	0.021	0.004
	$R^2 = 0.261, F = 5.286, n = 33$			

Note: The dependent variable is average daily mortality rate per thousand slaves per voyage.
Source: Data are drawn from PRO T70/1225. See text and Appendix B.

2.8. Again controlling voyage duration, the tonnage of a ship is found to have a positive and statistically significant effect on mortality rates. The estimated effect is considerable in magnitude, for it implies that a ship 100 tons larger than another would have had an average daily mortality rate 0.85 deaths higher per thousand slaves carried, an amount equivalent to more than 40 percent of the sample mean daily mortality rate. Equation 2 of Table 2.8 furthermore shows that this effect of ship size on mortality persists when the number of slaves carried is added as an independent variable, whereas the latter variable has no significant effect on mortality rates when tonnage is held constant.[48]

This positive relationship between ship size and mortality rates has not been a general finding of other studies.[49] The possibility must be kept in mind that in a sample as small as the one analyzed here, a few ships with unusual experiences can potentially produce results that would not persist in a larger sample, and evidence on the relationship from other sources on mortality in the slave trade should be examined before this is accepted as characteristic of the Middle Passage. Yet it does raise the possibility that some difference in conditions or practices on larger ships might have raised the mortality rates of slave cargoes. It is possible, for example, that higher mortality rates among slaves on large ships could have resulted from a greater incidence of epidemic outbreaks of serious diseases. To some extent this could have been caused by the presence on a ship of communicable diseases brought from Europe to which the Africans had not previously been exposed, and to which they consequently had no acquired immunities.[50] The probability of having such a disease on board would be expected to increase with the number of Europeans on the ship, and therefore with the size of the ship's crew. In equation 3 of Table 2.8, the size of a ship's crew is included as an independent variable, together with voyage duration. Its coefficient indicates a positive and statistically significant impact on mortality rates, with a magnitude closely comparable to that estimated for ship tonnage in equation 1.[51] This result is consistent with the possibility that the presence of larger crews was the mechanism tending to raise mortality rates on larger ships. Another related possibility is that the higher slave mortality rates on larger ships resulted from a greater incidence of epidemic outbreaks of communicable diseases that were endemic among African populations.[52] The crowded conditions and poor sanitation of the ships encouraged the spread of disease, as did the frequent mixing of Africans from normally separate disease environments. The probability of bringing a slave on board who carried a potentially dangerous disease would increase with the absolute number loaded. Because cargo size was highly correlated with ship tonnage, the probability of having an outbreak of such a disease would then be positively correlated with ship size. It should be noted that this interpretation is not necessarily inconsistent with the insignificant effect of cargo size on mortality rates shown by equation 2 in Table 2.8, for this latter result applies only within the relatively limited range of variation observed in the numbers of slaves carried after controlling ship tonnage; cargo size and ship tonnage varied together closely within the sample, making attempts to separate their effects on mortality for large variations in either of questionable validity.[53]

It might be thought that the positive observed association between ship size and mortality rates implies error or irrationality on the part of the Royal African Company, for it could be argued that the company should not have continued to use larger ships in view of their higher observed mortality rates. Yet this is not necessarily the case, for there could have been economies of scale involved in either the shipment or the sale of large slave cargoes sufficient to compensate traders for the greater loss of slaves in passage.[54]

A number of other variables have been discussed in studies of the Middle Passage as possible influences on slave mortality. The seasonality of voyages is considered in equation 1 of Table 2.9, by introducing seasons of departure from Africa as a series of dichotomous independent variables while controlling voyage duration. The results indicate that winter departures experienced daily mortality rates of more than one slave per day per thousand carried higher than did spring departures. Yet further investigation reveals that within the sample, ships that departed from Africa in winter were typically larger than those that left in other seasons; equation 2 of Table 2.9 shows that the

45

Table 2.9. *Effect of season of departure from Africa on mortality rates*

Equation	Independent variable	Estimated coefficient	Standard error	Significance level
1	Intercept	1.742	0.686	0.02
	Duration of			
	voyage (days)	−0.0040	0.0086	0.65
	Winter (Jan.–Mar.)	1.105	0.550	0.05
	Summer (July–Sept.)	0.874	0.608	0.16
	Fall (Oct.–Dec.)	0.280	0.553	0.62
	$R^2 = 0.172$, $F = 1.450$, $n = 33$			
2	Intercept	0.526	0.804	0.52
	Duration of			
	voyage (days)	−0.0043	0.0079	0.59
	Winter	0.749	0.527	0.17
	Summer	0.761	0.562	0.19
	Fall	0.379	0.511	0.46
	Ship tonnage	0.0074	0.0030	0.02
	$R^2 = 0.322$, $F = 2.565$, $n = 33$			

Note: The dependent variable is average daily mortality rate per thousand slaves per voyage. Spring (April–June) is the omitted category for the season variables.
Source: Data are drawn from PRO T70/1225. See text and Appendix B.

estimated impact of winter departure is reduced in magnitude, and becomes statistically insignificant, when ship tonnage is added as an independent variable. This result of course does not negate the finding that mortality rates on the Middle Passage varied seasonally within the sample analyzed. What it does suggest, however, is that mortality rates might have been higher in winter because larger ships were used then, perhaps because sailing conditions were worse.

The African place of origin of slaving voyages has also been mentioned as a potentially significant influence on passage mortality rates. Four specific places appear a sufficient number of times as places of origin in the sample analyzed here to allow statistical analysis.[55] Equation 1 of Table 2.10 indicates that voyages originating in Whydah had average daily mortality rates nearly 1.7 slaves per thousand higher than did those leaving from Cape Coast. Yet once again the difference appears to have resulted from a correlation within the sample between ship size and departure from Whydah, as the inclusion of tonnage as an independent variable in equation 2 of Table 2.10 reduces the magnitude of the effect on mortality of originating in Whydah, as well as reducing it to statistical insignificance. When both voyage duration and ship size are controlled, no significant differences appear across voyages owing to differences in place of origin.[56]

The lack of statistically significant effects of the seasonal and regional variables on passage mortality rates might result from the imprecision of

Table 2.10. *Effect of African place of origin on mortality rates*

Equation	Independent variable	Estimated coefficient	Standard error	Significance level
1	Intercept	1.397	0.668	0.05
	Duration of voyage (days)	−0.00042	0.0079	0.96
	Gambia	0.412	0.531	0.44
	Whydah	1.677	0.498	0.003
	Cabenda	0.729	0.564	0.21
	$R^2 = 0.335$, $F = 3.154$, $n = 30$			
2	Intercept	0.274	0.832	0.75
	Duration of voyage (days)	−0.000082	0.0074	0.99
	Gambia	0.351	0.500	0.49
	Whydah	0.804	0.632	0.22
	Cabenda	0.603	0.534	0.27
	Ship tonnage	0.0072	0.0035	0.05
	$R^2 = 0.435$, $F = 3.695$, $n = 30$			

Note: The dependent variable is average daily mortality rate per thousand slaves per voyage. Cape Coast is the omitted category for the place of origin variables.
Source: Data are drawn from PRO T70/1225. See text and Appendix B.

measurements made with the small numbers of observations available in the sample analyzed here. Yet a lack of significant effects from these variables may not be surprising, for the actions of slave traders might systematically have eliminated them. As noted earlier in this chapter, traders preferred not to purchase cargoes of slaves during the African rainy season because of the higher levels of disease among the West African population from June through August, and there was a decline in trading activity during these months. In addition, since traders were acutely aware of the danger posed by contagious diseases, to the extent that they did continue to make purchases in these months, they might have been more careful than at other times in selecting their cargoes and in provisioning their ships. This increased selectivity would of course be consistent with their lower observed levels of slave shipments. The forces leading them to this behavior would be strong, for if slave prices in Africa and the West Indies did not vary seasonally but passage mortality rates did, traders' profits would have been lower in the seasons of higher mortality.[57] The traders might therefore have been expected to continue shipping throughout the year only if, through relatively inexpensive means, they could successfully eliminate seasonal variations in passage mortality; otherwise they would have increased their rate of profit by simply not trading during part of the year. The statistical evidence presented here suggests that they may have been able to reduce or eliminate seasonal variation in passage mortality. Similar arguments apply to differences among African regions. Traders would have been expected to avoid regions with less healthy slaves, and consequently tendencies toward higher passage mortality, unless they could compensate for this, again perhaps by being particularly selective in their purchases. If they did continue to buy slaves from these regions, it might be because through their precautions they had been able to eliminate differences in passage mortality rates across places of origin of the slaves purchased.[58]

Several general points might be kept in mind concerning this quantitative analysis of mortality in the Middle Passage. One is that the frequently low proportion of the variance in mortality explained in the regressions presented here and the small number of statistically significant relationships result in part from the choice of the average daily mortality rate as the dependent variable. This should not be taken to imply that variations in mortality in the Atlantic slave trade were due only to random events, and that there were no systematic factors that affected the extent of mortality. That strong and consistent quantitative relationships existed can be seen by analyzing instead the total percentage of a ship's cargo lost in the course of a voyage. This was of course the mortality variable of primary interest to slave traders, for their profits and losses depended directly on the total numbers of slaves who died in transit. As shown in equation 1 of Table 2.11, the positive relation between the length of a voyage and mortality alone accounted for 14 percent of the variance of the percentage of slave cargoes lost in transit, and the proportion of the variance explained rises to 28–33 percent when the tonnage of the ship, the size of the crew, or the size of the slave cargo is added as an independent variable (equations 2–4, Table 2.11).

Another important point is that slave traders would often have had information unavailable to us that could have allowed them to exert considerable additional control over the mortality experienced on their ships. The skill and judgment of a captain could affect the length and rigor of a crossing, the choice of a crew and of a ship's surgeon could significantly affect the care and treatment given to the slaves during a voyage, and many other decisions taken both in preparation for the voyage and during its course could have an impact on the condition of the slaves and the mortality rates they experienced. Occasional glimpses of some of these mechanisms and their effects come to us from correspondence between the Royal African Company and its agents. In one instance in 1721, a ship hired by the company delivered its cargo to Barbados with the death of 15 (4 percent) of the 350 slaves it had taken from Africa. The company's agent in the colony reported approvingly: "I cannot perceive but that Capt. Mitchell has taken great care of the Negros in the Voyage by keeping his Ship clean, feeding them well, and diverting them with Musick, the Negroes being all in good order except 8 which are sickly."[59]

In a contrasting case, the company's factors at Cape Coast Castle wrote to alert the company about the behavior of the captain of another hired ship, the

Table 2.11. *Analysis of mortality per voyage*

Equation	Independent variable	Estimated coefficient	Standard error	Significance level
1	Intercept	0.0498	0.0330	0.14
	Duration of			
	voyage (days)	0.00104	0.00046	0.03
	$R^2 = 0.142$, $F = 5.125$, $n = 33$			
2	Intercept	−0.0397	0.0430	0.36
	Duration of			
	voyage (days)	0.00116	0.00042	0.009
	Ship tonnage	0.00045	0.00016	0.007
	$R^2 = 0.328$, $F = 7.322$, $n = 33$			
3	Intercept	−0.0481	0.0450	0.29
	Duration of			
	voyage (days)	0.00105	0.00041	0.02
	Size of crew	0.00336	0.00116	0.007
	$R^2 = 0.330$, $F = 7.371$, $n = 33$			
4	Intercept	−0.0110	0.0396	0.78
	Duration of			
	voyage (days)	0.00094	0.00043	0.04
	Number of slaves	0.00023	0.00009	0.02
	$R^2 = 0.283$, $F = 5.924$, $n = 33$			

Note: The dependent variable is the percentage of slaves dead in passage per voyage.
Source: Data are drawn from PRO T70/1225. See text and Appendix B.

Generous Jenny, in 1720. They complained that he had disregarded his sailing orders by delaying his departure from Africa without due cause, and charged that they suspected him of attempting to exchange slaves that had been furnished to him by the factors for inferior slaves provided by other traders for his own profit, after refusing to let the factors' messenger mark the slaves on his ship to guarantee that slaves of lower quality would not be substituted. The factors further observed that discipline on the ship was poor, as "Capt. Lamberth has no command over his Mates, & as little over the Sailors," and they predicted that in consequence the voyage would not do well for the company:

The absurdity of this behaviour is not to be so much admired at considering the little order & command that is to be observed among the Capt. & his Officers, with those before the mast, the ill management of which, we have too great reason to suspect, will be of ill consequence to the Voyage, & wish your honours may not feel the ill effects, in want of their care of the Slaves.[60]

The factors' gloomy forecast proved warranted, as in the event the *Generous Jenny* arrived in Maryland after a a voyage of 96 days, with the death of 42 (16.2 percent) of the 260 slaves it had taken from Cape Coast. Captain

2. Shipping and mortality

Lamberth wrote to the company blaming his large losses on an outbreak of smallpox, and the company's agent in the colony reported that the ship's long voyage, and consequent arrival late in the summer, had hurt the market for the slaves on board.[61] In contrast with the *Generous Jenny*'s experience, in the following year two company ships made the voyage from Africa to Virginia in the considerably shorter times of 77 and 50 days, with the smaller losses of 6.8 and 8.5 percent of their cargoes, respectively.

In 1706 Sir Dalby Thomas provided a forceful statement concerning the importance of employing high-quality captains and crews on company ships. Thomas argued that a captain with experience "shall have his negroes live and Do well, when the others that are unaquainted with the method of managing them shall have theirs sickly with great Mortallity." In Thomas's view the reasons for this were clear:

Notwithstanding all the care that can be taken both in Europe, Africa & America, if the Captns., Mates, Surgeons & Cooks are not honest Careful & Diligent & see that the Slaves have always their Victualls well Drest, well fed, well washt, Cleanly kept & kindly used ye Voyage will not be worth a farthing.

Thomas argued that with only one exception high mortality on slaving voyages could be traced to a single underlying cause: "When yor. ships have great Mortality unless occasioned by ye Small Pox, you may be assured its thro Carelessness of yor. Captns., Mates, Surgeons & Cooks usage who ought to answer to yor. Honors for it."[62]

Thomas was a knowledgeable observer of the transatlantic slave trade, and his emphasis on the importance of the experience and diligence of the captain and crew of a slaving vessel in avoiding high mortality among their cargoes deserves our attention, just as it received that of the company. His words undoubtedly found a receptive audience in London, for the company had earlier expressed similar views. In a letter to a factor written 20 years before, the company remarked on the poor health of a cargo of slaves delivered to the West Indies,

wch. Wee attribute very much to the Masters Negligence in Not looking well after them in their Passage for Wee find that those Masters that looke well after the Negroes bring them in Good Condition Though the Small Pox & Flux doe/happen among them whereas others that are not Carefull do loose the greatest part of the Negroes.[63]

Dalby Thomas's purpose in the comments quoted here was to spur the company to act on his advice to improve the quality of the captains and crews it hired, and to accomplish this end he might have exaggerated somewhat. It is likely that, as the company had argued in 1686, a good captain could minimize the mortality that resulted from an outbreak even of smallpox; care in preventing the contamination of food and in maintaining good sanitary conditions could also help prevent the spread of such contagious diseases as dysentery and yaws. It would appear unreasonable, however, to deny that chance played a significant role in determining mortality rates in the early transatlantic slave trade. Mortality rates among slave cargoes could rise sharply when stormy seas or the calm of the doldrums hindered a ship's progress, when smallpox or bacillary dysentery broke out during a voyage, or when a ship was harassed or captured by foreign privateers or pirates. Yet as in other branches of ocean trade in the same period, the influence of measurable variables acting in systematic ways can be discerned in the quantitative analysis of mortality in the slave trade, and the skill and experience of those involved in the trade enabled them to exploit some of these relationships, as well as others now beyond our ability to detect, in order to improve their economic fortunes.

The Atlantic slave trade was a major industry of the seventeenth and eighteenth centuries, and during the roughly five decades of its participation the Royal African Company was one of the largest enterprises involved in that trade. It should come as no surprise that the company's records reveal evidence of reasoned and systematic responses designed to minimize the economic costs of the risks and difficulties characteristic of the industry in which it was involved. Outbreak of war in the Atlantic caused the company to shift away from the use of medium-sized ships, toward both larger, more heavily armed craft able to defend themselves and smaller ships that could more easily evade enemies. The numbers of slave ships dispatched varied by season, as the company apparently attempted to avoid purchasing unhealthy slaves during the West African rainy season, and to avoid having its ships arrive in the West Indies during the hurricane season. Differences in the seasonality of arrivals among West Indian destinations furthermore suggest the use of strategies in marketing slave cargoes aimed at maximizing revenues; company ships bound for the Leeward Islands or more distant Jamaica might sometimes have stopped along their course in Barbados to try the market there before continuing on. The absence of a significant correlation between the length of a ship's voyage and the average daily mortality rate of its slaves might point to generally successful planning of slaving voyages, with ships' captains anticipating the time of their passage, and provisioning their ships accordingly. A lack of observed correlation between daily rates of passage mortality and such other variables as the ratio of slaves carried to ship size, the African place of origin of a voyage, and the season of travel after allowance for voyage duration and ship size might similarly point to the success of ships' captains and Royal African Company factors in acting so as systematically to counteract the tendencies of these variables to influence mortality in transit. An observed correlation between ship size and slave mortality might point to

51

2. Shipping and mortality

error on the part of company officials in using the larger ships that appear to have produced higher mortality rates among their slave cargoes, but alternatively it is possible that the higher costs from slave mortality on larger ships might have been offset, wholly or in part, by benefits in the form of scale economies in the shipment or sale of the larger slave cargoes.

3

Slave prices in the Barbados market, 1673–1723

The significance of slave prices

The overwhelming predominance of slaves in the labor force of the sugar islands of the West Indies in the late seventeenth and early eighteenth centuries makes information about levels and trends in slave prices of obvious importance for an understanding of the early economic history of this richest region of British America, and the role of the Royal African Company as the foremost supplier of slaves to the islands makes its records the best existing source of such information. This chapter provides annual estimates of slave prices in Barbados, the West Indies' largest market for slave imports during the early part of the period considered here, and the colony for which coverage of the company records is consequently best overall for the full span of decades covered. These prices can be used to illuminate a number of important issues in the economic history of the slave trade and of the growth of slavery elsewhere in colonial English America. Some of these issues will be explored in the latter sections of this chapter, and others will be treated in Chapters 4 and 5.

Estimation of slave prices

The major source of quantitative evidence used in this chapter is the homeward bound invoice account books of the Royal African Company.[1] Specifically, the estimation of slave prices is based on the records of all sales conducted by company factors in Barbados that are included in the surviving volumes of these accounts. The sample analyzed consists of the records of all slaves included in these volumes who were delivered alive and sold in Barbados.[2] The principal categories of slaves accounted for in the invoices that are not included in the analysis of prices are those described as having died on board ship or on shore prior to sale, and those described as having been "given away" for any reason by the company (i.e., for whom prices were not recorded), normally to pay either freight charges or the commissions of ships' captains.

3. Slave prices in Barbados, 1673–1723

The company's invoice account books covering the West Indies contain a separate record of each sale reported. Each such record was made by the company's factors in a particular colony to account for their disposition of the slaves delivered to them by a single ship. With relatively few exceptions, the format of these records remains standard throughout the volumes. Following information detailing the place and date of the sale and the names of the ship and its captain, the bargains are listed by transaction. The name of each individual who bought slaves was recorded, along with the number of slaves he purchased in each of four categories – men, women, boys, and girls – and the amount he paid.

The sums of money recorded in the accounts do not appear to represent spot or current prices for slaves, but rather the sums to be paid by purchasers to the company's factors at agreed dates in the future. They would therefore implicitly include some unspecified interest premium in addition to the spot price. K. G. Davies concluded that "the selling of slaves in the English West Indies had everywhere one common characteristic: virtually all buyers, whatever form their eventual payment might take, demanded and got credit."[3] Although the records of many entire sales do not mention the length of credit given to purchasers, this might simply have resulted from the use of standard payment dates for many purchasers. Indeed for sales in which factors did record the time of payment, a future date appears for nearly every transaction, and in each such case the number of different future payment dates is small. Because no information is generally recorded on either interest rates charged or length of credit, no attempt will be made to separate the spot prices of slaves from the interest charges that would have been included in the total amounts owed by purchasers for future payment. In the absence of significant changes over time in the conditions of credit, the slave price series to be presented should closely follow trends in spot prices, and in view of the apparent prevalence of credit in slave sales in the West Indies more generally, their levels should be basically comparable to those of slaves sold by other traders in the period.

In principle, with data recorded in the format described earlier, it would be possible to estimate the mean price of slaves in each of the four demographic categories enumerated separately by estimating a regression equation in which the total amount to be paid in each transaction was expressed as a linear function of the number of slaves in each of the four categories in the transaction. The estimated coefficient of each independent variable would then represent the mean price paid for slaves in the respective category in a given sale, or year. Yet when such regressions are actually estimated for particular sales, or annually pooled sales, the estimated coefficients tend to be erratic, with some unreasonably large, and others extremely small, in some cases even negative. The basic source of this problem appears to be the presence, in virtually all sales, of a downward trend in the price of slaves over the course of the sale. A number of factors might have produced this phenomenon, and a consideration of the specific causes in these sales will follow in Chapter 4. Here it may be sufficient to suggest that the outcome responsible for the trend appears to have been the sale of the highest "quality" slaves within each category early in the sales, with progressively declining quality as the sales went on, until only the slaves frequently described as unhealthy or "refuse" were left to be sold at very low prices. If this were the case, the quality of the slaves within each demographic category sold could be considered as an unobserved independent variable omitted from the regression equation described earlier. Negative correlation between this omitted quality variable and the number of slaves sold in any of the four categories – in the form of disproportionate sales of slaves in a particular category late in a sale – could then result in a downward bias in that category's estimated price, producing the very low and occasionally negative coefficients mentioned earlier, whereas a positive correlation with the omitted quality variable could bias a category's estimated price upward.

Although slave quality cannot be measured directly from the available evidence, the order of the transactions within each sale is known from the agents' listings. Under the hypothesis that the order in which slaves were sold was systematically related to their quality, the order of sale of the slaves can be used as a proxy for the unobserved quality variable. Experimentation with trend variables indicates that the downward movement of prices over the course of entire sales is not normally well approximated by a linear trend. More elaborate specifications, including trends of second or higher degree, can be used to fit the observations of any given sale, but pose problems both of interpretation and of occasional instability in the estimated prices of particular categories. To avoid these problems, the approach employed was to limit the specifications to linear trends, and to estimate price series on subsets of the samples. Specifically, it was observed that the downward trend in prices grew both more severe and more erratic later in sales than in the earlier stages, and as a result the decision was made to divide the observations of each sale by transaction rank, and to estimate prices separately for the transactions that occurred in the first and second halves of the sales.

The absence of strong trends in price in the early stages of many sales led initially to the specification used to estimate the prices presented in Table 3.1, for which regressions of the first form described earlier were estimated. Thus the transactions that occurred within the first half of each sale in a given year were pooled, and the amount paid per transaction was expressed as a linear function of the number of men, women, boys, and girls sold in the transaction.[4]

In some years the distributions of slaves sold in the four categories were dissimilar over the course of even the first halves of sales. In order to determine the extent to which this might have affected the estimated prices, a

3. Slave prices in Barbados, 1673–1723

Table 3.1. *Estimated annual mean prices of slaves sold in first halves of auctions*

Year	Men £	Men n	Women £	Women n	Boys £	Boys n	Girls £	Girls n
1673	19.85	45	20.73	18	—	—	—	—
1674	20.53	230	19.48	63	17.36	35	16.55	2
1675	20.60	238	20.31	72	10.20	8	18.50	6
1676	19.45	310	15.68	67	15.44	17	13.63	13
1677	18.55	131	16.12	43	17.46	22	11.23	16
1678	19.27	470	18.04	129	14.04	74	15.90	22
1679	19.28	57	16.85	23	13.67	13	—	—
1680	18.84	289	16.34	110	15.49	49	12.88	33
1681	21.60	281	22.79	135	15.74	102	6.51	59
1682	20.66	158	18.38	83	14.94	23	13.47	19
1683	21.98	12	17.07	12	13.95	11	8.29	9
1684	19.71	302	15.10	84	13.72	102	12.37	51
1686	20.28	286	15.64	113	14.92	97	12.01	38
1687	20.11	114	13.62	37	13.21	40	10.65	12
1688	18.72	263	14.38	148	15.15	94	11.59	40
1689	20.45	251	18.53	85	15.40	62	14.18	40
1690	23.24	117	19.06	29	17.86	18	16.28	1
1691	21.43	199	15.82	53	16.40	28	11.54	11
1692	25.06	221	21.06	102	16.52	41	16.57	19
1693	27.79	51	18.93	16	17.88	5	13.50	3
1694	24.62	186	16.88	71	21.93	47	19.26	15
1695	28.60	161	25.60	103	22.82	36	17.36	18
1696	35.85	144	35.50	79	26.13	24	25.91	5
1697	25.20	229	23.34	84	30.94	13	23.90	7
1698	19.21	42	25.61	26	19.86	14	23.15	3
1699	31.50	245	11.72	153	18.65	21	19.43	16
1700	44.08	201	—	—	23.25	48	16.59	26
1701	36.69	38	30.18	13	26.40	36	19.23	13
1702	44.09	87	—	—	26.42	53	10.34	23
1703	35.25	144	27.05	33	25.15	50	26.31	13
1704	39.65	180	37.10	50	26.28	127	29.64	46
1705	46.16	128	39.15	56	34.38	84	35.13	19
1706	36.88	154	40.15	51	32.19	87	33.46	36
1707	36.91	92	22.80	27	29.17	36	23.67	11
1708	32.45	232	25.16	42	23.12	92	29.26	23
1709	32.75	139	27.31	26	24.58	34	22.97	17
1710	34.64	109	30.41	36	23.69	62	24.42	24
1711	25.60	35	37.74	14	27.09	10	24.91	1
1715	31.30	43	24.22	12	24.08	14	23.85	5
1719	23.53	222	12.70	78	—	—	—	—
1723	32.86	74	21.61	18	29.76	29	—	—

Note: See text for source and method of estimation. The units of the price estimates in this and subsequent tables (except where explicitly noted) are local Barbados currency, with fractions converted to decimal equivalents.

56

Table 3.2. *Estimated annual prices of slaves sold in first transactions of auctions*

Year	Men £	n	Women £	n	Boys £	n
1673	20.83	45	20.19	18	—	—
1674	21.11	228	19.48	62	17.12	34
1675	21.84	238	21.47	72	—	—
1676	19.77	284	16.12	66	14.74	13
1677	22.23	110	16.07	36	15.35	12
1678	19.62	388	17.94	106	13.70	51
1679	17.27	57	21.13	23	14.75	13
1680	22.09	241	21.66	87	9.66	27
1681	20.07	179	17.12	92	14.50	25
1682	20.75	143	20.43	71	—	—
1683[a]	22.12	7	15.84	7	16.65	3
1684	20.55	261	18.88	71	14.09	48
1686	20.41	260	17.80	93	14.63	77
1687	21.58	99	17.96	34	13.70	23
1688	19.00	222	17.84	118	14.04	52
1689	20.10	234	24.08	74	16.15	33
1690	24.61	117	14.54	29	18.77	16
1691	23.67	190	16.94	48	14.45	22
1692	23.08	207	20.02	95	19.85	34
1693	28.85	51	22.33	16	17.68	5
1694	26.87	174	21.29	67	22.57	40
1695	29.17	153	25.29	93	23.79	25
1696	38.35	117	35.62	72	16.98	7
1697	31.82	229	33.08	84	32.00	12
1698	21.68	42	28.34	23	22.60	12
1699	31.48	233	30.45	150	16.44	17
1700	37.56	94	37.85	37	27.01	19
1701	38.82	38	47.87	10	24.63	24
1702	39.51	86	32.92	48	29.69	32
1703	38.53	133	27.38	33	26.65	25
1704	40.67	118	17.36	30	28.26	84
1705	46.83	109	37.50	50	35.56	72
1706	45.03	111	36.61	35	37.39	68
1707	36.67	82	32.79	23	33.10	17
1708	35.65	216	30.00	38	23.46	85
1709	33.76	121	26.36	25	14.72	18
1710	36.20	97	32.22	36	25.36	52
1711	36.12	35	27.50	14	29.91	9
1715	31.62	41	—	—	—	—
1719	26.04	76	22.55	17	—	—
1723	37.11	74	26.34	18	24.35	27

Note: See text for source and method of estimation.
[a]For 1683 transactions involving girls were included to provide sufficient observations to obtain estimates. The price estimated for girls is not reported.

second set of regressions was estimated on the same samples, in which explicit account was taken of the order of the transactions. The specification allowed for separate linear trends in the price of slaves in each category. Prices were estimated for only three of the categories; the fourth, girls, had to be dropped because of insufficient observations.[5] The price estimates for the other three categories were evaluated at the first percent of the transactions, and therefore notionally represent the prices of prime-quality slaves according to the hypothesis of ordering by quality suggested earlier. The results are shown in Table 3.2.

The general similarity of the results presented in Tables 3.1 and 3.2 lends support to the validity of the estimated price series. The simple correlation coefficient between the two price series for men is 0.94; the women's series yield a correlation of 0.63, and the boys' series a correlation of 0.89.[6]

Estimation of prices from the second halves of the sales posed greater difficulties for reasons noted earlier. Explicit recognition of the pronounced downward trend in slave prices late in the sales was necessary in virtually all years to avoid instability of the estimated coefficients. Linear trends were used in estimating the prices of slaves in the two categories, men and women, that most often had enough observations to derive reasonably precise estimates.[7] The estimated annual prices of slaves in these categories, evaluated at transactions midway through the second halves of sales, are presented in Table 3.3.

A separate set of regressions was estimated on the sample underlying the estimates of Table 3.3 in order to check their robustness in view of one other characteristic of the data. Frequently in the latter stages of a sale, transactions occurred in which large numbers of slaves were sold at extremely low prices. In order to assess the impact of these apparent "distress" sales on the estimated prices, variables were added to the equation used to estimate the prices shown in Table 3.3 which controlled for the effects on the prices of both men and women of individual transactions involving a total of 10 or more slaves.[8] The results of this procedure are shown in Table 3.4; the estimates given there represent the annual average prices of slaves in transactions midway through the second halves of sales, based on transactions involving nine or fewer slaves.

Once again, there is considerable similarity between the movements of the price series of Tables 3.3 and 3.4. Thus the correlation coefficient between the two men's series is 0.89, and that for the women's series is 0.77.[9]

The relationships among the estimated prices of Tables 3.1–3.4 generally conform to those that would be predicted by the hypothesis of declining prices over the course of auctions. Thus in 33 of 41 annual observations the estimated price of men in Table 3.2, which represents the price of the men sold at the beginnings of all sales held in each year, is higher than the price of men in Table 3.1, which represents the annual mean price of all men sold in the first

Table 3.3. *Estimated annual prices of slaves sold at midpoints of second halves of auctions*

Year	Men		Women	
	£	n	£	n
1673	12.89	7	—	—
1674	16.30	211	14.11	159
1675	16.14	277	14.38	129
1676	16.36	234	12.54	205
1677	13.90	217	27.61	161
1678	10.87	234	15.32	240
1679	25.40	122	—	—
1680	13.62	221	10.87	296
1681	11.05	222	10.13	233
1682	12.43	176	14.49	171
1683	16.52	70	2.01	45
1684	14.01	379	9.46	284
1686	12.35	222	12.61	185
1687	13.48	127	8.34	82
1688	14.07	110	12.06	209
1689	12.55	212	14.03	190
1690	12.34	147	19.65	57
1691	14.20	157	13.35	125
1692	10.40	206	14.71	185
1693	14.39	31	15.91	30
1694	16.71	186	18.86	146
1695	23.58	128	19.37	193
1696	21.56	62	20.12	132
1697	18.79	129	12.01	207
1698	18.28	27	12.38	19
1699	9.39	77	13.70	172
1700	26.85	57	12.04	149
1701	17.14	31	16.98	29
1702	21.48	42	14.77	123
1703	21.27	83	21.05	97
1704	27.59	128	28.00	124
1705	38.32	67	27.64	77
1706	18.40	113	30.91	98
1707	27.01	171	8.94	64
1708	23.24	199	24.41	63
1709	27.97	81	21.74	33
1710	26.67	94	24.64	78
1711	24.16	29	26.56	10
1715	29.40	7	23.23	5
1719	20.56	27	13.18	29
1723	23.20	77	27.40	20

Note: See text for source and method of estimation.

3. Slave prices in Barbados, 1673–1723

Table 3.4. *Estimated annual mean prices of slaves sold at midpoints of second halves of auctions, with effects of large transactions eliminated*

	Men		Women	
Year	£	n	£	n
1674	15.83	106	14.33	51
1675	16.62	85	16.65	27
1676	16.79	80	14.48	59
1677	13.78	71	19.56	35
1678	15.09	114	12.79	113
1679	13.51	28	—	—
1680	15.15	102	12.66	112
1681	13.93	53	9.40	50
1682	17.03	56	10.68	49
1683	11.74	11	7.20	4
1684	13.67	119	10.32	53
1686	13.62	119	13.18	107
1687	13.35	47	11.72	39
1688	15.20	61	12.22	85
1689	13.51	167	14.47	145
1690	15.62	88	16.63	34
1691	15.79	105	15.38	92
1692	16.98	98	15.59	92
1693	14.78	25	16.33	22
1694	18.86	109	16.31	64
1695	22.28	53	22.25	92
1696	24.34	35	22.24	45
1697	17.51	72	17.39	76
1698	18.95	12	13.51	9
1699	11.89	41	14.30	72
1700	23.06	18	19.04	16
1701	16.79	15	23.31	13
1702	19.36	18	17.39	39
1703	23.41	57	22.31	71
1704	29.94	68	26.65	74
1705	37.67	41	31.91	31
1706	20.29	72	28.64	72
1707	29.41	33	30.46	18
1708	24.66	84	23.70	33
1709	30.45	20	27.13	13
1710	28.41	55	26.77	45
1711	26.76	11	25.83	6
1715	29.40	7	23.23	5
1719	20.53	22	14.82	22
1723	29.39	26	28.48	10

Note: See text for source and method of estimation.

halves of the sales. In 40 of 41 years the estimated men's price of Table 3.1 is in turn higher than that of Table 3.3, which represents the price of men sold three-quarters of the way through the respective sales. There is furthermore some tendency for the men's prices of Table 3.4 to be higher than those of Table 3.3; in 26 of 40 cases the series in which the effect of larger transactions that occurred late in sales had been removed showed higher prices. The women's price series show similar tendencies for the entries of Table 3.2 to be higher than those of Table 3.1 (24 of 38 years), for the series of Table 3.1 to be higher than that of Table 3.3 (31 of 37), and for the series of Table 3.4 to exceed that of Table 3.3 (28 of 39). The boys' prices of Table 3.2 are higher than those of Table 3.1 in 21 of 36 years.

Comparing the categories, in Table 3.1 the price of men is higher than that of women in 34 of 39 years, the price of women is higher than that of boys in 29 of 37, and the price of boys exceeds that of girls in 26 of 37. For Table 3.2, men's prices are higher than women's in 34 of 40 cases, and women's are higher than boys' in 29 of 36. The price of men is higher than that of women in 24 of 39 cases in Table 3.3, and in 30 of 39 in Table 3.4.

The approach used here to produce estimates of slave prices in the Barbados market during 1673–1723 is an empirical strategy aimed at coping with observed outcomes generated by an imperfectly known underlying structure. Both the division of the samples into halves of sales by the order of transactions and the use of several different regression specifications on the resulting subsamples were intended to produce a variety of estimates in order to gain an indication of the robustness of the results. The basic similarity and consistency of the estimates obtained in these ways are reassuring, for they indicate that within this range of specifications and procedures the results obtained are not artifacts of particular samples or estimation procedures. The price series therefore appear to provide reliable estimates of slave prices in the West Indian market with which to approach questions concerning the operation of the slave trade and the changing cost of slave labor to the planters of colonial America. A number of these will be addressed both in the remainder of this chapter and in the following two chapters.

The structure of slave prices by age and sex

The estimates presented here have a number of significant advantages over previously published price series for slaves in this period. Their derivation from a single source based on sales held in a single location provides a greater comparability over time than has been attained from some previous combinations of scattered price quotations, and their information on prices by category allows greater control of the demographic characteristics of the slaves covered than has previously been possible.[10]

One important issue on which these price series bear is the structure of the relative prices of slaves by age and sex in the Barbados market. Some caution is necessary in interpretation, however, because of the lack of information on the specific ages of the slaves listed in the invoice accounts. The normal definitions of the categories by which they were classified are known. In the course of a negotiation in 1720, a company committee pointed out to a prospective buyer that "the Ages he had putt down did not agree with those wch. the Compy. usually contract for," and they

therefore gave him a Copy of theirs, as follows, Vizt
    Men from 16 to 40 years
    Women from 15 to 35
    Boys from 10 to 15
    Girls from 10 to 14.[11]

Althogh minor variation in the definitions of the four demographic categories used in the invoices could have occurred over time, these definitions appear to be basically consistent with references to slave ages that appear in correspondence between the company and its agents in Africa and the West Indies.

The price series of Tables 3.1 and 3.2 produce similar results concerning the relative values of slaves by sex. Calculating the mean of the annual ratios of women's to men's prices from Table 3.1 yields a value of 0.85; the same procedure for the price series of Table 3.2 gives a value of 0.88. Similar calculations of the value of women relative to men from Tables 3.3 and 3.4 produce somewhat higher values, of 0.96 and 0.94, respectively. That these are higher than the ratios from the price series based on transactions from the first halves of sales appears to imply that the extent of price differentation among the slaves by sex declined late in sales as the level of prices, and quality, declined.

For purposes of computing the overall relative prices of sex of all slaves sold, a more informative procedure is to weight the first- and second-half sale prices of both men and women by the relative numbers of slaves in each category actually sold in the first and second halves of sales before calculating the relative prices. The annual price series for adult men and women obtained by this weighting procedure are presented in Table 3.5; these represent the mean values of all men and women, respectively, sold by the Royal African Company in Barbados each year.

The weighting of the component price series has a significant impact on the calculation of the relative prices of male and female slaves, for the distribution of the two sexes over the course of sales was quite different: Whereas adult men were equally likely to be sold within the first or second halves of transactions in a sale, adult women were more than 2.5 times more likely to be sold in the second half. Calculating the mean of the annual ratios of women's to men's prices from Table 3.5 reveals that overall the adult women sold in Barbados in the period considered here were an average of 81 percent as valuable as the adult men.[12]

Table 3.5. *Estimated mean prices of slaves sold in Barbados*

Year	Men	Women	Year	Men	Women
1673	£18.91	£20.73	1695	26.37	21.54
1674	18.51	15.63	1696	31.55	25.88
1675	18.20	16.50	1697	22.28	15.28
1676	18.12	13.31	1698	18.85	20.02
1677	15.65	25.19	1699	26.21	12.77
1678	16.48	16.27	1700	40.27	12.04
1679	23.45	16.85	1701	27.91	21.07
1680	16.58	12.35	1702	36.73	14.77
1681	16.94	14.77	1703	30.14	22.57
1682	16.32	15.76	1704	34.64	30.61
1683	17.32	5.18	1705	43.47	32.49
1684	16.54	10.75	1706	29.06	34.07
1686	16.81	13.76	1707	30.47	13.05
1687	16.62	9.98	1708	28.20	24.71
1688	17.35	13.02	1709	30.99	24.19
1689	16.83	15.42	1710	30.95	26.46
1690	17.17	19.45	1711	24.95	33.08
1691	18.24	14.09	1715	31.03	23.93
1692	17.99	16.97	1719	27.21	12.83
1693	22.72	16.96	1723	27.93	24.66
1694	20.67	18.21			

Note: Both series in this table were constructed as weighted averages of the appropriate price series of Tables 3.1 and 3.3, with weights equal to the *n* values given in those tables.

Although the lack of precise information on the ages of the slaves sold in Barbados means that comparisons to other evidence can be only suggestive, it is interesting to note that Robert Fogel and Stanley Engerman found that female slaves were worth 85 percent as much as males at age 20 in the American South in 1850, and that the value of women relative to men fell to 80 percent at age 25, and 75 percent at 30.[13] The mean ages of the adult men and women slaves sold by the Royal African Company in Barbados probably fell within this range, and the mean annual price ratio of 81 percent for women's prices relative to men's obtained from the company's sales would therefore be consistent with the absence of any major differences in the relative values of adult slaves by sex between Barbados during 1673–1723 and the American South in 1850.

Calculating the mean of the annual ratios of girls' prices to those of boys from Table 3.1 yields a value of 0.90. Comparison to Fogel and Engerman's prices by age again suggests a basic similarity; the value of female relative to male slaves in the nineteenth-century South fell from about 96 percent at age 11 to 92 percent at 14.[14]

3. Slave prices in Barbados, 1673–1723

Considering the relative prices of slaves in the Barbados market by age, the mean of the annual ratios of boys' to men's prices is 0.76 in Table 3.1 and 0.72 in Table 3.2; the analogous value for girls' prices relative to women's is 0.84. The higher price of girls relative to women than of boys relative to men is consistent with the nineteenth-century evidence that the price of female slaves rose less steeply than that of males after childhood, producing higher relative prices of teen-aged females relative to adults than of males.[15] The magnitudes of these Barbados price ratios by age do not appear surprising in comparison with the nineteenth-century evidence; although precise comparison is again precluded by the lack of specific ages for the slaves sold in Barbados, it is interesting to note that Fogel and Engerman's data for the Old South produce ratios of the price of 14-year-old slaves to 21-year-olds of 0.76 for males, and 0.83 for females.

Trends in Barbados slave prices, 1673–1723

Changes in slave prices were a key influence on the performance of the economy of the early English West Indies. During the final quarter of the seventeenth century slaves had come to dominate the labor forces of all the English islands, so that by 1700 all had substantial black majorities among their populations. The harsh demographic regime of the region furthermore meant that over the course of a typical decade planters would have to buy total numbers of new slaves equivalent to 30 percent of those present at the decade's beginning simply to prevent their slave populations from decreasing. As a result, slave prices received a scrutiny from both planters and traders that was rivaled in intensity perhaps only by their attention to the state of the market for the islands' dominant product, sugar.

In order to facilitate an examination of trends in prices over time, Table 3.6 presents an annual index of Barbados slave prices derived from the series of Tables 3.1 and 3.3. The price index of Table 3.6 was constructed as a weighted average of the prices of slaves in each of the four demographic categories sold in both the first and second halves of sales, with constant weights across years equal to the share of each category in total deliveries by the Royal African Company to Barbados during 1673–1723.[16] After conversion to sterling to eliminate the effects of fluctuations in the value of Barbados's currency over time, the index serves to emphasize some important features of the history of slave prices in the West Indies in this period.

The early portion of the index indicates that slave prices in Barbados fell from the 1670s to the 1680s. The mean annual sterling index value for the 1670s, £15.28, is about 16 percent greater than the mean of £13.17 obtained from the annual values from the 1680s. The component price series presented earlier furthermore suggest that the prices of the 1670s might in turn have been considerably lower than slave prices several decades earlier. Richard

Table 3.6. *Annual index of Barbados slave prices, 1673–1723*

	Index			Index	
Year	Barbados currency (£)	Sterling (£)	Year	Barbados currency	Sterling
1673	14.93	13.44	1695	23.50	20.44
1674	17.01	15.31	1696	26.32	23.16
1675	16.71	15.04	1697	19.86	17.48
1676	15.80	14.22	1698	17.75	15.80
1677	18.66	16.80	1699	17.07	15.19
1678	15.00	13.50	1700	27.76	24.71
1679	20.66	18.59	1701	23.78	20.21
1680	14.46	13.01	1702	26.88	21.77
1681	14.68	13.21	1703	25.45	20.87
1682	15.64	14.08	1704	31.29	26.28
1683	13.79	12.41	1705	36.93	26.22
1684	14.20	12.78	1706	29.34	17.90
1686	14.75	13.28	1707	24.37	13.65
1687	13.65	12.42	1708	25.91	19.17
1688	14.61	13.15	1709	26.87	19.88
1689	15.57	14.17	1710	27.96	20.97
1690	17.88	16.27	1711	26.31	21.05
1691	15.88	14.29	1715	26.99	21.59
1692	16.66	14.49	1719	18.18	14.18
1693	18.64	16.22	1723	26.65	20.79
1694	19.47	16.94			

Note: The index in Barbados currency was contructed by weighting the price series of Tables 3.1 and 3.3 by the shares of the respective categories in the first and second halves of auctions in total deliveries to Barbados during 1673–1723. The weights were as follows:

	Men	Women	Boys	Girls
First half	0.2559	0.0956	0.0644	0.0265
Second half	0.2621	0.2470	0.0310	0.0174

Missing values for women's, boys', and girls' prices were interpolated using the following values relative to men's prices: women = 0.86 men; boys = 0.76 men; girls = 0.68 men. The prices were converted to sterling using the exchange rates of John J. McCusker, *Money and Exchange in Europe and America, 1600–1775* (Chapel Hill: University of North Carolina Press, 1978), pp. 240–2, with linear interpolation for missing years.

Ligon, who lived in Barbados during 1647–50, wrote that "Thirty pound sterling is a price for the best man Negre; and twenty five, twenty six, or twenty seven pound for a Woman."[17] The price series of Table 3.2 – for slaves sold at the beginning of sales – indicate that the best adult men sold by the Royal African Company in Barbados during the 1670s brought estimated prices in the range £17–22 and the best women £16–21, levels substantially below those reported by Ligon; in addition, unlike Ligon's quotations, the company sales were recorded in local currency, which during the 1670s exchanged against sterling at a discount of roughly 10 percent.[18] If Ligon's figures are accurate, therefore, they point to a very substantial decline in slave prices in Barbados between about 1650 and the 1670s.[19]

Quantitative evidence from the 1660s, however, suggests that there may have been no decline in slave prices from the middle of that decade through the 1670s, and perhaps even a moderate increase. Table 3.7 presents estimates of slave prices in Barbados during 1663–4 from the one known surviving volume of accounts listing specific slave sales made by the Company of Royal Adventurers, the predecessor of the Royal African Company.[20] The overall estimated mean price of men in 1663–4, of £21.22, was equivalent to about £15.90 sterling, and the mean women's currency price of £18.26 was equivalent in sterling to £13.70.[21] This men's sterling price is 4 percent less than the sterling value of the mean of the men's prices from the 1670s in Table 3.5, whereas the women's sterling price for 1663–4 is fully 14 percent lower than the mean sterling value of the annual price observations for women from the 1670s. This evidence therefore suggests that Barbados slave prices might have changed very little between 1663–4 and 1673–9, and that what trend did exist in the period might have been upward.

Additional evidence from decades prior to the 1660s will be necessary before long-term trends in West Indian slave prices during the seventeenth century can be described with confidence. The available quantitative evidence suggests that prices may have risen moderately from the mid-1660s to the mid-1670s, before falling more sharply from the 1670s to the 1680s. Richard Ligon's report on the Barbados slave market during the late 1640s furthermore suggests the possibility that a major decline in prices had occurred between about 1650 and 1663, with a possible drop of nearly one-half in the level.[22]

The mid-1680s therefore appear to have been the lowest point of a decline in West Indian slave prices of at least a decade in duration, and perhaps as long as three decades. Although the causes of these movements remain to be explored in detail, the secular decline could have been the consequence of falling labor productivity in sugar production in South America as well as the West Indies due to steadily falling European sugar prices; sugar prices in Amsterdam fell by more than 50 percent between the early 1640s and the late 1670s, then continued to fall thereafter before reaching the bottom of a deep trough in the late 1680s.[23]

The decline observed here in West Indian slave prices might have been an important factor in bringing large-scale slavery to the North American mainland, for slave traders who were dissatisfied with the low and falling prices they were receiving in the 1670s and 1680s might as a result have begun to bring the tobacco planters of Maryland and Virginia a steady supply of Africans at low prices. The Royal African Company did express dissatisfaction

Table 3.7. *Estimated annual prices of slaves in Barbados, 1663–4*

Year	Men £	Men *n*	Women £	Women *n*	Boys £	Boys *n*
1663	20.55	151	17.35	119	11.76	8
1664	21.70	315	18.46	230	12.76	27
1663–4	21.22	466	18.26	349	12.69	35

Note: The prices for 1663–4 were estimated on the pooled sample from both years.
Source: PRO T70/646. See text for method of estimation.

with the level of West Indian slave prices during the 1680s, not only in public declarations, which might be discounted to some extent because of their role in the political struggle discussed in Chapter 1 between the company and West Indian planters over the continued existence of the company's legal monopoly, but also in private correspondence, which did not contain this propaganda element. The company wrote to its Barbados factors in 1687 complaining of a recent cargo, "some of wch. Negroes, according to the accot. of Sales turne miserably to accot." Although the letter did go on in a more positive vein to note "though those by Capt. Buttram came out well in Refference to the bad Sales Wee have of late yeares mett with," it closed plaintively: "but they doe not reach such Prices as you know Wee have sold Negroes for when the Returnes did produce much better then they now doe."[24] The company certainly had ample evidence with which to measure the decline in slave prices, most notably the same invoice accounts on which the price estimates of this chapter are based.[25]

The low slave prices of the 1680s, following a period of declining prices that spanned its trading career, might have prompted the Royal African Company as well as other smaller slave traders to take positive action to find new markets for their cargoes, for there was no obvious end in sight to the falling prices in their usual markets in the West Indies. And to the extent that the low slave prices were perceived to be linked to the slump in international sugar markets, these traders would have been expected to look for new markets for their cargoes based on the production of crops other than sugar. In English America at the time, the likeliest alternative was clearly the tobacco colonies of the Chesapeake Bay.

Although records of Royal African Company activity in the Chesapeake colonies during the seventeenth century are poor, fragmentary evidence does indicate an apparent increase of company interest in the region during the 1680s. Russell Menard has documented the company's dispatch of at least seven ships, capable of carrying a total of 1,300–1,400 slaves, to Virginia and Maryland during that decade.[26] Total slave imports to the two colonies were considerably greater than this, whether from undocumented company deliveries or those of independent slave traders, as estimates of net migration to the Chesapeake indicate that the region received more than 7,000 blacks during the 1680s, a sharp increase over figures of less than 2,000 in each of the preceding three decades.[27] The increase in slave imports had a dramatic impact on market conditions in the region. Already in 1679, the Royal African Company's agents warned the central office not to expect much from the sale of a cargo of slaves who had arrived in poor health, remarking that "now good Negroes are so plenty that few will buy bad though at Low Prices."[28]

Chesapeake planters were willing to buy larger numbers of slaves in part because of a substantial increase in the price of white indentured servants; the price of an adult male with at least four years to serve rose from levels of £8–9 in the late 1670s to £10.5–11.5 during the 1680s, and reached £12 by 1690. But the planters' decisions were obviously also influenced by a decline in local slave prices, from a range of £23–25.5 for prime males during the 1670s and early 1680s to a low of £22 by the late 1680s.[29] The Chesapeake's rapid transition in the 1680s from primary reliance on white servants to the large-scale use of black slaves, in the course of which Maryland planters' holdings shifted from a ratio of 3.9 servants to 1 slave in the late 1670s to one of 3.6 slaves to 1 servant in the early 1690s, was therefore fueled by a steady and substantial fall in the price of slaves relative to servants that was in progress by the mid-1670s and continued until 1690, as a result of both rising prices for white labor and falling prices for black labor.

The end of the 1680s brought a sudden halt to the secular decline in West Indian slave prices. Table 3.6 confirms that the outbreak of war between England and France in mid-1689 produced higher slave prices for Barbados planters, as the cost of shipping in the Atlantic rose sharply.[30] Already in December 1689 the company wrote to its factors in Barbados complaining of the low prices they had submitted in their accounts for a cargo of slaves sold in September, admonishing them that

you had a good argument to have advanced their prices to answere the difficultie must be during the warr to gett Negroes to yor. markett, & as freight is advanced with you, so it is here for all places, & as ships of late have not gott out on any termes, so that the buyers have the Advantage which ought to have been ours.[31]

The company went on in the same letter to instruct the agents that "as any more comes to yor. markett you must stand upon £20 to £25 per head or wee shall loose of our principle." Whereas the estimates of Table 3.1 suggest that the agents were successful in following these instructions for adult males of good quality, Table 3.5 indicates that several more years passed before the average price for men reached the level desired by the company.

The end of King William's War in 1697 brought about a reduction in slave prices, but the interlude was brief. A widespread increase in the demand for slave labor in the Americas, apparently related to an upswing in the price of sugar in Europe, produced an increase in slave prices beginning in 1700, and high shipping costs due to the resumption of Anglo–French war in 1702 contributed to fluctuating but generally high prices over the course of the following decade.[32] The paucity of price evidence among company invoice accounts from Barbados following the conclusion of Queen Anne's War in 1713, which reflects primarily the dwindling level of company involvement in the transatlantic slave trade and secondarily the declining importance of Barbados as a destination for slave shipments owing to the rise of Jamaica, makes generalization about trends in the Barbados market in the final decade of company activity there difficult. Yet Table 3.6 does capture the sharp drop in slave prices that occurred in Barbados in 1719, and the subsequent recovery of the early 1720s.[33]

This chapter has provided evidence on the prices of slaves sold by the Royal African Company in Barbados during 1673–1723. The importance of slaves in the economy of the West Indies during this period makes this information valuable for a variety of uses, some of which will be explored in the following chapters. Examination of the prices suggested that the structure of relative prices of slaves by age and sex observed during this period in Barbados might have been very similar to that which existed in the American South in the nineteenth century. A consideration of trends in the price series indicated that low and declining slave prices prevailed in the West Indies during the 1680s, the decade in which slave labor was first adopted on a large scale on the North American mainland, and that higher slave prices subsequently faced West Indian planters in the periods of war that dominated the 1690s and the first decade of the eighteenth century.

4

On the order of purchases by characteristics at slave sales

Chapter 3 described a set of econometric procedures that were used to estimate the prices of slaves in different demographic categories from the Royal African Company invoices in the face of an unexpected problem. The problem, which had not previously been discussed in the historical literature on the slave trade, was that the prices of slaves within given demographic categories were consistently found to decline throughout the course of sales of individual cargoes of slaves. The procedure followed in Chapter 3 was to assume that this decline implied that slaves were ordered within sales by quality, with the best slaves sold early in a sale, and the quality of slaves declining thereafter as the sales progressed. The order of transactions within a sale could then be used as an independent variable that functioned as a proxy for the unobserved quality variable.

This procedure yielded plausible results; yet the validity of those results depends on the validity of the assumption that slave sales were ordered by quality. Further investigation of this phenomenon is therefore called for, in order to determine whether this assumption is accurate. If it is correct, the result is an intriguing one, for both historical and theoretical reasons. Historically, little is known about the conduct of slave sales in this early period of the history of the slave trade. An investigation of this conduct, and why it might have resulted in a systematic ordering of the sale of slaves by quality, can provide previously neglected information about the nature of relations between buyers and sellers in early American slave markets. Theoretically, economists have long been interested in the behavior of auctions and other organized sales, and have analyzed a number of characteristics of the outcomes produced by some variants of these markets. Yet one significant feature of sales has been relatively neglected, that of the order in which goods will be sold in an organized market with flexible prices.

This chapter presents evidence from a previously unexploited source on the order of purchases in a market resulting from the operation of the early transatlantic slave trade, and it investigates some economic forces that could have produced the observed outcomes in this, as well as other, markets.

4. On the order of purchases

Characteristics of slave sales in Barbados

The typical size of Royal African Company sales held in Barbados did not vary greatly over the course of the period considered here. A sale in which between 185 and 300 slaves were sold in 35–75 transactions remained typical throughout the period covered by the invoice accounts,[1] although sales with as many as 600 slaves and more than 100 transactions and with as few as 50 slaves or less and only a dozen transactions could occur. The records of transactions make it clear that standard lot sizes were never used for slave sales in Barbados, and that considerable variation occurred in both the number of slaves sold and their composition by demographic category from transaction to transaction.

Evidence on the duration of sales was not recorded systematically in the account books. Those cases in which notations of specific sale dates were made suggest that sales might typically last from two to four days. They could last considerably longer in some instances, however, with some slaves remaining unsold at the end of a week or more. In 1694 the company's chief agent in Barbados reported that "sometimes the agents have been ten daies or more in selling & disposing two hundred & fifty or three hundred negroes."[2]

Although its typicality cannot be judged, an account of the timing of the sales of one ship's slaves comes from a journal kept by Peter Blake, captain of the *James,* in 1676. Blake arrived in Barbados with a cargo of slaves for the Royal African Company on Sunday, May 21. On Monday the company's two local agents, Edwin Stede and Stephen Gascoigne, inspected the slaves on board, and the following day they ordered Blake to prepare the slaves for sale on Thursday. On Wednesday Blake recorded that "this day our Slaves being shaved I gave them fresh water to wash & Palme Oyle & Tobacco and Pipes." The agents had evidently mustered the slaves during their inspection on Monday, for Blake also noted that on Wednesday Gascoigne had delivered his commission slaves to him, following the company's normal practice of making partial payment to ships' captains for their services in the form of slaves. On Thursday Blake noted that "this day about 8 of the Clock Mr Steed & Mr Gascoyne came on boord to sell our Slaves" and that during the day 163 were sold. Sales continued on Friday, when 70 slaves were sold, and on Saturday 118 more were sold. The remaining slaves were apparently of poor quality, and no further sales occurred until Wednesday of the following week, when Blake managed to sell five slaves to a planter. Finally, on Tuesday, June 6, Blake noted that "Mr Gascoyne fetcht a shoar the remaining Slaves being 7 men & 10 Woemen." Thus in this case the sale began four days after the arrival of Blake's ship in Barbados, and 351 of the company's 373 slaves in the cargo were sold within the first three days of sales. Sales then virtually ceased, however, and 17 slaves remained unsold nearly two weeks after sales had begun.[3]

The company insisted that their agents use a specific method in reporting the sales of slaves, and as a result the sale records listed in the invoice accounts follow a standard format. After information detailing the place and date of the sale, the name of the ship by which the slaves were delivered, and the name of the ship's captain, the transactions of the sale are listed individually. In a tabular format the name of each person who bought slaves is listed in the order of the original sales,[4] along with the number of slaves he purchased in each of four demographic categories – men, women, boys, and girls – and the amount he paid, or promised to pay. At the conclusion of each sale, the agent would total the amount due to the company, and sign an oath stating that he had acted to the best of his ability in selling the slaves and that the account was accurate.

The behavior of prices over the course of slave sales

From evidence of the type described, systematic direct information on the characteristics or "quality" of slaves within each of the four demographic categories is not available.[5] Yet what can be done with the available evidence is to make a closer examination of the behavior of the prices of slaves within particular categories over the course of sales, and to make inferences about the ordering of the quality of the slaves purchased from the observed prices. Some of these inferences can then be tested against other types of evidence, including the reports of the company agents who ran the sales.

The econometric specification used in estimating slave prices by demographic category in this analysis is again based on the view that the price paid in a particular transaction can be approximated as a linear function of the numbers of slaves in each demographic category purchased in that transaction. The problem of observing the behavior of prices by category over the course of entire sales could potentially be solved by including trend terms as explanatory variables, but this solution was not adopted here, primarily out of a desire not to impose particular functional forms on the observations of whole sales. Instead, the transactions from each sale were divided into sections determined by transaction order within the sale – for example, into fifths – and a separate regression equation was estimated on each of the resulting sections. The use of relatively fine divisions is dictated by a desire to chart the behavior of prices as closely as possible. In order to provide adequate sample sizes, the records of sales that occurred in Barbados in a given year were pooled and only the 18 years in which 800 or more slaves were delivered to the island were analyzed. Two of the demographic categories – boys and girls – together accounted for less than 14 percent of total slave deliveries to Barbados during 1673–1723, and in many years offered insufficient numbers for reliable estimation using the procedure described here; in order to make estimating procedures standard across years, all transactions involving these two categories were eliminated from the sample analyzed.

4. On the order of purchases

The general specification of the estimating equation used was as follows:
$$P_{ij} = b_{1j}M_{ij} + b_{2j}W_{ij} + e$$
where

P = total amount paid per transaction
M = number of men
W = number of women
i = index of transaction
j = index of "section" of sale, defined as $x < j < y$, where x and y are percentiles of transaction rank within an individual sale (i.e., the sale of a single cargo of slaves)

The estimated coefficients $\hat{b}_1$ and $\hat{b}_2$ can then be interpreted as the mean prices of adult male and female slaves, respectively, sold in a given section – for example, the first fifth, or the first 20 percent of the transactions – of each of the sales that occurred in Barbados in a particular year.

To gain an indication of the robustness of the results to different divisions of the transactions into sections, the specification stated here was applied to a series of different divisions of the annual observations. Specifically, the transactions from each year were divided sequentially into fifths, sixths, and eighths.

The estimated regression coefficients from each of these three divisions for each year are shown in index form in Tables 4.1–4.3, with the estimated coefficient of each category within each section of each year's sales expressed as a percentage of the estimated coefficient for the category for the first section in the year. For example, Table 4.1 shows that in 1674 the mean price of men was the same in each of the first two fifths of all sales held in that year, whereas the mean price in the third fifth was 96 percent as high, in the fourth fifth 94 percent as high, and in the final fifth 56 percent as high.

The final rows of each table show the means of each section index for men and women across all years. These means are graphed in Figure 4.1. The profiles shown clearly point to a basic pattern that, although subject to some variation in specific shape across years, appears for both demographic categories in nearly all years analyzed. The downward slope of these profiles indicates a tendency for the prices of slaves in each demographic category to decline over the course of sales, while the typical concavity of the profiles indicates that this decline was normally gradual in the earlier stages of the sales, and accelerated in the later stages.

Although as noted earlier systematic evidence is not available on many aspects of the quality of the slaves sold, including such obviously relevant variables as age, state of health, size, and strength, the consistent downward trend in prices over the course of sales suggests that the highest "quality" slaves – those with the highest expected productivity on West Indian plantations – were sold early in the sales, with progressively declining quality as the

Table 4.1. *Relative prices of slaves sold by section: five divisions*

Year	Sex	Section number				
		1	2	3	4	5
1674	M	100	100	96	94	56
	F	100	93	82	51	74
1675	M	100	89	87	85	64
	F	100	87	64	64	40
1676	M	100	94	98	83	74
	F	100	106	99	92	56
1677	M	100	96	83	79	38
	F	100	95	94	96	75
1678	M	100	99	89	93	33
	F	100	100	90	75	64
1680	M	100	97	68	79	35
	F	100	105	94	46	66
1681	M	100	98	85	65	30
	F	100	103	82	56	37
1684	M	100	90	93	72	63
	F	100	89	79	49	28
1686	M	100	98	90	70	30
	F	100	96	82	74	62
1688	M	100	97	96	88	44
	F	100	99	96	71	56
1689	M	100	98	87	82	44
	F	100	83	75	61	51
1692	M	100	92	51	67	15
	F	100	112	81	95	74
1697	M	100	85	78	75	47
	F	100	90	54	70	39
1699	M	100	93	75	33	13
	F	100	90	64	53	37
1700	M	100	96	96	114	56
	F	100	90	78	32	13
1704	M	100	88	89	80	62
	F	100	91	100	83	53
1706	M	100	100	75	54	30
	F	100	94	93	85	82
1708	M	100	81	82	78	60
	F	100	96	83	87	38
Means: all years						
	M	100	94*	84*	77	44*
	F	100	96*	83*	69*	53*

Note: An asterisk in this table and Tables 4.2 and 4.3 indicates that the mean is significantly different from that of the previous column at the 0.10 level.

4. On the order of purchases

Table 4.2. Relative prices of slaves sold by section: six divisions

		Section number					
Year	Sex	1	2	3	4	5	6
1674	M	100	100	95	98	79	58
	F	100	87	96	72	73	57
1675	M	100	91	87	84	76	63
	F	100	81	88	63	71	41
1676	M	100	95	95	92	79	59
	F	100	103	99	84	74	60
1677	M	100	99	82	85	65	29
	F	100	101	100	91	112	81
1678	M	100	104	94	87	85	34
	F	100	103	95	90	74	65
1680	M	100	101	78	84	77	35
	F	100	91	89	87	45	63
1681	M	100	109	90	41	78	27
	F	100	100	113	90	39	40
1684	M	100	96	96	72	78	76
	F	100	94	73	80	40	8
1686	M	100	100	92	86	66	32
	F	100	95	83	90	68	52
1688	M	100	93	97	104	78	45
	F	100	98	102	93	75	56
1689	M	100	97	100	83	66	36
	F	100	87	66	74	63	51
1692	M	100	89	81	51	67	10
	F	100	114	117	80	101	76
1697	M	100	95	76	85	64	48
	F	100	80	76	43	62	38
1699	M	100	93	82	65	20	13
	F	100	96	60	56	56	39
1700	M	100	96	93	96	111	55
	F	100	91	86	73	32	14
1704	M	100	104	90	91	83	66
	F	100	105	91	100	80	52
1706	M	100	97	77	69	52	20
	F	100	100	91	81	84	89
1708	M	100	79	85	76	83	60
	F	100	98	75	92	84	37
Means: all years							
	M	100	97*	88*	81	73	43*
	F	100	96*	89*	80*	69*	51*

sales progressed, until the lowest-quality slaves were sold last.[6] The extent of the decline over the course of a sale was typically considerable; on average both men and women sold in the final stages of a sale yielded only about half the prices of their counterparts sold at the sale's beginning.

Some fragmentary evidence from the accounts directly supports part of this

76

Table 4.3. *Relative prices of slaves sold by section: eight divisions*

Year	Sex	Section number							
		1	2	3	4	5	6	7	8
1674	M	100	103	102	98	100	108	75	48
	F	100	100	95	94	80	38	76	67
1675	M	100	97	86	89	86	83	66	58
	F	100	73	100	83	64	77	72	40
1676	M	100	98	97	94	87	94	78	56
	F	100	84	100	96	103	76	70	59
1677	M	100	96	91	75	83	77	64	26
	F	—	—	—	—	—	—	—	—
1678	M	100	100	100	93	84	89	89	—
	F	100	116	102	98	96	86	67	117
1680	M	100	96	96	76	88	78	69	35
	F	100	92	104	92	91	96	48	65
1681	M	100	103	99	86	52	57	64	—
	F	100	104	105	91	75	78	44	58
1684	M	100	94	89	92	85	61	66	—
	F	100	39	105	72	81	57	34	30
1686	M	100	98	94	90	85	70	59	32
	F	100	102	96	82	96	87	56	44
1688	M	100	83	92	88	91	93	51	41
	F	—	—	—	—	—	—	—	—
1689	M	100	100	98	102	83	78	53	35
	F	100	79	81	60	70	57	63	45
1692	M	100	85	90	78	50	72	58	—
	F	100	111	117	115	81	91	76	62
1697	M	100	111	85	77	87	74	52	—
	F	100	55	75	63	35	58	40	28
1699	M	100	95	89	77	74	49	26	—
	F	100	100	103	65	54	57	42	41
1700	M	100	94	99	91	94	105	—	66
	F	100	89	82	83	66	32	—	—
1704	M	—	—	—	—	—	—	—	—
	F	—	—	—	—	—	—	—	—
1706	M	100	96	94	75	68	52	45	—
	F	100	114	107	113	100	93	84	106
1708	M	100	99	80	85	78	77	56	41
	F	100	89	93	75	91	87	109	51
Means: all years									
	M	100	97*	93*	86*	81	77	61*	44*
	F	100	90*	98	85*	79	71	63	58

Note: Estimates insignificant at the 0.10 level have been treated as missing information.

interpretation. The company's agents in the colonies would occasionally write into the invoices they sent to the company in London specific descriptions of the slaves sold in particular transactions. These descriptions, which might note that the slave had a disease or particular disability, or less specifically

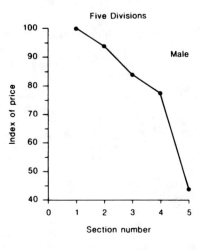

Five Divisions

Male

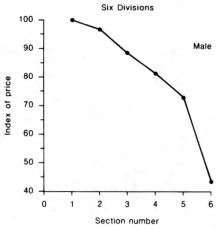

Six Divisions

Male

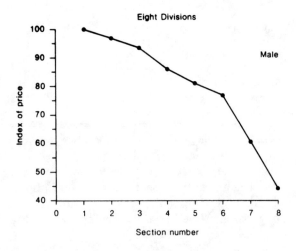

Eight Divisions

Male

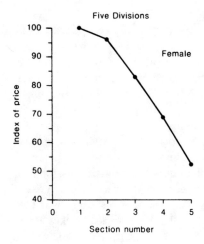

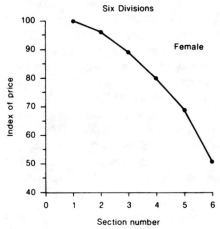

Figure 4.1. Relative prices of slaves sold by section of sales. *Source:* See Tables 4.1–4.3, means.

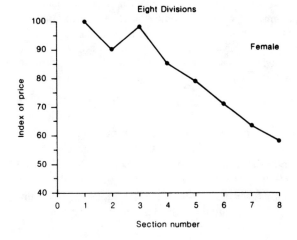

was a "refuse" slave, invariably appear for only the lowest-priced slaves. The purpose of these notations was apparently to indicate to the company's main office that these slaves were sold for exceptionally low prices not because the agent was dishonest or incompetent, but because the slave was deemed virtually worthless by purchasers, usually for obvious reasons of health. These descriptions of refuse slaves appear only in the final stages of the sales, most often the final few transactions.

It was common knowledge among the company's West Indian agents that the poorest slaves were the last to sell, and references to this often appeared in letters they sent to the main office, in the course of explanations for their failure to have completed and submitted the accounts for particular cargoes of slaves. In 1691 the agents in Barbados wrote of a ship's cargo that they "could not finish ye accott. of the Kendall's being many Sickly Poore Negroes that took up much Time to put them off [sell] and yet have two Negroes remaining [unsold] in Badd Condition."[7] Similarly, in 1680 the Barbados agents had written that the sale of a cargo of only 59 slaves from Gambia had not been completed after more than three weeks because "those brought were very ordinary Slaves both Old some Poore & Blind and many burst ones, Which with the little esteeme those Negroes have here, made them ly long on our hands & goe off at low prices."[8] In 1707 the company's agent in Virginia reported the arrival of a slaving ship but noted that "ye Small pox being aboard . . . has retarded ye Sale."[9] A sale in Barbados that remained unfinished after two weeks in 1712 prompted the explanation: "The Slaves are young. Several are sick, and they go off but slowly."[10] The company's agent in Nevis wrote in 1714 of the delay in selling some slaves that resulted from the need to allow them to recover from the effects of illnesses and rough treatment they had suffered on shipboard:

I have yet remaining Unsold of both Cargoes of Negroes Forty One my utmost Endeavours shall not be wanting to Compleat theire Sales as soon as it's Possible, having a Plenty of Provisions to feed them has Improved a Considerable Number of them, since there being on Shore, that were very feeble & weak at their Landing and many having such a Contraction of their Nerves by being on Board, and Confined in Irons that were hardly Capable to walk have perfectly recovered by which Occasions in some part does Oblige their Laying on hand the Longer, but hope in the Conclusion may prove of advantage to yor. Honors, by ye different Vallues made in their Sales.[11]

In an extreme case, the company's agents in Jamaica in 1681 wrote that one woman who long remained unsold "was betweene mad & Foole soe that noe body would give any thing for her or accept of her for nothing being dangerous to be Kept on Port Royall or any Plantation where fyre may doe hurt," and congratulated themselves that "yett at last she was sold for 20s.," which they noted had been roughly the cost of maintaining her while trying to find a purchaser.[12] Finally, in a case discussed earlier, Peter Blake, a ship's captain, recorded in his journal in 1675 his attempts to expedite his departure from

Barbados after delivering a cargo of slaves. Five days after sales had begun aboard his ship, with only 22 of the 273 slaves he had delivered to the company agents remaining unsold, Blake grew impatient with the local agents' efforts to dispose of his remaining cargo, and on two successive days he personally brought planters on board to try to sell them "some of our refuse Slaves." His first attempt was unsuccessful, for the planter would not buy, saying of the slaves "hee did not like them," while on the second day Blake reported that he had "sould 5 of ye refuse Slaves." Perhaps as a result of Blake's action, two days later the company's agents removed the remaining slaves from his ship.[13]

One other aspect of the econometric results appears worthy of note. The considerable dispersion of slave prices within each category, witnessed by average prices for both men and women in the final stages of a sale that were only about half as high as those in the initial stages, points to considerable variation in the quality of the slaves sold. This does not appear surprising; in part it would be expected from the differing quality of the slaves purchased in Africa. Beyond this initial variation, the rigor of the transatlantic voyage, which produced mean slave mortality rates per voyage falling from levels of nearly 25 percent in the 1680s to a still substantial 10 percent by the 1730s,[14] introduced considerable additional variation in the health and physical condition of the slaves who survived the voyage. The more gradual decline of slave prices in the early stages of sales than later indicates that there was less heterogeneity among the higher-quality slaves than among those of lower quality. This would imply that there was less variation in the expected productivity of relatively healthy than of unhealthy slaves; some slaves would survive the voyage without illness, whereas those who did suffer disease could range from only moderately ill to near death.

The format of Royal African Company slave sales

Research on a variety of auction markets has shown that outcomes are potentially sensitive to the particular rules and institutions under which these markets operate. In trying to explain the ordering of the sale of slaves observed in the previous section, it would be desirable to begin with a precise description of the normal way in which the sales were conducted, and of how bargains were made. Unfortunately, the existing body of Royal African Company records and correspondence yields no such description, nor have accounts of these procedures been found in other contemporary sources. Yet the company's records do contain correspondence relating to an abortive attempt to change the normal procedures, and this episode provides revealing indirect evidence on the normal methods.

In late 1690 the company wrote to its West Indian agents to direct them to change their procedures in conducting slave sales. Noting that "Wee find that the Planters are very much dissatisfyed with the methods wee have hitherto taken in the Sale of our Negroes,'' the company described new procedures designed "to prevent their clamours, and to give them satisfaction as much as in us lyes." The new format was to be that of a formal auction, to begin at a previously announced time, with each slave sold separately. The company notified its agents that

we do hereby order and direct you, that such Ships as shall arrive with Negroes for our Accots. after the receipt hereof that they be sold by the Inch of Candle each negro apart, & to this purpose you must publish a day of Sale for them, giveing such convenient time as shall be necessary for all Buyers to come in.

The particular auction method specified, sale by the inch of candle, was a common one in which an ascending-bid auction was conducted on each lot, with the time for bidding on each one determined by the time a candle took to burn an inch. This method was generally considered fair because it guaranteed a minimum time available for bidding, preventing an auctioneer from making quick sales to favored customers. The method was known to produce disputes, however, for disagreements could arise over who had been the final bidder before the flame flickered out. To help assure the planters of the auctions' fairness, the company informed the agents that it had asked the governor of each island to nominate referees who would help them settle any disputes:

wee have wrote the Governor to whom applie yourselves that wee have given you such directions . . . And wee have desired the Governor to joyne with you an equall number of persons to decide differences if any should happen amongst the Buyers about the Negro then upon Saile & when any Lott cannot be decided suche Lott must be put up againe.

Finally, the use of the formal auction involved one other important departure from the company's usual method of selling slaves: Whereas previously nearly all sales had been credit transactions, the company now instructed the agents "that you sell for money[,] Goods or Bills of Exchange with Securitie and not give further Creditt."[15]

The company's expression of sensitivity to planters' dissatisfaction was probably sincere, for this episode occurred at a time when planters' lobbying played a significant political role in debate over the continuation of the company's legal monopoly of the slave trade to English America. In fact, in the same letters that instructed them to use formal auctions in selling slaves, the company informed its West Indian agents that a committee of the House of Commons currently had under consideration the company's request for confirmation of its charter, which had effectively lapsed with the flight of James II in 1688. The company wrote that the committee had not yet reported to the House, but that when it did "wee intend more fully to plead our right to that trade and the necessity of managing it in a joynt Stock & doubt not of making it out to their Satisfaction." This confidence of success resulted from the company's belief in the strength of its case, of which the formal auctions open to all comers were to be an element. The company contended that it served all the English planters of the West Indies, not only the wealthiest, and it noted that "the cheife endeavours against us seeme to be from the Interest of some Planters who (if opportunity of an open trade should permit) would serve their owne occasions without accomodating their meaner [i.e., poorer] neighbours as wee have done."[16]

The company clearly also believed that the use of formal auctions would be in its interest financially, as it was quick to point out when the governor of Barbados expressed his suspicion of the new arrangement. The company was asking for no favors, it assured him, for

What wee desired from your Lorp. [Lordship] was onely that some persons whom yor. Excellcy. should appoint, might be joyned with our factors to sit as judges at the Candle who should be the fairest Buyer thereby to satisfie the Planters they should have justice done them by that way of Sale.

By this means, the company maintained, "wee & our ffactors" would be

cleared from the charge against us that none of the best Negroes are sold to the Planters and them which are sold are at extravagant prices & that the best are privately disposed of which if practised is against our Interest & wee never approved thereof.

The company's argument was therefore that the formal auction might increase its revenues by preventing a number of possible abuses by its factors. However, another important motivation for the proposed change in practice was also disclosed in the same letter, as the company went on to complain that "As to the Planters wee have suffered more by their ill payment then wee have got by dealing with them," for "their Debt goes annually increasing which concerns us to put our ffactors on more vigorous measures to prevent its further increase and to reduce it to a more moderate sume." Protesting that "where wee give time wee find wee are at the Planters mercie when wee shall be paid," the company stated its desire to introduce standardized sale procedures that would publicly be seen to be fair, in the hope that quicker payment would be forthcoming from the planters: "by selling by the Candle no man can be imposed upon in the price, so wee hope that clamour will thereby cease & we get quicker payment for the future."[17]

The company's agents reacted unfavorably to the order to introduce the new sale procedures. Two years later, in November 1692, the company wrote angrily to its agents in Barbados, rebuking them for their failure to reply to the original order after acknowledging its receipt, and for their failure to use the new method in their recent sales.[18] In answering a specific complaint from its agents in Jamaica the previous year, the company had rejected their objection to the new method's "tediousnesse," responding that an auction of a typical cargo by the inch of candle could be carried out in two or three days, which was no more than a customary sale would have taken if the agents were conscientious. The letter emphasized that the purpose of the new method was to protect the agents from "aspersions" that they had frequently engaged in a variety of unfair practices. It then returned to the problem of credit:

present payment is the life of our businesse & the great debt on your and other Plantations much injures us in our managerie of the Affrican trade, neither are wee obleiged to give credit to the Planters & as neare as you can you must prevent it by selling what you can for ready mony Goods or Bills of Exchange. [19]

The company's abandonment of these efforts came suddenly. In December 1692, only a month after criticizing its Barbados agents for failing to obey its earlier instructions, it abruptly reversed its position, writing to these same agents:

The Method wee proposed for ye sale of our Negroes by ye Candle, as it proved difficult to you, so wee find it prejudiciall to us in regard it excluded such able Buyers as had not ready mony to pay for them[.] Wherefore to prevent the like inconveniencys Wee have thought fitt to leave it to your discretion to dispose of such Negroes as shall for the Future come to your hands for our Accounts in such wayes and Methods as you shall judge most for our Interest and Advantage. [20]

The company's advocacy of the formal public auction was thereby dropped. In a letter to the governor of Barbados written later the same month, the company explained that it had been disappointed by the results of a sale held under the new auction format; because the sale did not coincide with the sugar harvest, "few men had ready Goods or mony to pay presently by which means the greatest number of Planters were disappointed." The conclusions the company drew from this, and their indicated course of action, were therefore straightforward:

to prevent such Inconveniencyes for the future Wee judge it not reasonable to proceed strictly in such a Method as Limitts our Factors to persue what seems so Strange and prejudiciall to the Planters, and also to our selves espetially at a time when so many Interlopers take the Opportunity to sell their Negroes as seems most advantageous to them. We have therefore thought fitt for the present to recall our said Orders, and to give our Factors liberty to sell in such manner and way as they shall judge most practicable & best for us. [21]

This episode has several important implications for our knowledge of the normal methods of selling slaves that were used by the company's agents. Under normal conditions virtually all transactions involved credit of varying lengths,[22] and the need to evaluate the default risk of each buyer separately meant that this required individual bargaining between buyer and seller over each transaction. The records of the Barbados sales show clearly, as noted earlier, that at no time in the company's trading on the island were slaves placed into lots of uniform size or demographic composition; the records also show that uniform prices were never assigned to slaves by demographic categories.[23] This would again point to the importance of negotiating each bargain individually.

Explaining the order of purchases in the slave sales

Lacking specific knowledge of the methods and rules by which sales were conducted, a full explanation of the outcomes observed here is not possible. Yet what can be done is to point to some factors, the presence of which is supported by contemporary testimony, that are consistent with the observed results; for motives consistent with the observed outcome of slave sales in descending order of quality were potentially present on the parts of both buyers and sellers.

For the company's agents, a strong motivation to sell the lowest-quality slaves last was potentially present in some cases. Specifically, when ships arrived with cargoes that included slaves suffering from virulent contagious diseases, the agents had an incentive to keep this information from potential buyers, for knowledge that an entire cargo had been exposed to a disease like smallpox would depress the bidding of planters for otherwise apparently healthy slaves.

The frequency and success of such attempts cannot be determined, and in general both frequent attempts and success would seem problematic. Aware of the problem of contagious disease in the transatlantic slave trade, with its high mortality rates among large numbers of people crowded into restricted quarters for long periods, planters in the West Indies appear to have demanded the right to examine thoroughly all the slaves put up for purchase from the earliest years of the slave trade. Richard Ligon wrote in 1657 of Barbados slave sales that "the Planters buy them out of the Ship, where they find them stark naked, and therefore cannot be deceived in any outward infirmity."[24] Chance references in Royal African Company correspondence indicate that slave sales might be held either on shore or on board the ship that delivered the cargo.[25] In either case, however, some slaves could have been concealed from the view of buyers, perhaps more easily under the former arrangement, by simply leaving unhealthy slaves on board ship when the others were brought on shore to market, but also by placing them on a ship's lower decks if the sales were held on board.

The company's agents were well aware of the problem that buyers' judgments of quality were influenced by the health of all the slaves on board a ship, and high mortality on a voyage generally, and the presence of specific diseases in particular, were common explanations sent back to the central office for low proceeds from sales. An example was reported from Barbados in 1679 when the agents wrote of a cargo that "as they were few in Numbr. so were they very bad slaves and sold at meane rates people being fearfull to buy

4. On the order of purchases

them there having bin so great a mortallity amongst them.''[26] In another case the company's agent at Nevis reported on one sale that "the Rumor of the Small Pox being aboard deterd severall persons from buying at ye Sale.''[27]

One explicit example of an agent's attempt to act in the way described here – albeit apparently not very successfully – survives in a company minute book. A company clerk recorded of a sale held in Virginia in 1708 that "Coll. Gavin Corbin writes that ye Slaves per ye Bridgewater had ye Small pox wch tho' he concealed as much as possible was very prejudiciall to their Sale.''[28]

It is clear from a number of references that in many cases in which slave sales were conducted on shore, slaves in very poor condition were left on board ship when the others were taken to market. However, it cannot be determined in most of these cases whether this was done to conceal them from buyers. Another common reason for leaving unhealthy slaves on board had to do with the determination of freight charges owed to the ship's captain. As noted earlier, freight was paid as a flat sum per slave delivered alive in the West Indies. The company's agents might refuse to pay freight on slaves who were so seriously ill that they might die shortly after delivery. The criterion used was the slave's ability to walk off the ship; those unable to "go over the side" would be left on board until they had either died or recovered.[29] In the latter case they would then be taken ashore for sale, and the freight on them paid. An example of this comes from a letter quoted earlier from the company's agent in Nevis, who reported to the central office that he had "Delivered [84 slaves] to the Capt. in part of his freight & Commission and the rest assoone as they [unhealthy slaves] are fitt to be brought on Shoar.''[30]

These two reasons for leaving unhealthy slaves to be sold last need not have been mutually exclusive, if buyers had not been told whether any slaves had been left on board the ship, and therefore were not present at a sale. It should be noted that either reason alone, as well as both in conjunction, would have tended to produce the phenomenon of the lowest-quality slaves being sold in the closing transactions of a sale. Company correspondence clearly shows that some unhealthy slaves were left on board ship for some time in numerous instances, although as noted earlier the reason normally cannot be determined from the references. For example in 1715 the company's agent in Barbados reported that he had sold 200 slaves from a ship recently arrived from Africa; he then added that "Six more [slaves] remains yet on board the Ship so lame and Ill that twas not fitt to bring them ashore with the other Negroes to the House of Sale but shall use my best Endeavours to make the most I can of them.''[31]

As noted earlier, it is unlikely that knowledge of the presence of contagious disease among slave cargoes could often successfully have been kept from slave buyers. West Indian planters would have been cautious purchasers, for they were well aware of the common hazards posed by disease on the Middle Passage. Company agents resident in a colony for periods of years might also have hesitated before risking damage to their reputations by deceiving their purchasers. Yet the frequency of illness among the slaves delivered might have made it difficult to determine when agents had purposely misled planters about the condition of their slaves, as opposed to having themselves been ignorant, and the difficulty of deceiving planters might not always have deterred agents from attempting to deceive, particularly when the potential gains were large. However neither such attempts to conceal diseased slaves nor the practice of leaving unhealthy slaves on shipboard to determine whether they would survive before paying for their transport would appear capable of accounting for more than a small part of the pattern of ordering identified earlier. Whereas either of these effects from the supply side could have resulted in the lowest-priced slaves being sold last, neither would have produced the consistent downward trend in slave prices that was observed throughout the course of entire sales. Yet this full pattern could have been due to a different, probably much more important, effect that entered on the demand side of this market.

The convenience of buyers would have tended to result in the sale of the highest-quality slaves first, and for transactions to have proceeded in descending order of quality thereafter. This follows from a combination of three factors: the characteristics of the format of the Royal African Company sales, of slaves as a commodity, and of the economics of production. The lack of a formal auction format, and of fixed lot sizes for purchases, meant that the rate at which slave sales would proceed was very uncertain. In addition, as remarked earlier, there was substantial variation in the quality of the slaves being sold. In any sale in which goods can be sold rapidly, there will be a strong incentive for many or all of those potentially interested in making purchases to arrive at the beginning of a sale of heterogeneous commodities to ensure a relatively wide range of choice. If buyers of widely differing wealth and status assemble at the beginning of a sale, it would be expected that the order of transactions would be closely associated with the wealth of the purchasers, for wealthier buyers, who would place a high value on their time, would tend to demand, and to receive, first service from sellers. This might particularly be expected to occur in such informal sale formats as those of the Royal African Company slave sales, for the agents who negotiated the transactions might naturally be expected to accommodate the wealthier and more important planters first, and to proceed thereafter in roughly descending order of planters' wealth.[32]

Some standard hypotheses concerning the economics of production could then account for the positive correlation between the wealth of a purchaser and the quality of the slaves he purchased. In a market for a productive input, such as slaves, this would be predicted if, as would be expected, the quality of the various inputs used were complementary in production – that is, if there were a positive association between the quality of each input and the relationship between the quality and marginal productivity of each of the others – as long as wealthier planters tended to use other inputs of relatively high quality.[33] Richard Dunn has observed that during the 1670s the largest plantations in Barbados – those owned by the wealthiest planters – were located on the island's best land.[34] Complementarity in sugar production between the quality of land and the quality of labor would imply that wealthier planters would tend to buy higher-quality slaves to work their more valuable land, with poorer planters buying progressively lower-quality slaves. The combination of an ordering of transactions within sales by the descending wealth of planters and a positive association between the wealth of planters and the quality of the slaves they purchased would therefore be expected to yield the result observed in the Royal African Company accounts, of descending quality of slaves over the course of sales.

Evidence of the relevance of these effects to the Barbados slave market appears in the company records at a number of points. One particularly interesting example occurs in a letter from the company's agents in Barbados in 1684 complaining that their efforts to obtain the best prices for the company's shipments of slaves were hindered because the captains of the ships delivering the cargoes were allowed to sell the slaves assigned to them in partial payment of their commissions and freight charges whenever they pleased after the slaves had been delivered to them.[35] These deliveries were made prior to the opening of the company's sales, and the agents complained that this created direct price competition between the captains and themselves. The agents went on to observe that the captains further lowered company receipts because, unlike the agents, they did not have to wait to make sales until all the purchasers had assembled. The agents wrote that buyers who had been notified of a company sale to be held in several days' time might board the ship to inspect the cargo, and "when finding the Capt. at Liberty to sell his Negroes they buy of him rather then to come down again to buy in a Croud." Significantly, the agents not only complained that this loss of potential customers cost them much of the benefit of the expenses they incurred in the form of "our Labour & Cost in sending up & downe the Countrey to Invite Customers to our day of Sale" because it lost them some buyers in general, but they specifically argued that they "thereby also loose the advantage of ready mony Customers & bill of Exchange men, & none left us to deale withall but ill pay Masters & such as buy but few Negroes at a time."[36] Therefore in the agents' view, those buyers who made deals with the ships' captains in advance of the company's sales in order to avoid the trouble of remaining in town and buying in a crowd were those who bought large numbers of slaves with cash and bills of exchange – in short, the wealthiest customers – whereas poorer purchasers who bought only small numbers of slaves for lower prices waited to make their purchases later.

Evidence that the company's agents were sensitive to the status of purchasers in ordering bargains is afforded by the invoice records of sales. One striking feature of these is that they reveal that it was common in the West Indies for the initial purchases at sales to be made by a colony's governor. While this occurred only occasionally in some places, in some colonies it appears to have been routine. The company's sale accounts indicate that Sir William Stapleton, the governor of the Leeward Islands, was the first purchaser in four of the five sales held by the company in Nevis during 1674–5, the company's first two years of trading there; Stapleton was also the first purchaser in nine more sales that took place on the island in the eight years that followed. In Jamaica the colony's governor, John Lord Vaughan, made the first purchases at three of nine sales held during 1675–6. In three of the others, this distinction went to the buccaneer Sir Henry Morgan, the colony's lieutenant governor.

Quantitative evidence on the ordering of transactions by the wealth of purchasers at Royal African Company sales in Barbados can be obtained by linking the names of purchasers given in the sale invoices to a unique census of property taken by Sir Jonathan Atkins, the colony's governor, in late 1679.[37] The census provides information on the amount of land and numbers of slaves owned by the colony's planters. Together these two assets clearly made up a large share of the colony's wealth, and therefore constitute a useful measure of the wealth of individuals. Furthermore, because the ratio of acres to slaves varied little across plantations, either can be used alone as an index of planters' relative wealth.

Table 4.4 presents evidence on the mean numbers of acres of land in Barbados owned by those slave purchasers successfully traced to Atkins's census of property from each of six years of the invoices, categorized according to the quarter of each sale (by transaction rank) within a given year in which their purchases occurred. The results are somewhat erratic, for the sample sizes and mean numbers of acres of purchasers fluctuate over time. Some patterns do emerge clearly, however. In all 18 possible cases, the mean number of acres owned by purchasers in the second through the fourth quarters of the slave sales is less than that of those buying in the first quarter of sales in the respective years, although as indicated in the table in only six cases is the difference in means statistically significant. Yet the tendency for the wealth of planters to decrease as the sales progressed is clear. In three of the six years, the mean acres owned by planters declined monotonically over the successive quarters of the sales. Furthermore, not only were the mean acres owned by first-quarter purchasers highest within the respective year in each of the six years, as already noted, but the most frequent ranking for the second-quarter means was second (four of six years), the most common for the third-quarter means was third (three of six), and the most common for the fourth-quarter means was fourth (four of six). This quantitative evidence therefore lends strong support to the hypothesis that it was the wealthiest

Table 4.4. Mean acres of land owned by purchasers at Royal African Company sales in Barbados, by transaction order within sales, 1677–82

Quarter of sale, by transaction rank	1677		1678		1679		1680		1681		1682	
	Mean acres	n	Mean acres	n	Mean acres	n	Mean acres	n	Mean acres	n	Mean acres	n
1	191	18	165	36	152	6	196	30	90	15	183	16
2	142	21	152	40	68	10	79*	25	70	20	139	12
3	101	20	100*	33	26	6	95*	26	33	19	93	9
4	147	12	62*	32	51	15	71*	22	30	18	21*	15

Note: An asterisk indicates that the mean shown is significantly different from the mean for the first quarter of the respective year at the 0.10 level for a two-tailed t-test with an assumption of unequal variances.
Source: See text.

planters of Barbados who opened the slave sales, paying the highest prices for the highest-quality slaves, and that subsequent transactions tended to be ordered according to the descending wealth of the purchasers.[38]

This chapter has provided detailed evidence on the behavior of slave prices over the course of sales conducted by the Royal African Company in Barbados, and it has suggested that systematic economic forces could have produced the observed outcomes. The finding that the prices of slaves within given demographic categories tended to decline over the course of sales was taken to indicate that the quality of the slaves sold declined as the sales progressed, and this inference was supported by literary evidence drawn from company correspondence. It was argued that this ordering could have resulted in part from the initial withholding of very unhealthy slaves from sales, in some cases in apparent attempts by agents to conceal the fact that a cargo of slaves had been exposed to a contagious disease, and in others because company agents might wait to accept delivery of unhealthy slaves from ships' captains until it could be determined that those slaves would survive. Yet these effects could at most explain only part of the observed pattern of prices, and it was suggested that a more important cause probably followed from the format of the sales. Bargains were made between buyers and sellers in roughly descending order of the wealth of the buyers, and this implied that the slaves were sold in descending order of quality because in general wealthier planters desired to purchase higher-quality slaves.

Some questions remain unanswered about both the specific market examined here and the broader applicability of this analysis to other sales. For this historical case, it would be valuable to have actual descriptions of the method by which the ordering of the slaves sold by company agents was decided, and of how transactions were negotiated, in order to evaluate more directly the accuracy of the explanations offered here of the observed behavior of slave prices. In drawing wider lessons from this market, the questions of the generality of this ordering of goods by quality at sales with flexible prices, and of the possible significance of the motives discussed here in other markets and for sales of other types of commodities remain to be pursued. The opportunity cost of the buyer's time would clearly become a less important consideration when some or all buyers need not be present at a sale, perhaps because they are represented by agents. The seller's interest in concealing the condition of some of his goods for the reasons suggested here is also obviously diminished or absent when the nature of the commodities being sold means that the condition of any given item is unlikely to be influenced by the condition of other goods, and it would similarly disappear when, for legal or other reasons, the seller allows potential purchasers to inspect all the goods to be sold before a sale begins.[39] Yet these factors remain of potential importance in a number of markets in both the past and the present. The questions of when the

4. On the order of purchases

outcome of ordering of purchases by quality will appear, and of its source in those cases when it does, would therefore seem of continuing interest to those concerned with understanding the behavior of prices in a wide variety of economic markets.

5

The demographic composition of the slave trade

An economic investigation

Variation in the age composition of the slave trade

The demographic composition of the population of slaves carried from Africa to America is a topic that has attracted considerable attention from historians of the slave trade. Variation in the age and sex composition of the slave trade has been discussed as a factor with significant implications for such issues as the potential for slave populations in the Americas to be able to sustain stable families, the economic productivity of American slave populations, and the potential for black populations to grow in both the sending regions of Africa and the receiving regions of America.[1] Yet in spite of the recognition of its significance, the demographic composition of the slave trade has received little systematic analysis. This chapter presents an economic model of the age composition of the slave trade, and explores some of its implications in light of evidence drawn both from the records of the Royal African Company and from earlier research on the structure of internal African markets for slaves.

The age composition of the slaves carried by the Royal African Company varied considerably within the period covered by the account books. Table 5.1 presents listings by colony of destination of the numbers of slaves carried annually by the company within each of the four enumerated demographic categories. These figures show that the share of boys and girls in total annual deliveries to Barbados, Jamaica, and Nevis ranged from negligible levels of 4 percent or less for each colony to maximum levels of more than 25 percent in each case; in 1725 children made up fully one-third of all slaves carried to Jamaica. The age composition of the slaves carried by the Royal African Company during 1673–1725 therefore varied considerably over time, and provides ample opportunity for statistical testing of the economic hypothesis to be presented here.

Table 5.1 also indicates that considerable variation occurred in the composition of annual cargoes by sex. Each of the company's major destinations received shares of females of less than 20 percent of total shipments in some years and of more than half in others. Although the sex composition of the

5. Demographic composition of the slave trade

Table 5.1. *Demographic composition of Royal African Company slave shipments by destination, 1673–1725*

Year	Men		Women		Boys		Girls		Total	
	n	%	n	%	n	%	n	%	n	%
Barbados										
1673	157	71	54	25	8	4	1	0	220	100
1674	731	62	366	31	72	6	16	1	1,185	100
1675	955	65	468	32	29	2	28	2	1,480	101
1676	834	58	499	35	78	5	24	2	1,435	100
1677	498	59	260	31	61	7	28	3	847	100
1678	1,063	55	686	35	134	7	58	3	1,941	100
1679	271	50	221	40	44	8	11	2	547	100
1680	679	49	532	39	103	8	58	4	1,372	100
1681	674	45	587	39	160	11	82	5	1,503	100
1682	37C	49	313	42	36	5	33	4	752	100
1683	86	50	62	36	13	8	10	6	171	100
1684	796	55	467	32	127	9	64	4	1,454	100
1686	638	49	428	33	150	12	74	6	1,290	100
1687	280	56	150	30	53	11	15	3	498	100
1688	469	40	486	42	138	12	72	6	1,165	100
1689	480	54	290	32·	78	9	49	5	897	100
1690	280	70	93	23	20	5	5	1	398	99
1691	367	60	193	32	32	5	15	2	607	99
1692	453	51	341	38	66	7	34	4	894	100
1793	92	60	52	34	7	5	3	2	154	101
1694	440	55	261	33	72	9	23	3	796	100
1695	300	42	313	44	61	9	32	5	706	100
1696	208	46	213	47	27	6	7	2	455	101
1697	424	51	362	44	31	4	13	2	830	101
1698	99	42	99	42	22	9	15	6	235	99
1699	376	43	426	49	46	5	28	3	876	100
1700	378	43	380	43	79	9	42	5	879	100
1701	111	32	134	38	69	20	35	10	349	100
1702	168	28	307	52	73	12	45	8	593	100
1703	234	52	139	31	51	11	22	5	446	99
1704	369	44	219	26	175	21	73	9	836	100
1705	222	42	164	31	111	21	31	6	528	100
1706	377	42	307	34	148	16	72	8	904	100
1707	271	61	99	22	53	12	19	4	442	99
1708	535	59	176	20	140	16	49	5	900	100
1709	273	57	83	17	85	18	38	8	479	100
1710	249	47	162	31	80	15	40	8	531	101
1711	67	60	27	24	14	13	3	3	111	100
1715	123	60	42	20	34	17	7	3	206	100
1719	257	64	109	27	26	6	9	2	401	99
1723	305	73	53	13	56	13	4	1	418	100
Total	15,959		10,623		2,862		1,287		30,731	

Table 5.1. *(cont.)*

Year	Men n	Men %	Women n	Women %	Boys n	Boys %	Girls n	Girls %	Total n	Total %
Jamaica										
1674	235	58	169	42	0	0	0	0	404	100
1675	761	60	458	36	43	3	16	1	1,278	100
1676	576	55	426	41	27	3	13	1	1,042	100
1677	658	57	413	36	56	5	30	3	1,157	101
1678	419	42	447	45	92	9	39	4	997	100
1679	181	43	185	44	46	11	9	2	421	100
1680	751	49	552	36	159	10	78	5	1,540	100
1681	482	42	484	42	106	9	71	6	1,143	99
1682	886	45	785	40	227	11	88	4	1,986	100
1683	242	41	228	39	76	13	39	7	585	100
1684	807	49	603	36	170	10	73	4	1,653	99
1685	157	44	155	44	32	9	9	3	353	100
1686	1,887	49	1,315	34	418	11	215	6	3,835	100
1687	105	46	83	37	24	11	14	6	226	100
1688	309	43	229	32	109	15	70	10	717	100
1689	312	46	298	44	44	6	28	4	682	100
1690	219	61	101	28	26	7	13	4	359	100
1691	327	56	167	29	63	11	22	4	579	100
1692	322	55	169	29	77	13	15	3	583	100
1693	637	65	234	24	82	8	24	2	977	99
1694	538	57	254	27	118	13	26	3	936	100
1695	488	51	357	37	79	8	38	4	962	100
1696	90	80	22	19	1	1	0	0	113	100
1699	42	33	54	43	15	12	16	13	127	101
1700	329	48	291	42	26	4	42	6	688	100
1701	317	41	286	37	120	16	45	6	768	100
1702	257	45	196	34	94	16	25	4	572	99
1704	405	51	240	30	113	14	43	5	801	100
1705	732	53	406	29	164	12	90	6	1,392	100
1707	134	68	35	18	18	9	9	5	196	100
1708	1,044	66	363	23	116	7	53	3	1,576	99
1723	667	52	188	15	296	23	122	10	1,273	100
1724	576	59	189	19	135	14	76	8	976	100
1725	226	49	84	18	133	29	20	4	463	100
Total	16,118		10,466		3,305		1,471		31,360	
Nevis										
1674	204	46	193	43	30	7	20	4	447	100
1675	255	53	191	40	28	6	7	1	481	100
1676	215	39	284	51	29	5	26	5	554	100
1677	285	58	167	34	20	4	23	5	495	101
1678	233	47	200	41	43	9	15	3	491	100
1679	263	49	219	40	48	9	12	2	542	100
1680	325	40	363	44	84	10	48	6	820	100
1681	308	35	403	46	107	12	64	7	882	100
1682	28	30	53	58	7	8	4	4	92	100
1683	42	40	36	35	15	14	11	11	104	100

5. Demographic composition of the slave trade

Table 5.1. *(cont.)*

Year	Men n	Men %	Women n	Women %	Boys n	Boys %	Girls n	Girls %	Total n	Total %
1686	128	50	114	44	7	3	9	3	258	100
1687	75	80	12	13	5	5	2	2	94	100
1688	195	61	91	29	22	7	11	3	319	100
1689	202	70	73	25	8	3	6	2	289	100
1695	237	77	65	21	5	2	2	1	309	101
1698	146	43	152	45	22	7	16	5	336	100
1699	228	62	127	35	10	3	3	1	368	101
1700	147	43	153	45	17	5	21	6	338	99
1701	119	48	82	33	33	13	12	5	246	99
1704	327	52	208	33	69	11	27	4	631	100
1705	66	40	72	43	21	13	7	4	166	100
1708	32	63	13	25	6	12	0	0	51	100
1709	32	62	20	38	0	0	0	0	52	100
1716	39	49	24	30	16	20	1	1	80	100
Total	4,131		3,315		652		347		8,445	
Antigua										
1679	65	40	95	58	1	1	2	1	163	100
1693	68	79	18	21	0	0	0	0	86	100
1702	200	53	130	34	34	9	13	3	377	99
1707	269	44	217	35	90	15	36	6	612	100
1708	78	71	28	25	3	3	1	1	110	100
1709	306	53	183	32	56	10	33	6	578	101
1721	94	90	10	10	0	0	0	0	104	100
1723	107	75	14	10	21	15	0	0	142	100
Total	1,187		695		205		85		2,172	
Montserrat										
1688	79	87	8	9	2	2	2	2	91	100
1689	237	91	24	9	0	0	0	0	261	100
1700	63	37	79	46	22	13	7	4	171	100
1704	26	50	20	38	6	12	0	0	52	100
1705	32	28	57	50	17	15	7	6	113	99
1706	74	29	89	35	60	24	29	12	252	100
1724	29	63	9	20	8	17	0	0	46	100
Total	540		286		115		45		986	
St. Kitts										
1721	206	70	49	17	30	10	11	4	296	101
Virginia										
1705	65	98	1	2	0	0	0	0	66	100
1708	67	51	31	23	21	16	13	10	132	100
1721	309	73	57	13	38	9	22	5	426	100
Total	441		89		59		35		624	

Source: PRO T70/936–59. See text for procedures.

slave trade will not be the primary focus of the economic analysis of this chapter, some important features of the determination of sex ratios in the slave population carried to America will emerge in the course of the investigation of its age composition.

The age composition of the slave trade: an economic analysis

The proximate determination of the demographic composition of the slave population that would be carried on the Middle Passage was done by the European traders who purchased the slaves in Africa. In the case of the Royal African Company's trade, this purchaser would be either an agent resident at a company factory on the African coast or the captain of a ship. In either case, the purchaser would typically buy slaves directly from an African trader.

In choosing slaves for the voyage, the purchaser would obviously wish to select those who would yield him a profit. Slaves would therefore be carried from Africa to America only if the prices the trader expected to obtain for them in America exceeded their African prices by at least the full cost of transportation, where the latter would include not only the direct pecuniary cost of passage but also an allowance for the probability of mortality, with complete loss of the slave's value, on the voyage. Under the assumption that large numbers of slave traders in both African ports and American markets made the Atlantic slave trade a competitive industry, in long-run equilibrium pure profits would be eliminated from the slave trade, and American slave prices would exceed African prices by just this full cost of transportation.[2] For any trader, therefore, total revenue would equal total cost:

$$P_B Q(1 - m) = P_A Q + (1 - m)Qt \tag{5.1}$$

where

P_A = African price of slaves at coastal markets, by age and sex

P_B = American price of slaves upon delivery

Q = total number of slaves purchased in Africa

m = proportion of slaves lost due to passage mortality

t = freight charges per surviving slaves

In equation (5.1) the left-hand term is the trader's total revenue, defined as the product of the appropriate American prices of the slaves upon delivery and the number surviving the voyage. The right-hand side is the total cost, made up of the sum of the cost of the slaves initially purchased in Africa – the product of slave prices and the quantity purchased – and the charges incurred for the transportation of the slaves, here stated as the product of freight charges per slave and the number of slaves delivered alive to America.[3]

Annual evidence on the African prices of slaves by demographic category for the period under consideration here is not available. Yet equation (5.1) can

5. Demographic composition of the slave trade

be used to derive the African price of a slave that would be warranted by any given American price, transportation costs, and passage mortality rate. Specifically, solving equation (5.1) for the African slave price yields the expression:

$$P_A = (P_B - t)(1 - m) \tag{5.2}$$

Equation (5.2), which expresses the African price of a slave as a function of its American price, freight charges, and passage mortality rates, is an equilibrium condition that applies only to categories of slaves actually traded from Africa to America. This is an important qualification, for the equilibrium upon which it depends need not exist for categories of slaves that did not enter the trade. More generally, P_A in equation (5.2) should define a lower bound of the actual prices of all slaves in Africa, for the existence of the Atlantic trade would guarantee that a slave's value in Africa would be at least equal to its American price less the full cost of transport. For slaves actually traded under competitive conditions, this inequality would become an equality, and in equilibrium equation (5.2) would yield the actual African price. It is possible, however, that owing to demands for slaves from sources other than the Atlantic trade, a slave might have a price in Africa higher than that warranted by its American price. In this case, a significant example of which will be discussed later in this chapter, the slave would be retained in Africa.

The analysis will initially be carried out for the conditions that faced the Royal African Company in the period considered here for hired shipping. In this case the company paid a flat sum to the ship's owners for each slave delivered alive to the West Indies, so the cost of shipping slaves from West Africa to destinations in the West Indies was the same for slaves in all demographic categories at a given time.[4] Lacking detailed evidence on age-specific mortality rates for the Middle Passage, a provisional assumption will be that mortality did not vary significantly by age within the actual range of ages carried by the Royal African Company.[5] Given these premises the full cost of transportation would have been constant across demographic categories.

Equation (5.2) can be used to consider the relationship between American (or hereafter, for relevance to the present case, West Indian) slave prices and the age composition of the slaves carried across the Atlantic. Evidence on West Indian slave prices by age considered in Chapter 3 suggests that these followed the same basic pattern found for slaves in the nineteenth-century United States, with relatively low prices for children, rising with age to a peak, typically in early adulthood, then falling with age thereafter. The level of these profiles has been found to differ by sex, and the empirical analysis of this chapter will therefore consider males and females separately. The following theoretical analysis will be stated with reference to males, but the basic

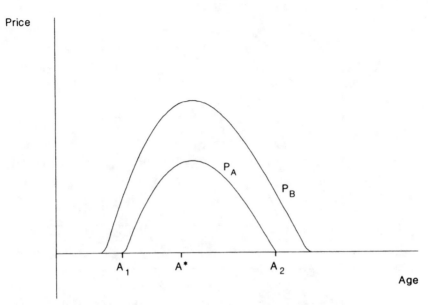

Price

A$_1$ A*   A$_2$

Age

Figure 5.1. Determination of minimum and maximum ages of slaves eligible for shipment to America. *Note:* The age–price profile P_B was constructed by fitting a sixth-degree polynomial to the mean prices by age of slaves in the Old South in 1850; these data are shown in Robert William Fogel and Stanley L. Engerman, *Time on the Cross: The Economics of American Negro Slavery* (Boston: Little, Brown, 1974), p. 72. P_A was constructed by shifting P_B downward by a constant vertical distance.

similarity of the shapes of the age–price profiles of the two sexes makes its predictions equally applicable to females.

Assuming West Indian male slave prices to be represented by the schematic age–price profile P_B in Figure 5.1, equation (5.2) can be used to derive the warranted African age–price profile P_A, with the vertical distance between the two profiles equal to the full average cost of transporting a slave from Africa to the West Indies. Because actual African prices cannot be observed directly, the least restrictive reasonable assumption about them will be made, that they would be bounded from below by zero (if not some higher price).[6] Given this assumption, lower-bound ages for boys who traders would have been willing to purchase for shipment to America, as well as upper-bound maximum ages for men, would be determined in each year as the range in ages in which the warranted African prices of male slaves was positive; in the case of Figure 5.1, this would be the range from A_1 to A_2. The trader would not find it profitable to purchase boys younger than A_1 or men older than A_2 simply because the difference between their African and expected West Indian prices would be less than the expected cost of transporting them.[7] The ages

5. Demographic composition of the slave trade

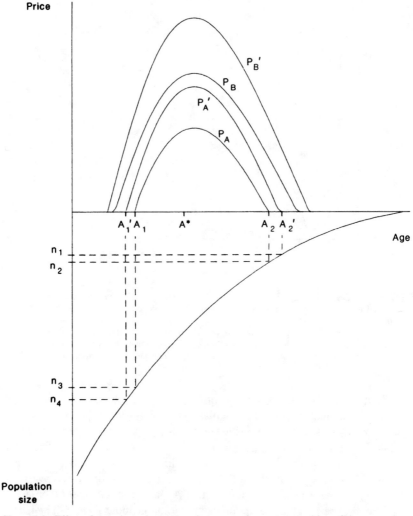

Figure 5.2. Effect of American slave price changes on the age composition of the transatlantic trade. *Note:* For the age–price profiles P_B and P_A, see Figure 5.1. The African population profile by age is based on Model South, Level 4, with an annual growth rate of 10 per thousand; Ansley Coale and Paul Demeny, *Regional Model Life Tables and Stable Populations* (Princeton, N.J.: Princeton University Press, 1966), pp. 782–3. On the selection of this model, see John Thornton, ''The Slave Trade in Eighteenth-Century Angola: Effects on Demographic Structures,'' *Canadian Journal of African Studies*, Vol. 14, No. 3 (1980), p. 420. P_B' was constructed by increasing all the prices of P_B by a constant proportion; P_A' was then constructed by shifting P_B' downward by a constant vertical distance.

A_1 and A_2 therefore bound the range of ages of male slaves that could profitably be shipped to America; if A^* in Figure 5.1 was the age used by the Royal African Company to divide boys and men, those from A_1 to A^* would make up those entered in the accounts as boys, and those from A^* to A_2 would be those recorded as men.[8]

Now consider the effect of a change in American slave prices, due for example to a rise in labor productivity in the West Indies caused by an increase in sugar prices. As shown in Figure 5.2, the curve P_B shifts upward to P_B'. The warranted African age–price profile therefore shifts upward, from P_A to P_A'. This has the effect of widening the range in the ages of slaves that can profitably be shipped from Africa to the West Indies, by lowering the minimum age (from A_1 to A_1' in Figure 5.2), and raising the maximum age (from A_2 to A_2').[9]

The next question concerns the effect of this widening of the range of ages at which slaves were eligible for shipment on the actual composition of the population of slaves transported. The widening of the eligible range of ages in Africa would generally have added a considerably larger number of boys than men to eligibility for the trade. This can be seen by adding a reasonable schematic African population age profile to the lower quadrant of Figure 5.2 (because the profile is placed in the lower quadrant, the numbers of males must be read as increasing as the vertical distance downward from the origin increases). The relevant African age pyramids of populations from which slaves were drawn were heavily skewed toward the younger ages. This was of course primarily because of the normal demographic conditions that prevailed among these preindustrial African populations, but another contributing source of the age imbalance might have been the further reduction of the adult African population resulting from the past activity of slave traders.[10] As a result, the number of young Africans added to eligibility for the trade by the price increase would tend to be much greater than the number of additional adults: As shown in Figure 5.2, the numbers of males at the ages between A_1' and A_1 are considerably larger than at the ages from A_2 to A_2'. This disproportionate increase in the number of children in the population of Africans eligible on economic criteria for shipment to America would have tended to increase the number of children actually carried relative to that of adults.[11]

Similar logic indicates that a decline in American slave prices would have had the symmetric effect of narrowing the range in the age of slaves that could profitably be shipped to America, thereby disproportionately reducing the share of boys among African males economically eligible for the trade, and tending to reduce the number of children carried relative to adults. Overall, then, this economic analysis predicts the existence of a positive association between changes in West Indian slave prices and changes in the share of children among total slaves carried from Africa to America, with higher prices producing larger shares of children, and lower prices resulting in smaller shares of children, with other things remaining the same.[12]

Before proceeding to an empirical test of this prediction, several important qualifications must be considered. Changes in transportation costs to the West Indies could have changed slave prices in that region in a way that could have had a different effect on the demographic composition of the slave trade. The freight rates charged for the shipment of slaves to the English West Indies could change for a variety of reasons, most dramatically due to wars in the Atlantic that increased the riskiness of carrying cargoes to and from the islands. An increase in freight costs to the region would have raised the supply prices of all slaves in the West Indies by the constant amount of the fare increase.[13] This would have had the effect of raising the West Indian prices of lower-priced slaves – that is, children and older adults – relative to those of the higher-priced adults of prime working age. West Indian planters would wish to buy fewer of these less productive slaves at their new higher relative prices, and the result would be that traders would find it profitable to carry slaves only within a narrower range of prime ages. Eliminating some children and older adults from eligibility for the trade would generally remove more young than old slaves from the population acceptable to traders in Africa, and the increase in freight charges would therefore tend to reduce the share of children in the trade, with all else remaining the same.

The presence of this effect implies that transportation costs should be included as an independent variable in an equation designed to explain variations in the age composition of the slave trade. Unfortunately, no annual time series of transportation costs is available. From K. G. Davies's discussion, however, it is clear that there was a sizable increase in the rate the Royal African Company paid shipowners for the transportation of slaves from Africa to the West Indies upon the outbreak of King William's War in 1689. Rates to Barbados rose from £4–5.5 in the prewar period to £10–11 during the war, fell to somewhat lower levels during the brief interwar period that followed, and returned to generally higher levels during the 12 years of Queen Anne's War beginning in 1702.[14] Davies's account indicates that fluctuation around these levels occurred, but neither the extent nor the precise timing is known. In order to investigate the effects of the major change in the level of freight rates that occurred at the end of the 1680s, a binary variable will be included in the empirical analysis that follows, separating the periods before and after the beginning of war in 1689.

Another important qualification of the analysis presented here concerns the assumption that freight charges were a constant amount per slave, and did not vary with any characteristics of the slaves. This was true for hired shipping throughout the Royal African Company's history: Rental contracts between the company and the owners of hired ships almost invariably specified freight charges as a flat sum to be paid per slave delivered alive at the ship's agreed destination. In the first few decades of the company's activity, it relied primarily on hired shipping.[15] Over time, however, the company increasingly invested in acquiring its own fleet, so that after 1700 a majority of the ships it dispatched from England were its own.[16] As the company recognized, on these ships it was less costly to transport children than adult slaves, for children required both less space and fewer provisions during the voyage.[17] Consequently, on company-owned ships, for young slaves transportation costs were positively related to age, since the younger the slave, the lower the full cost of transportation to the West Indies. The effect of this was to lower the minimum age at which slaves could profitably be carried to America. With other things equal, this would have tended to raise the share of children in the trade on company-owned ships.

In examining this effect empirically, it would be desirable to know whether each ship that carried slave cargoes from Africa to America was owned or rented by the Royal African Company. This information is not available in the company's invoice accounts of slave sales, however, or from any other sources for most of the company's history. In recognition that the proportion of company-owned ships engaged in its transatlantic trade rose over time, a time-trend variable will be included in the following empirical analysis to investigate whether the progressive shift from hired to company-owned ships over time tended to raise the share of children in the trade.

Evidence on the prices and quantities of slaves carried by the Royal African Company to the West Indies during 1673–1723 can now be used to test the predictions of the analysis presented earlier. These are three. The first is of a positive correlation between the level of West Indian slave prices and the share of children among the slaves carried, with other things equal. The second is that rising freight costs after 1689 would reduce the share of children, *ceteris paribus*. And the third is that the trend over time toward company ownership of its own fleet would raise the share of children, again with other things equal.

The empirical analysis will be performed separately by sex of the slaves, and therefore two separate regression equations are specified. The dependent variables are, respectively, the total number of boys recorded annually in the invoices of slaves carried to all listed destinations as a proportion of total male slaves carried, and the corresponding number of girls as a share of total females; the definition of these demographic categories is again based on the company's invoices.[18] Three independent variables are included in each equation: a variable that represents appropriate slave prices in the West Indies, a binary variable that separates the periods before and after the onset of war in 1689, and a time trend.[19]

When these two equations were estimated separately, the residuals of the two regressions were found to be highly correlated. This suggests the presence of systematic forces acting on both dependent variables that are not captured by the independent variables included in the equations. An estimation method known as the seemingly unrelated regression model has been developed that uses this additional information provided by the correlation between the residuals in two equations to produce estimates of the coefficients in them that have a smaller variance than those obtained when the two equations are estimated separately.[20] The results obtained by using this method are as follows (standard errors are given in parentheses):

$$
\begin{aligned}
\text{Share of boys} = \ & -0.2695 \ + \ 0.00400 \ \text{slave prices} \\
& (0.0924) \quad\ \ (0.00197) \\
& -0.08618 \ \text{wartime} \ + \ 0.00436 \ \text{time} \\
& (0.03089) \qquad\qquad\quad (0.00112) \\
\text{Share of girls} = \ & -0.3223 \ + \ 0.00100 \ \text{slave prices} \\
& (0.0733) \quad\ \ (0.00120) \\
& -0.07976 \ \text{wartime} \ + \ 0.00501 \ \text{time} \\
& (0.02423) \qquad\qquad\quad (0.00089)
\end{aligned}
$$

Weighted R^2 for system = 0.365, $n = 82$

With the exception of the estimated coefficient for the price variable in the equation for females, the results are similar for both sexes and strongly support the predictions made earlier. In both sets of estimates, the onset of war in 1689, with its associated higher freight rates to the West Indies, is associated with a decline in the share of children in the slave trade.[21] The estimated magnitudes of this decline, of 8.6 percentage points for the share of boys among all males and 8.0 points for that of girls among females, are nearly the same. Similarly, for both sexes there was a considerable upward trend over time in the share of children in the trade, and of similar magnitudes: 0.44 of a percentage point annually for males and 0.50 of a percentage point annually for females.[22] In all these cases, the sizable magnitudes and strong statistical significance of the estimated coefficients support the validity of the economic analysis presented earlier.

Other effects could of course have contributed to the outcomes observed here. For example, the positive estimated coefficient of the time-trend variable is also consistent with falling rates of slave passage mortality during the period examined. Falling mortality rates would have lowered the full cost of transportation in the analysis above, raising the African slave prices warranted by any given American prices, so increasing the range in ages eligible for the trade, and tending to increase the share of children in the trade. Although not allowed for explicitly in the regressions for lack of detailed time-series evidence, a significant decline in average mortality on the Middle Passage did occur within the period spanned by the data analyzed here.[23]

The results for the relationship between the share of children and the slave price variable differ by sex. For males the estimated coefficient suggests that an increase of £1 in the mean sterling price of adult slaves in Barbados was associated with an average increase of 0.40 of a percentage point in the share of boys among total males carried by the Royal African Company to the West Indies annually.[24] The effect suggested by this estimate is sizable, as moving from the minimum to the maximum price for the period would raise the share of boys among male slaves by more than 5.5 percentage points. In contrast, although the coefficient of the price variable estimated for females has the predicted positive sign, its magnitude is small, and the associated standard error is greater than the coefficient.

The absence for female slaves of a statistically significant association between West Indian slave prices and the share of children in the transatlantic trade is inconsistent with the analysis presented above of the age composition of the slave trade. A possible explanation for this inconsistency can be provided by elaborating the economic analysis in a way suggested by some independent historical evidence on internal African slave markets. Before doing so, it should be stated that although this elaboration is capable of providing a logical reconciliation of the model and the evidence examined here, it cannot be tested in detail using currently available data. It is undertaken here because of the importance of trying to understand the links that existed between African slave markets and the Atlantic slave trade, and in the hope that future research will produce evidence with which to test its validity.

Females in internal African slave markets and the Atlantic slave trade: a hypothesis

The first step is to return to an observation made earlier. The basis for the prediction examined above concerning the age composition of the slave trade was the equilibrium condition that African slave prices would mirror those of the West Indies, specifically that slave prices in the two locations would differ only by transportation costs. It was noted, however, that this need not be the case, and that slaves whose African prices were greater than the level warranted by American prices would not be traded, but would be retained in Africa. Why such African prices might have existed was not explored at that point, but one reason forms the basis for the hypothesis of this section concerning the behavior of the age composition of the female population in the Atlantic slave trade.

While the Atlantic trade was one major source of demand for African slaves in the seventeenth and eighteenth centuries, there were also two other major sources. The smaller of these, yet still an estimated 40 percent as large as the transatlantic trade in the sevententh century, was the Muslim market of the Arab world.[25] The larger, which may have been the largest of all three sources of demand, was the internal African market for slaves.[26] The existence of these other sources of demand for slaves, and the contrast of their demands with those of American planters, might explain the failure of the earlier analysis of the transatlantic market for female slaves.

As noted above, some demographic classes of slaves could have been absent from, or underrepresented in, the Atlantic trade if a high demand for them in internal African markets had raised their prices to a level that would have made their transportation to America unprofitable. Philip Curtin has argued that in the case of slaves shipped from Senegambia for export to the Americas in the seventeenth century this was true for women, as a higher valuation of women than men both within the region and in North Africa led local traders to retain women, while exporting men for purchase by the Europeans, who valued them more highly.[27] One source of evidence on the relative prices of slaves by sex in the region is a report sent by the explorer Cornelius Hodges to the Royal African Company in 1690, informing the company that at one slave market in Senegambia, "Men Slaves which they purchase for Sale they buy for 1 Ounce [of gold] Boys & ffemale Slaves wch. is for theire owne use 2 oz & sometimes more according to their features."[28] Recent research on systems of slavery in the seventeenth and eighteenth centuries in both African and Muslim societies has resulted in general agreement that female slaves greatly outnumbered male slaves in these societies, and that the prices of female slaves were typically greater than those of males.[29]

Yet these facts alone do not resolve the problem posed by the empirical analysis examined above. Curtin is correct that a high internal price for female slaves within Africa would have reduced the numbers of females exported, but the existence of a uniform premium in price for females at all ages, for example, should not have eliminated the positive correlation predicted above between changes in American prices and changes in the share of young females in the trade. A factor that could have done this, however, is a differential premium in the internal African market by age.

Figure 5.3 shows one way in which this could have occurred. P_B represents an American age–price profile for female slaves, and P_A is the African profile warranted by it. A^* is again the age dividing children from adults. Now suppose that the curve P_I represents the valuation of female slaves for use within Africa. European traders in this situation would buy females only between the ages of A_3 and A_2; they would not purchase slaves younger than A_3 because the internal African demand had raised their actual prices above those – the warranted prices P_A – that would allow their profitable shipment to America.

Figure 5.4 then illustrates the possible effect of an increase in American slave prices. P_B shifts upward to P_B', shifting the curve P_A upward to P_A'. The maximum age of female slaves that European traders can profitably purchase increases to A_2', as in the earlier example in Figure 5.2. But now, instead of the minimum age of eligibility falling by an amount as large as that from A_1 to

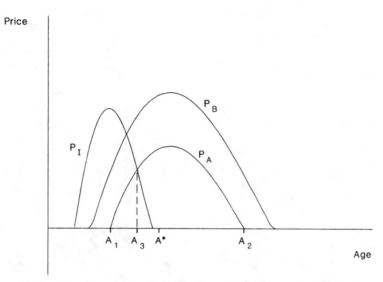

Figure 5.3. Possible effect of internal African demand for female slaves on the determination of minimum and maximum ages eligible for shipment to America. *Note:* For the age–price profiles P_B and P_A, see Figure 5.1. For the construction of P_I, see the text.

A'_1, the minimum age falls by only the smaller interval from A_3 to A'_3. This smaller decline in the minimum age is due to the fact that internal African demand continues to value females more highly than the Europeans at ages below A'_3; that is, the curve P_I remains above P'_A at ages below A'_3. The number of girls added to the pool of females eligible for the Atlantic trade is therefore smaller in this case than in that of Figure 5.2 for two reasons: Not only is the size of the interval of younger ages added smaller, as just noted, but also the numbers of African female slaves at these added ages are somewhat smaller than at the younger ages added in the case of Figure 5.2. The net change in the relative numbers of girls and adult women eligible for the slave trade is now less clear than in that previous case, and will depend on a number of factors, including the slopes of the two age–price profiles P_A and P_I in the regions near their intersection. For example, the steeper the profile P_I near its intersection with P_A, the smaller will be the increase in the range of ages of females eligible for the Atlantic trade caused by a given American price increase, and the smaller the expected increase in the share of girls among total females transported.

This result clearly depends critically on a particular configuration of the internal African valuation of females (P_I) relative to that warranted in Africa by American prices (P_A), with the former peaking at a lower age than the latter. Yet the origins of the internal age–price profile P_I are not completely

5. Demographic composition of the slave trade

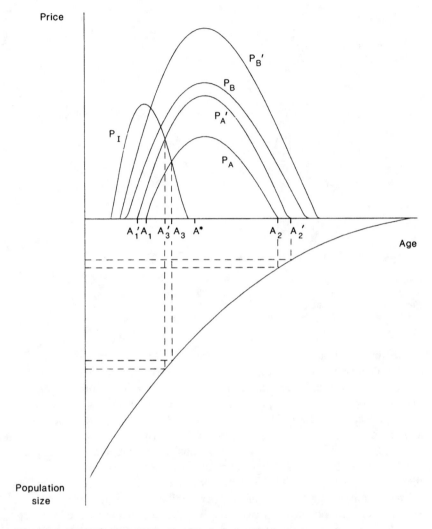

Figure 5.4. Possible effect of American female slave price changes on the age composition of the transatlantic trade. *Note:* For the age–price profiles P_B and P_A, see Figure 5.1; for P_B' and P_A' and for the African population profile, see Figure 5.2. For P_I, see Figure 5.3.

arbitrary. Few detailed records of slave prices in internal African or Arab markets survive from the seventeenth and eighteenth centuries. Later observations, however, appear to provide some basis for believing that the valuation of female slaves for internal African use produced an age–price profile with a relatively early peak. A recent study of the structure of slave prices in the nineteenth-century West African Sokoto Caliphate found not only that females were more highly valued than males, but also that "the value of females increased much more sharply between childhood and adolescence, and decreased much more sharply between young adulthood and later life, than did the value of males." The author argued that this difference might have resulted from "a demand for young females as concubines and child-bearers."[30] A number of surviving contemporary accounts of specific nine-teenth-century African and Muslim societies emphasize that a premium was paid for female slaves purchased as wives or concubines, and that this pre-mium was greatest at relatively young ages. One recent discussion of a society in Eastern Africa in the late nineteenth century reports that the Arabs there often purchased African concubines, for whom they typically paid prices considerably higher than for laboring slaves; furthermore, the author notes, concubines were usually chosen as young girls.[31] Similarly, a traveler in the southern Soudan in the 1870s quoted the typical price paid for slave children of both sexes there, then added that

particularly pretty women-slaves . . . fetch nearly double that price, and are very rarely procured for exportation, because they are in great demand amongst the numer-ous settlers in the country. Strong adult women, who are ugly, are rather cheaper than the young girls, whilst old women are worth next to nothing, and can be bought for a mere bagatelle. Full-grown men are rarely purchased as slaves, being troublesome to control and difficult of transport. Slaves in the East are usually in demand as *objets de luxe*, and consequently lead an idle life, and are not valued according to their ca-pabilities for labour.[32]

It is of course obvious that these accounts of nineteenth-century practices cannot simply be assumed to apply to societies that existed two centuries earlier. The precise extent to which the higher price of female slaves in African and Arab markets was a consequence of their procreative abilities rather than their capacity for physical labor is currently the subject of consid-erable controversy among scholars of African slavery.[33] Yet if the premium for female slaves that Curtin describes in seventeenth-century Senegambia had come from a demand for young females – those in the teen ages, whether they were to serve as concubines or as domestic laborers – that was not simply determined by the productivity of females in heavy agricultural field work, it could have produced an age–price profile like P_I in Figures 5.3 and 5.4, with a peak at an age lower than that of the American profile P_B, which did depend on productivity in heavy field labor and therefore rose, as strength increased, into adulthood. As Figure 5.4 illustrates, this could then account for the attenuation or even the complete absence of a significant positive correlation between changes in West Indian slave prices and the share of children in the female slave population transported to the islands by the Royal African Company.

Although this hypothesis cannot be tested directly with available evidence,

5. Demographic composition of the slave trade

one indirect implication of it can be tested through the use of the quantitative evidence presented earlier on the demographic composition of the Royal African Company's slave shipments. This involves the prediction of a difference in the relative numbers of children and adults by sex. Specifically, if an internal African age–price profile for slaves like that shown in Figures 5.3 and 5.4 as P_I had existed for young females, while the African age–price profile for male slaves had been of the form of P_A in Figures 5.1 and 5.2, the proportion of female slaves exported from Africa that was made up of girls should have been smaller than the proportion of exported male slaves that was made up of boys. The source of the difference, which can be seen from a comparison of Figures 5.1 and 5.3, is that whereas internal African demand would bid away young girls from the export trade, and girls younger than A_3 in Figure 5.3 would therefore be retained in Africa, this would not occur for boys, and all male slaves available to African traders whose export to America would yield a profit would in fact be exported. The reduction in the number of girls exported, without a parallel reduction in the number of boys, would be predicted to lower the share of girls among females exported relative to the share of boys among males. The quantitative evidence of Table 5.1 confirms this prediction: Whereas boys accounted for 15.8 percent of the 45,810 males transported by the Royal African Company who are categorized in Table 5.1, girls accounted for a lower 11.4 percent of the 28,804 females. This evidence therefore provides some indirect quantitative support for the validity of the hypothesis presented in this section.

The selection of cargoes and the demographic composition of the slave trade

The Royal African Company and its employees in both West Africa and the West Indies were of course well aware of the basic proposition underlying the economic analysis of this chapter, that slaves could be carried profitably only if their expected American prices covered their transportation costs. The failure of company factors to observe this principle in purchasing slaves in West Africa brought severe complaints, as on an occasion in 1683 when the company's Barbados agents wrote about the arrival of a cargo of slaves:

The 28th March Capt. Barton in the Delight togeather with Agent Wight – arrived here in abt. one mo. time bringing 169 slaves of 171 taken in at Cunho, Boson & Rio Grande . . . abt. 1/3d part of those he did bring were very small most of them noe better then sucking children nay many of them did suck theire Mothers that were on board . . . the most part of those small ones not worth above £5 per head Wee told agt. White wee wondred to see soe many small Children brought by him for that they were not worth theire Freight.

The one unusual aspect of this complaint is the reference to such a large number of very young children. White's reply to the agents is interesting, for he argued that his selection of the cargo had been influenced by a very unusual charter agreement for the ship: "he replyed they cost not much & the shipp had as good bring them as nothing she being paid by the month." Instead of the company paying the normal flat freight charges per slave delivered, White claimed that the whole ship had been rented by the month, and that under this arrangement, with excess space available in the ship, the sale of the slaves had only to cover a much lower marginal cost of transportation – principally provisioning – in order to be profitable. His reasoning was correct, and the same reasoning was applied by the company to the slave ships it owned in later years. The agents accepted White's explanation and paid his commission, but they were nonetheless uneasy at reporting the very low prices they received for the unusually young children. They therefore explained in their letter that they "thought it necessary to give the Comp. this accott. that soe they may not blame us for the small Prizes wee are forced to sell them for when they are truly Informed they are such Pittiful Children & not men & women are delivered to us."[34]

The company's concern with the selection of slave cargoes that would result in profitable voyages is witnessed in its correspondence on several occasions in rebukes it sent to the company factors in West Africa charged with purchasing the cargoes. One such case illustrates the analysis presented earlier of the effects of the wartime increase in freight charges for slaves, as in 1702 a factor was asked to be more selective:

Our ffactors at the West Indies complain much of the badness of the Negroes purchased by our ffactors upon the Coast . . . Wee hope better things from you, ffreight is now dear by reason of the Warr therefore an old decrepit Negro is by no meanes to be put aboard any of our Ships.[35]

Here the company explicitly stated that the higher wartime freight costs meant that slaves that might previously have been marginally profitable were no longer worth transporting, for their American prices would no longer cover their costs of transportation. With similar purpose, though more gently, in 1704 the company wrote to Dalby Thomas, its agent-general at Cape Coast, concerning a recent cargo delivered to Barbados:

the Edward & Francis was Arrived with 143 Slaves . . . We find there were 26 Boyes & 12 Girles in ye Complement Shipt which Wee should very well Approve on were they Sizeable But our Factors complain severall of them were not above 10 years of Age so that they did not sell for much more than their Freight. Procure as many Boyes & Girles as you can but lett them be of the Age of 14, 15, or 16 years and Avoid Sending Old Negros.[36]

Thomas did not take this admonition lightly. This is perhaps not surprising in view of his status, for he was well known in England for his scholarly writings on the West Indies, and he was knighted during his tenure in Africa. It is perhaps even less surprising because his appointment as agent-general at

111

5. Demographic composition of the slave trade

Cape Coast in 1703, which made him commander of the largest English fort in West Africa, also made him the highest-paid employee of the Royal African Company in Africa, with a salary of £1,000 per year plus commissions on all company profits from the Gold Coast. Even the slightest threat to his job might have been expected to attract his serious attention, and this one did. In early 1705 the company noted receipt of a letter from Sir Dalby in which he described in some detail his practices in buying slaves for the company, emphasizing the care he took in supervising the factors and ships' captains who came under his authority. In an interesting passage, Thomas made the point that he avoided buying potentially marginally profitable slaves at both ends of the age distribution when company ships alone were present on the Gold Coast, and those in small numbers, but he relaxed his age criteria to permit the purchase of both younger children and older adults when more ships, including those of the company's competitors, arrived:

when few or no Ships are on ye Coast then yors. & not many of them I direct [that the slaves purchased for the company] shale not Exceed 30 Years of Age Men, 25 Woomen, boys & Girls 15 at other times to advance 5 Years on Men & Woomen boys & Girls 14 or 13, large lusty & Strong.[37]

Thomas here demonstrated a clear understanding of the process of selection implied by the economic analysis suggested earlier of the slave trade's age composition. He described the adjustment of the range in the ages of slaves eligible for the trade as a means of moving to the margins of profitability: When local market conditions were favorable to the company, his policy was to remain cautiously within the bounds of the minimum and maximum ages that could profitably be shipped, whereas when the level of demand in the local market increased, he became willing to buy both older and younger slaves than before, with due care to selecting relatively choice ones at these marginal ages. His closing phrase in fact draws attention to an obviously important additional dimension of this process, implied by the same economic analysis but not subject to empirical test here for lack of recorded evidence, that the choicest and most valuable slaves at an existing marginal age would be selected for transportation before others of the same age.

Thomas's comment properly points up the importance of physical characteristics in the actual selection of slaves. The company would typically describe its criteria for choice in terms of a combination of age and physical characteristics. A detailed example appears in a letter to the king of Whydah in 1701 informing him what types of slaves his buyers should procure to satisfy the needs of the company:

We . . . do desire your Majestie and great Capasheens . . . will be pleased to direct ye Buyers never to buy a Negro to be offered to us to sale above 30 years of Age nor lower than $4\frac{1}{2}$ foot high . . . nor none Sickly Deformed nor defective in Body or Limb, for we want Negroes as Chargeable in Carriage as ye best. And ye Diseased and ye

Aged have often been ye Distruction of ye whole Adventure, so that we must desire that our Negroes be every way perfect & fit for Service and had much Rather at proportionate prices have a boy & a Girle not under 3½ foot high to every 5 Men and 5 Women than have any above 30, sickly & deformed.[38]

In the following year the company repeated the same criteria in the course of a cordial response to another African king's invitation to send their ships to trade with him. It then added the condition of trade "that whenever others not so well qualifyed are delivered or pretended to be delivered to our People for our use, that they be returned and the person selling them be obliged immediately to make satisfaccon."[39]

As in the case of the first letter quoted in this section, the demographic composition of the slave cargoes they received for sale was often a source of complaint for the company's West Indian agents. In part, no doubt, this was because reference to poorly chosen slaves was the principal way in which agents would attempt to justify unusually low prices when reporting sales to the company, arguing that the poor results were not due to their own incompetence or dishonesty but rather to the negligence of the company's factors in Africa. Age was a common cause for comment, as when the Barbados agents remarked of a cargo in 1683 that "The Negroes sent are but Indifferent being many elderly amongst them nigh ½ of the men being of 40 to 50 years old or more."[40]

Such complaints were sometimes relayed by the company to its factors in Africa. In a letter written in May 1703, the company's agent in Barbados reported of one cargo that

The Negroes were pretty good except 15 Men & Woomen which were old and most of ye Woomen were from 22 to 30 Years of Age. But young woomen from 15 to 22 will sell from 8 to 10£ per head more than those from 26 to 32 Years old.

The company's clerk then added: "he Complaines that ye Comp's Factors mind not what he Writes every opportunity, of sending more Boys then Girles & Men then Woomen & no old ones."[41] Both the final complaint and the information about the existing price differentials by age for women in Barbados were passed along almost verbatim in a letter dispatched by the company to its factors at Cape Coast in July 1703, together with an instruction to purchase more male than female slaves.[42] In a similar instance, in 1704 the company passed on a complaint from its agents in Jamaica to its factor in Whydah:

We hear ye ffaulconburgh is arrived at Jamaica with 466 Negroes pray for ye future procure as many Boys & Girls as you can of ye age of 14 or 15 Years Especially when Men are scarce & dear since our Jamaica Letters coming to hand our ffactors advise that there are a great many old men & Women and very small Boys & Girls amongst ye Faulconburgh's Negroes of which great care must be taken to prevent ye like Complaints.[43]

5. *Demographic composition of the slave trade*

As these examples illustrate, the age of slaves was the characteristic most often cited by the company and its agents in both Africa and the West Indies in discussions of the suitability of particular cargoes of slaves as well as of the selection of slaves for the trade in general.[44] That this could be done was due to the strong relationship between the ages of slaves and their prices in the West Indies; that it was important that it should be done was because it was profitable to carry a slave to America only if his or her price there exceeded the sum of the African price and the cost of passage.

This chapter has provided an economic framework for analyzing the age composition of the Atlantic slave trade. An empirical test of the analysis using evidence from Royal African Company records of slave shipments showed that two of its basic predictions were consistent with the results obtained for both males and females. The share of children of both sexes in the trade decreased when wars in the Atlantic raised shipping costs. The share of children otherwise tended to rise over time, as the Royal African Company came to own an increasing number of the ships that traded on its behalf. There was furthermore evidence that, as the analysis also predicted, the ratio of boys to men in the trade was positively related to the level of American slave prices. The analogous test for females did not support the analysis, however, and a further elaboration of the model based on independent evidence on African slave markets suggested that this could have resulted from the nature of the demand for young female slaves for use within Africa. Examination of literary evidence from Royal African Company correspondence indicated that the company and its agents in West Africa and the West Indies were well aware of the mechanisms implied by the economic analysis presented here, and that the factors in Africa did use the ages of slaves in the way implied by the analysis as a central criterion guiding their selection of the slaves they purchased for the transatlantic trade.

6

Estimating geographic persistence
from market observations

Population turnover among estate owners and
managers in Barbados and Jamaica, 1673–1725

The significance of mobility and the use of persistence studies

Economists and historians have long been interested in the amount of geographic mobility in a society for a number of reasons. The extent of geographic mobility can indicate the degree to which labor will move in response to
changing opportunities, and contribute to an efficient allocation of productive
resources in an economy. The amount of geographic mobility is often considered a determinant of the political and social stability of a society. And the
frequency with which the members of a population move can suggest the
extent of economic opportunity in a community. Although in each of these
cases the interpretation of mobility requires care, because the many causes
and effects of individual migration make its linkages in the aggregate to each
of these social and economic consequences varied and complex, the extent of
geographic mobility has nonetheless been considered a basic characteristic of
a society.

One common approach to the study of migration in American history has
been the measurement of geographic persistence. Since the pioneering studies
of migration in rural Kansas by James Malin, in Trempealeau County,
Wisconsin, by Merle Curti, and in Newburyport, Massachusetts, by Stephan
Thernstrom, a series of studies have been done that measure the persistence of
a population in a particular location by calculating the proportion of a sample
of individuals from a chosen base year that could still be found in that location
at some subsequent date, typically 10 years later.[1] The source most often used
in these studies has been the nineteenth-century manuscript federal census
schedules, but a variety of other sources, including records such as tax lists
produced by local governments and city directories compiled for private use,
have also been used to push the time periods studied both back into the
American colonial period and forward into the twentieth century.[2] Yet a
potentially important type of information has not previously been used on a
large scale to study persistence. Specifically, observations generated by the
functioning of economic markets have not been exploited to study the extent

of population turnover in the past. Following a discussion of some general advantages and disadvantages of the use of market observations for this purpose, this chapter uses evidence generated by the Royal African Company's sales of slaves to measure the persistence of estate owners and managers in Barbados and Jamaica between 1673 and 1725, a subject that has eluded systematic quantitative investigation from other sources.

Market observations and the measurement of persistence

The principle underlying the use of market observations to measure geographic persistence is a simple one, although it is subject to some qualifications. Records of the dates at which an individual participated in a market in a known location can be used as evidence of the individual's presence in that location, and in some cases this can be taken to imply the individual's residence in the vicinity of the marketplace. Certain obvious assumptions are basic to this formulation. One is that the market records must list the names of the individuals actually present at the transactions, rather than those of principals who may only be represented by agents present at the marketplace. Another is that presence at the marketplace can be taken to contain information about the individual's place of residence. If these assumptions prove to be valid, the names of market participants can be traced through records of transactions over time to produce estimates of the duration of their persistence in the vicinity of the market.

The first of these assumptions may be subject to indirect test from the evidence of the registrations. Evidence on the practices of the market recorders can be obtained by checking whether the names of individuals known to be agents for specific principals ever appear in the records. If the names of known agents (e.g., employees or associates) do appear, this might be presumed to indicate that the clerks did record the names of the individuals present at the marketplace, rather than those of absent principals on whose account the transactions were made.

Some evidence on the validity of the second assumption can generally be deduced from market characteristics. The more frequently the market convened, the less precisely its meetings could be anticipated, and the closer the location of alternative marketplaces, the more likely it would be that participation in the market indicated residence in the vicinity of the market. Great markets or fairs held annually on fixed dates might draw participants from a very wide area, and the same participants might make long journeys to return year after year. In such cases inferences about residence from evidence of appearance at the market would have little validity. In contrast, the appearance of an individual at a market at more frequent intervals might tend to indicate residence closer to the market. The same might be true of markets

116

whose meetings could not be well anticipated; in many periods the date of the sale of goods from a ship completing a long voyage could be anticipated only approximately, and if the sale occurred shortly after the ship's arrival, only those who lived near the port might be expected to attend. Similarly, the larger the number of markets in any geographic area that sold the same commodity, the greater would be the tendency for the market to serve only local customers.[3]

Definitive tests of these basic assumptions may not be feasible in many cases, and consequently evidence obtained from market observations may remain somewhat ambiguous concerning the geographic persistence of individuals in a particular region. Given this ambiguity, why should this type of data ever be used to study persistence?

Market observations have several important characteristics that argue strongly for their value in studying geographic persistence in some circumstances. The most basic of these is coverage, for records of market transactions are available for many times and places for which no other type of evidence that bears on migration may exist on a similar scale. As is the case in the study to be done in this chapter, records of market activity have survived from many early periods and many locations from which no systematic and regular forms of population enumeration were undertaken, with the latter defined broadly to include government censuses or tax records, church records of vital events, or other official registrations. The question of the value of market observations for studies of persistence in any particular case then initially concerns the extent of the information included in the records. Clearly the names of market participants are a necessary minimum in this respect, while additional information about the characteristics of individuals can improve the confidence that can be placed in linkages of names across time, and can also increase the knowledge of the correlates of migration or persistence that can be gained from the data.

Market observations also have some potential advantages over the other types of population enumerations on which persistence studies have typically been based. One is that they may appear more frequently than censuses or other official enumerations. This raises the possibility of more precise measurement of the actual interval in which an individual was present in a location than would be the case for records like decennial censuses. Another potential advantage is that if the market involved the sale of an expensive commodity, the recording of transactions might have been done with more care than such official enumerations as census registrations, in which little was directly at stake for the enumerators. In the case to be analyzed here, the market records were produced by a private company for the purpose of keeping track of sizable debts owed to it by purchasers buying valuable commodities, often in large quantities. Furthermore, the lucrative jobs of the recording agents, whose earnings were determined as a proportion of the value of the revenues collected for the commodities they sold, would be jeopardized if the accounts were poorly kept, and if the debts could consequently not be collected.[4]

Some potential difficulties involved in using market observations for studies of persistence should be mentioned at the outset. One is the problem of defining the population at risk to appear in the records, beyond the obvious statement that it consists of those who participated in the particular market under consideration. It will often be very difficult to define the size and attributes of this group precisely, and therefore to know their characteristics relative to larger populations from which they were drawn. The characteristics of the commodity traded, however, can give important indications of those likely to participate. Expensive commodities or luxuries will tend to be bought disproportionately by the wealthy, specialized inputs into particular industries will be bought primarily by practitioners of the relevant trades, and so on. A second potential problem is incomplete recording of transactions. As in the more familiar case of underenumeration in censuses, this will tend to lower measured persistence relative to true persistence rates. The use of market observations also entails a third potential problem, with an effect like that of incomplete recording, that is not shared by censuses. Whereas censuses are normally intended to be complete enumerations of the population resident in some location, the same is not true of market records; people present in a location might simply choose not to make purchases in a given market in that place within some time period. While the extent to which this occurs will vary with the commodity and location in question, voluntary abstention from participation will be a reason why a person actually present in a place will not be known to be present from market records. This will tend to lower persistence rates measured from market observations, and therefore reinforces the effect of incomplete recording in making persistence rates measured from such records lower-bound estimates of true persistence rates.

The Royal African Company invoice accounts and the market for slaves in Barbados and Jamaica

The data for this study are drawn from the records of 129 slave sales held by a succession of agents of the Royal African Company in Barbados between March 1673 and September 1723, and of 119 slave sales held by company agents in Jamaica between November 1674 and October 1725. The recorded names of the individuals who purchased slaves form the basis of this investigation. In all, 2,886 different names of purchasers appear in a total of 6,458 transactions recorded in Barbados over the five decades spanned by the registrations, while the names of 1,587 purchasers appear in a total of 4,802 transactions recorded in Jamaica.[5] The distribution of these transactions over time is uneven, owing to both temporary fluctuations and a downward secular trend in the level of the Royal African Company's trading activity; the effects of this will be discussed in some detail later, in assessing the impact of the temporal distribution of the transactions on the persistence estimates obtained from these data. Perhaps the most important preliminary issue to be considered here concerns an issue raised earlier, of defining the population under study.

The Royal African Company invoices to be analyzed here record the sales of slaves in Barbados and Jamaica. The presumption might be that those who made purchases in these markets were primarily those residents of Barbados and Jamaica who were in a position to buy slaves. Two significant questions arise about this formulation. One concerns the possible presence of buyers from islands other than Barbados and Jamaica, while the other has to do with defining more precisely the group of those in a position to buy slaves.

Barbados was the largest market for slaves in the late seventeenth-century English West Indies, and as a result its sales undoubtedly attracted some purchasers from the other English islands in the region. Several factors, however, suggest that these purchasers would not generally have made up a large proportion of buyers at sales held in Barbados. One of these was the cost to planters of traveling to Barbados. The distance of 300 miles from Barbados to the nearest English colonies, the Leeward Islands of Antigua, Montserrat, Nevis, and St. Christopher, represented a three-day voyage, while the trip to Jamaica, more than 1,000 miles, was more than twice as long.[6] In addition, the dates of slave sales could not be very precisely anticipated. Although as seen in Chapter 2 there was a pronounced seasonality in shipping to the West Indies, the main season for the arrival of slave ships spread over six months or more, and even in active trading years, only half a dozen Royal African Company cargoes might arrive in Barbados, with perhaps an equal number from other sources. The spacing of sales was not even, and long periods could pass without sales. Sales generally began within three or four days of a ship's arrival in port, in most cases leaving inadequate time for information of a slave ship's arrival in Barbados to bring a contingent of purchasers from the Leewards. And finally, although complaints were frequently made by planters in the Leewards and Jamaica concerning Barbados's favored position in the slave trade, direct shipments of slaves from Africa to all of these islands were made throughout this period, both by the company and by smaller independent traders. The combined effects of the cost of travel to Barbados's market, the difficulty of anticipating sales, and the availability of markets in the other islands must have resulted in an overwhelming majority of purchasers in Barbados being residents of the island. To the extent that purchasers did come from other islands, however, these considerations might be expected to have made regular or frequent attendance of these "strangers" at the Barbados market unlikely. Inclusion of these purchasers in this study would therefore probably tend to lower measured persistence rates, by adding disproportionately to the group of purchasers who appeared at only a small number of auctions.

The presence of nonresident purchasers at slave sales is likely to pose even less of a problem for Jamaica than for Barbados, for Jamaica was the most geographically isolated of the English colonies in the West Indies. In combination with the same difficulties discussed for Barbados that raised the cost to outsiders of coming to the island to purchase slaves, the thousand-mile voyage that separated Jamaica from the Leewards must have reduced to a very small minority the number of purchasers present at slave sales on the island who lived elsewhere.

The second question raised earlier concerns in part the practices followed by Royal African Company agents in recording the sale outcomes. Specifically, a critical issue is whether the name of the purchaser recorded was always that of an individual actually present at the sale, or whether it might be the name of an absentee plantation owner on whose account slaves were purchased by an employee. Considerations involving the purpose of keeping the records suggest that the former might have been more likely. Although information about the conditions of payment is often not specified in the records, nearly all transactions involved credit,[7] and the primary purpose of the invoice accounts was to preserve records of debts owed to the Royal African Company. Nearly all transactions appear as sales to a single person. If company agents were to record the names of absentee plantation owners as purchasers rather than those of the employees actually present, it might be expected that debts could be more easily denied by the plantation owners, for the latter could claim the company had falsely debited their accounts in the absence of any actual purchases. A record of the name of the individual actually present at the sale would constitute more concrete evidence of the circumstances of a sale.

Although limited in number because of the difficulty of identifying managers working for absentee plantation owners, some cases drawn from the Royal African Company invoices do support the view that the individual recorded as the purchaser in the invoices was actually present, whether or not he owned the plantation for which he was buying the slaves. Some relatively detailed evidence comes from the experience of Bybrook Plantation in Jamaica.[8] Although the plantation was owned by the absentee William Helyar between its formation in 1669 and 1697, Helyar's name never appears in the invoices as a purchaser of slaves. William Whaley, a part owner who managed the plantation during 1672–6, appears as a purchaser of slaves in invoices of three different company sales held in Jamaica during 1674–6. Edward Atcherly, who became manager after Whaley's death, appears as a purchaser at a company sale held in Jamaica in 1677. Thomas Hillyard, who managed Bybrook during 1678–87, is similarly recorded as a purchaser at a sale held in Jamaica in 1682. After William Helyar's death in 1697, his sons employed

Robert Hall as an overseer, and that name appears in the account of a Jamaica sale in 1704.

In another case Christopher Jeaffreson, a planter in St. Kitts, is recorded as making purchases on four occasions at company sales in nearby Nevis during 1678–81. During this period Jeaffreson employed a manager named Edward Thorn, and a purchaser of that name appears in a Nevis sale of 1679.[9]

Although limited, this evidence does demonstrate that plantation managers could be listed in the Royal African Company invoices as purchasers. Although strong generalizations about the company's recording practices are not warranted, it seems reasonable that it would have been the general practice to record the name of the person present at the sale, who actually agreed to the terms of the bargain. If this were the normal practice, the population represented in the sale invoice accounts from a given colony would consist primarily of those individuals resident in the colony who were responsible for the operation of estates or plantations, whether they were owners or hired managers or overseers.[10]

All resident estate owners and managers in Barbados and Jamaica of course do not appear in the Royal African Company's records. In part this is because throughout this period there were many estates too small to warrant the ownership of slaves. According to a census of property taken in Barbados during December 1679, 703 of the island's 2,724 property holders did not own any slaves.[11] In addition, those who bought slaves need not have purchased them from the Royal African Company, for there were other shippers who brought slaves to the islands; slaves could also be purchased from other resident slave owners, or from the estates of deceased owners. The purchasers who appear in the company invoices would therefore have made up only some subset of the island's planters and overseers. The characteristics of this group relative to that larger population cannot be known with precision, but some outlines can be given. Specifically, the amount of land and numbers of slaves owned by all purchasers from the Royal African Company invoices whose names appear in the 1679 census of Barbados can be compared to the holdings of property owners listed in that census whose names do not appear in the invoices. This comparison clearly indicates that those planters who bought slaves from the Royal African Company were disproportionately drawn from Barbados's wealthier planters.[12] This is not surprising, for as noted earlier most of the company's transactions involved credit, and larger planters might generally have been regarded by the company as better clients, with lower risk of default; in part this is because, as will be shown later, there was a positive association between a planter's wealth and the length of his stay in the colony.

Persistence in Barbados and Jamaica

Geographic persistence was measured in this study by tracing the names of purchasers over time through the invoice accounts of slave sales held by the

Royal African Company in Barbados and Jamaica. The actual tracing was performed by computer. In preparing the evidence of the invoices for computer analysis, each transaction was coded separately. Along with the date of the sale, the number of slaves purchased, the amount paid, and other details of the transaction, a number was recorded that corresponded to the name of a specific purchaser; for example William Bulkey, the first purchaser at the first sale that appeared in the company invoices from Barbados, was assigned the number 1. This identifying number was then recorded for every subsequent transaction in which the name of William Bulkey appeared as the purchaser. The measurement of persistence was then done by having the computer determine the intervals of time over which each purchaser's identifying number appeared; this was done separately for Barbados and Jamaica.

A familiar problem appears with this use of nominal record linkage. The presence in the invoices of different individuals with the same first and last names – for example, two different men named William Bulkey – will result in false linkages being made between their appearances on different occasions. This will tend to raise the measured persistence rates relative to those true rates that would be obtained if the appearances of the different individuals could be accurately distinguished. For example, if one William Bulkey had made a purchase in 1673 and then soon left Barbados, while a different William Bulkey had arrived in the colony and made a purchase in 1683, the tracing procedure would falsely indicate that "William Bulkey" had persisted in Barbados from 1673 to 1683.[13]

The estimates of persistence in Barbados and Jamaica that are presented in Tables 6.1 and 6.2 have been adjusted in an attempt to eliminate the effects of the problem posed by common names, by means of a procedure discussed in Appendix C. The entries in these tables indicate the proportion of the total number of purchasers in each base year whose names reappear in an invoice at least some specified number of years later. For example, the first line of Table 6.1 indicates that 33 different individuals appeared as purchasers in Barbados in the first year of the invoices, 1673; the names of 25 of these same individuals (76 percent) reappeared as purchasers in 1674 or subsequent years, whereas 16 (49 percent) reappeared in 1683 or later, and 9 (27 percent) reappeared as purchasers in 1693 or later.[14] These estimates use sale invoices from as late as 1725, but the dwindling levels of activity of the Royal African Company in the early eighteenth century make the use of base years later than 1700 of questionable value; throughout this analysis, the base years used will therefore be those from 1673 to 1700.

If the one-year persistence rates for Barbados from Table 6.1 are averaged by decade, with weights equal to the number of individuals in each of the base-year samples, the mean persistence rate from base years in the 1670s is 60 percent, that for the 1680s is 53 percent, and that for the 1690s is 44 percent. Calculating weighted means in the same way for the five-year per-

Table 6.1. *Persistence of purchasers in Barbados (all common names eliminated)*

Base year	N: 1	2	3	4	5	10	15	20	No. of buyers in base year
				Percent present sometime after N years					
1673	76	73	73	67	61	49	33	27	33
1674	64	59	56	55	49	41	27	20	162
1675	63	60	57	50	50	32	22	16	178
1676	60	57	49	49	48	37	22	12	164
1677	65	58	57	51	48	37	23	15	99
1678	51	49	44	42	40	30	22	14	223
1679	60	55	52	45	45	31	19	11	62
1680	63	58	54	54	49	35	26	18	156
1681	59	53	53	42	42	26	20	13	121
1682	53	52	43	43	37	25	18	11	95
1683	58	42	42	37	37	16	11	11	19
1684	42	42	35	33	31	21	13	9	154
1686	53	50	44	39	36	26	18	14	180
1687	51	43	41	38	36	21	12	5	81
1688	56	49	48	44	42	28	23	11	164
1689	50	48	42	36	35	21	12	3	193
1690	35	31	25	24	22	14	10	5	88
1691	47	37	36	34	32	21	11	2	152
1692	46	46	40	38	35	27	11	2	189
1693	47	35	35	29	18	12	9	0	34
1694	43	38	34	27	26	14	4	1	160
1695	56	49	43	42	35	27	5	1	102
1696	52	41	38	31	30	17	4	3	81
1697	40	38	32	31	29	18	4	3	114
1698	40	30	30	28	25	10	3	3	40
1699	37	36	34	33	31	13	3	2	120
1700	47	43	36	32	30	6	2	0	47

Note: See text and Appendix C for method of construction.

sistence rates yields means of 47 percent for the 1670s, 39 percent for the 1680s, and 30 percent for the 1690s; the same procedure applied to the 10-year persistence rates yields means of 35 percent for the 1670s, 25 percent for the 1680s, and 19 percent for the 1690s. Interestingly, in each case the means of the rates decline consistently over time. In part this results from changes in the level of the Royal African Company's activity in this period; the extent to which the declining rates indicate real declines in the persistence of planters over time is an important question, and will be considered in some detail in the next section of this chapter.

Averaging the one-year persistence rates of Table 6.2 for Jamaica by decade, with weights again equal to the number of purchasers in the respective

6. Estimating geographic persistence

Table 6.2. *Persistence of purchasers in Jamaica (all common names eliminated)*

Base year	Percent present sometime after N years								No. of buyers in base year
	N: 1	2	3	4	5	10	15	20	
1674	74	63	59	52	46	35	20	13	54
1675	61	54	45	43	42	27	13	6	136
1676	62	53	50	49	45	29	15	9	117
1677	60	55	55	50	48	15	10	7	134
1678	54	53	47	44	37	15	10	5	126
1679	60	53	53	42	40	26	16	12	57
1680	58	57	40	38	33	16	11	9	170
1681	69	50	50	47	44	23	8	6	64
1682	45	44	37	36	23	14	9	4	201
1683	57	48	48	33	33	17	14	5	42
1684	48	47	28	26	23	12	10	7	105
1685	60	43	40	40	29	17	11	6	35
1686	35	32	27	21	20	9	7	3	203
1687	48	36	32	29	26	16	7	0	31
1688	30	28	26	23	23	11	6	4	53
1689	33	30	25	25	22	12	3	0	60
1690	44	25	19	6	6	6	6	0	16
1691	44	44	24	20	16	8	4	0	25
1692	70	60	40	40	40	30	10	0	10
1693	48	35	33	33	33	18	10	5	40
1694	40	37	37	37	37	27	7	7	62
1695	43	43	43	43	37	33	10	10	30
1699	50	42	33	25	25	8	8	8	12
1700	36	29	25	25	22	7	7	7	77

Note: See text and Appendix C for method of construction.

base-year samples, yields a mean rate of 61 percent for the 1670s, 47 percent for the 1680s and 45 percent for the 1690s. The same procedure applied to the five-year rates produces weighted means of 43 percent for base years in the 1670s, 26 percent for the 1680s, and 30 percent for the 1690s, while the weighted means of the 10-year persistence rates are 23 percent for the 1670s, 14 percent for the 1680s, and 21 percent for the 1690s. The weighted mean persistence rates for Jamaica do not show the same consistent tendency to decline from decade to decade as do the Barbados rates, although in each case the mean persistence rate for the 1670s is greater than that for each of the two following decades.

An interesting difference appears in the structure of persistence rates from Barbados and Jamaica for base years in the 1670s and 1680s, then disappears for base years in the 1690s. Barbados planters who purchased slaves from the Royal African Company during the 1670s and 1680s appear to have been considerably more likely to remain in their colony for long periods, particularly of 10 years or more, than their counterparts in Jamaica. The weighted mean persistence rates for 10, 15, and 20 years calculated for Barbados from Table 6.1 for base years in the 1670s (35, 23, and 16 percent, respectively) are in each case more than half again as large as the analogous rates for Jamaica in the same periods calculated from Table 6.2 (23, 13, and 8 percent, respectively). The relative differences are even larger for the 1680s, as the mean Barbados rates for the same 10-, 15-, and 20-year periods (25, 18, and 11 percent, respectively) are in each case more than 80 percent greater than the rates for Jamaica (14, 9, and 5 percent, respectively). For base years in the 1690s, however, these differences disappear, as the weighted mean 10-, 15-, and 20-year persistence rates for Barbados (19, 7, and 2 percent, respectively) are virtually the same as those for Jamaica (21, 8, and 5 percent). Relative differences in persistence rates between the two colonies for shorter periods are generally smaller or altogether absent; both had practically the same weighted mean one-, three-, and five-year persistence rates for base years in both the 1670s and 1690s, whereas in the 1680s Barbados had mean one- and three-year persistence rates only moderately higher than those of Jamaica, with a mean five-year rate about half again as large as that of Jamaica.

This evidence points strongly to a tendency for Barbados planters present in the 1670s and 1680s to have been substantially more likely to remain in the colony for 10 years or longer than were planters present in Jamaica during the same periods. This tendency may have disappeared subsequently, for there was no difference in long-term persistence rates for the two colonies measured from the 1690s. The possible causes of the early difference in the structure of persistence between colonies, as well as of its later disappearance, will be considered in the final section of this chapter.

Trends in persistence over time

The estimates of Table 6.1 show a decline over time in measured persistence rates in Barbados during the period for which observations are available and, although somewhat less consistently, the estimates of Table 6.2 display a downward trend in persistence rates in Jamaica during a large part of the period they cover. This poses an important question for our understanding of the economy and society of the English West Indies in the last quarter of the seventeenth century: Were these declines in persistence real, or are the measured declines simply artifacts of the method of analysis or of the data employed in this investigation? That the latter might be the case is suggested by the decline of Royal African Company trading activity in Barbados and Jamaica over time. Information from the invoices indicates that both the number of sales held annually by the company in Barbados and Jamaica and the number of slaves sold declined sharply in the 1690s, and then declined further after the first decade of the eighteenth century. Since falling numbers of

Table 6.3. *Persistence of planters in Barbados*

Base year					Percent present in a given year after N years						No. of buyers in base year
N:	1	2	3	4	5	6	7	8	9	10	
1673	45.4	39.4	33.3	30.3	27.3	3.0	15.2	15.2	18.2	6.1	33
1674	26.5	24.1	14.8	25.9	6.8	17.3	7.4	9.3	1.2	10.5	162
1675	21.9	19.1	26.4	7.3	19.7	8.4	6.7	0.6	15.7	—	178
1676	16.5	29.3	9.1	16.5	12.2	9.8	1.8	11.0	—	15.2	164
1677	21.2	15.2	27.3	15.2	13.1	2.0	15.2	—	15.2	10.1	99
1678	4.5	17.0	10.3	9.4	1.8	13.9	—	12.1	4.5	6.7	223
1679	16.1	12.9	14.5	1.6	17.7	—	21.0	4.8	4.8	14.5	62
1680	10.9	12.2	2.6	16.7	—	20.5	7.1	10.3	12.8	6.4	156
1681	10.7	1.7	16.5	—	13.2	5.0	6.6	12.4	4.1	7.4	121
1682	4.2	10.5	—	16.8	8.4	6.3	12.6	4.2	8.4	8.4	95
1683	26.3	—	21.1	5.3	10.5	10.5	10.5	10.5	10.5	0.0	19
1684	—	8.4	2.6	9.7	9.7	5.2	5.2	7.1	2.6	7.1	154
1686	3.3	10.6	7.8	3.9	7.8	10.6	3.3	10.6	7.8	5.0	180
1687	13.6	9.9	2.5	11.1	7.4	2.5	13.6	6.2	3.7	6.2	81
1688	11.6	3.0	7.9	10.4	1.2	11.6	6.7	6.1	6.7	1.8	164
1689	3.6	9.3	8.3	2.1	11.9	5.7	6.2	6.2	2.1	5.2	193
1690	6.8	9.1	3.4	4.5	3.4	5.7	6.8	2.3	3.4	2.3	88
1691	11.8	2.0	5.3	5.3	5.3	5.3	2.6	7.9	0.7	1.3	152
1692	1.6	6.3	5.3	5.8	4.2	3.2	9.0	3.2	3.7	4.8	189
1693	11.8	5.9	11.8	8.8	0.0	0.0	0.0	2.9	0.0	2.9	34
1694	4.4	2.5	5.6	2.5	5.0	1.9	5.0	3.1	5.0	3.7	160
1695	6.9	3.9	2.0	10.8	3.9	2.9	4.9	8.8	7.8	2.9	102
1696	9.9	0.0	11.1	4.9	2.5	8.6	6.2	9.9	2.5	6.2	81
1697	1.8	5.3	2.6	2.6	2.6	1.8	0.0	4.4	2.6	0.9	114
1698	7.5	0.0	5.0	5.0	2.5	2.5	2.5	2.5	5.0	7.5	40
1699	1.7	0.0	3.3	2.5	5.0	5.0	5.8	3.3	6.7	5.8	120
1700	0.0	6.4	6.4	8.5	4.3	10.6	6.4	6.4	2.1	4.3	47

Note: See text and Appendix C for method of construction.

Table 6.4. *Persistence of planters in Jamaica*

Base year	Percent present in a given year after N years										No. of buyers in base year
N:	1	2	3	4	5	6	7	8	9	10	
1674	48.1	24.1	33.3	16.7	9.3	20.4	20.4	29.6	9.3	16.7	54
1675	31.6	30.1	15.4	6.6	19.9	7.4	22.1	4.4	13.2	1.5	136
1676	36.8	18.8	11.1	28.2	12.0	29.1	5.1	18.8	2.6	21.4	117
1677	23.9	6.7	24.6	14.2	30.6	3.7	16.4	3.0	21.6	1.5	134
1678	14.3	31.0	11.9	27.0	6.3	12.7	6.3	26.2	0.8	7.1	126
1679	40.4	24.6	38.6	10.5	10.5	8.8	24.6	1.8	10.5	8.8	57
1680	17.1	37.6	5.3	14.1	2.9	22.4	1.8	8.2	6.5	0.6	170
1681	57.8	9.4	21.9	10.9	37.5	4.7	12.5	9.4	4.7	10.9	64
1682	9.0	18.4	7.5	27.9	2.5	5.5	6.0	2.0	4.5	2.5	201
1683	31.0	14.3	38.1	7.1	11.9	9.5	11.9	11.9	4.8	7.1	42
1684	9.5	40.0	7.6	11.4	9.5	3.8	6.7	2.9	6.7	6.7	105
1685	48.6	17.1	11.4	20.0	11.4	11.4	5.7	14.3	5.7	8.6	35
1686	6.4	10.8	11.8	3.0	6.4	3.4	6.9	7.4	3.9	—	203
1687	29.0	19.4	12.9	19.4	9.7	16.1	3.2	9.7	—	—	31
1688	15.1	5.7	11.3	7.5	15.1	13.2	1.9	—	—	—	53
1689	6.7	13.3	5.0	11.7	8.3	5.0	—	—	—	1.7	50
1690	37.5	12.5	18.8	6.3	6.3	—	—	—	0.0	0.0	16
1691	12.0	36.0	8.0	12.0	—	—	—	4.0	4.0	0.0	25
1692	50.0	40.0	10.0	—	—	2.5	0.0	20.0	20.0	0.0	10
1693	25.0	10.0	—	—	—	—	12.5	15.0	5.0	—	40
1694	16.1	—	—	—	1.6	14.5	8.1	6.5	—	14.5	62
1695	—	—	—	6.7	20.0	10.0	6.7	—	6.7	20.0	30
1699	41.7	8.3	33.3	—	16.7	8.3	—	0.0	16.7	—	12
1700	14.3	9.1	—	15.6	15.6	—	1.3	5.2	0.0	—	77

Note: See text and Appendix C for method of construction.

transactions over time would tend to reduce the probability that an individual would appear as a purchaser even if he were still present in a colony, an investigation of whether the decline over time in slave sales is responsible for the observed decline in persistence rates is in order.

This problem can be simplified both conceptually and computationally by beginning with a new set of persistence estimates. Unlike the rates shown in Tables 6.1 and 6.2, each of which was derived from tracing individuals from a single base year to an interval consisting of a number of years – specifically, any year after the passage of a stated number of years – each persistence rate in Tables 6.3 and 6.4 was obtained by tracing individuals from a single base year to a single subsequent year.[15] As would be expected, the persistence rates obtained with this procedure are considerably lower than those of Tables 6.1 and 6.2. The significant feature for the present investigation, however, the decline in persistence rates over time, reappears in these estimates. Indeed for Barbados the proportional decline in the rates of Table 6.3 over time is even more severe than that noted above for the estimates of Table 6.1. The weighted mean 10-year persistence rate from Table 6.3 is 10.5 percent for base years in the 1670s, 5.6 percent for base years in the 1680s, and 3.6 percent for base years in the 1690s. The same increase in the magnitude of the proportional decline over time appears in comparing the rates for Jamaica in Tables 6.2 and 6.4, as the weighted mean 10-year persistence rates of Table 6.4 fall from 8.3 percent in the 1670s to 4.0 percent in the 1680s.

The problem is to devise a method of adjusting these rates in order to make them comparable over time, in view of the fact that they are calculated using different numbers of observations in each terminal year. Some consideration of the nature of the persistence calculations suggests how the measured rates can be adjusted to accomplish this.

The general form of this problem concerns the effect on a measured persistence rate of tracing individuals present in a place in a chosen base year to a terminal year for which only a partial population listing for that place exists. What must consequently be taken into account is the possibility that an individual actually present in the place in the terminal year might not appear in the partial listing, or sample, of names available from that terminal year.

The probability that an individual present in any population will be drawn into a sample taken from that population can be expressed as the ratio of the size of the sample s to the size of the population p – that is, the ratio s/p.[16] Measured persistence rates r_m, which are obtained by tracing specific individuals from a particular base year to a sample drawn from a population in a specific terminal year, can therefore be expressed as the product of the underlying "true" persistence rate r_t, the true probability that an individual present in the base year will still be present in the terminal year, and s/p, the probability that, if present, he will be drawn into the terminal year sample:

$$r_m = r_t \cdot \frac{s}{p} \tag{6.1}$$

This equation can be solved for the true persistence rate r_t:

$$r_t = r_m \cdot \frac{p}{s} \tag{6.2}$$

Equation (6.2) shows that in order to convert a measured persistence rate into an estimate of the true underlying rate that takes into account the incompleteness of the population listing available for the terminal year, the measured rate must be multiplied by p/s, the multiplicative inverse of the sampling probability in the terminal year.

This result provides a more formal statement of a familiar theme in the historical literature on the measurement of geographic persistence.[17] The expression for r_t in equation (6.2) is a general one, and is bounded by the case in which a completely accurate census of the entire population in the terminal year is used to find the individuals drawn from the population in the base year. In the latter case, p/s becomes unity, and the measured and true persistence rates are equal. That real censuses and city directories are not complete listings of actual populations, as noted by Stephan Thernstrom and others, can easily be seen to translate into the statement that in practice, even with the use of population censuses, $s < p$, and as a result measured persistence rates understate true ones by the proportion $[1 - (s/p)]$.[18]

Two pieces of information for each terminal year would therefore be needed in order to convert the measured year-to-year persistence rates of Tables 6.3 and 6.4 into estimates of true persistence rates; this would solve the problem faced here, because the latter would obviously be comparable over time. One of these pieces of information, the size of the sample in the terminal year (s), is available from the sale invoices from which the persistence estimates were calculated. The other, however, the size of the total population at risk to appear in the invoices in each terminal year (p), is not known with precision, for reasons discussed earlier in this chapter. Lack of this information means that reliable estimates of the true persistence rates cannot be derived from these year-to-year persistence estimates.

The available estimates of persistence from Tables 6.3 and 6.4 can be used, however, to consider the question of whether there was a genuine downward trend in persistence rates over time, under certain assumptions. This can be done by multiplying the rates of Tables 6.3 and 6.4 by $1/s$, where s is again the size of the sample from the terminal year. The magnitudes of the resulting estimates do not in themselves have direct interpretations; as shown in equation (6.2), they would have to be multiplied by the sizes of the appropriate terminal-year populations to be converted into actual persistence rates. Yet the resulting estimates do constitute an index of persistence that has been adjusted for differences in the sizes of the terminal-year samples to which individuals are traced, and their behavior over time can therefore be examined for trends if certain possible biases are kept in view. These possible biases result from the missing information on population size. If the relevant population at risk to appear in the invoices had not changed over time, the trend of the index derived here would constitute an unbiased estimate of the true trend in persistence rates; the index and the true rates would differ by only a constant multiplicative factor, equal to the constant population size. If the relevant population had been declining over time, however, the trend of the index would be biased upward – that is, the extent of any decline in the true persistence rate over time would be understated by the index. An upward trend in the size of the relevant population would result in a downward bias of the trend of the index relative to that of the true persistence rates. Since the white populations of both Barbados and Jamaica were declining significantly during the period under consideration here, it might seem unlikely that the relevant population of estate owners and managers would have been increasing; the behavior of the indexes for these colonies, which implicitly assume constancy of the relevant population over time, might therefore be biased against the finding of a decline in persistence rates over time.

The indexes derived from the 10-year persistence rates of Tables 6.3 and 6.4 are shown in Table 6.5. The results for the two colonies contrast sharply. For Barbados, the index does appear to provide clear evidence of a secular decline in persistence rates in the period considered. The rate of decline is far from constant, however, as the index shows a major decline in roughly the first decade of the period, with a continuing decline at a much slower rate during the following two decades. This can be seen by grouping the index values into averages for semidecennial periods, weighted by the number of individuals in the respective base-year samples. The means obtained in this way decline from a value of 0.111 in 1673–4 to 0.073 in the second half of the 1670s, a drop of more than one-third, and they decline further by more than one-quarter to 0.052 in the first half of the 1680s. Thereafter the rate of decline is much smaller, as the means fall to 0.051 in the second half of the 1680s, to 0.044 in the first half of the 1690s, and to 0.040 in the second half of the 1690s. The size of the early relative decline is obviously substantial, as the estimates imply that persistence rates measured from base years during the 1680s were on average only about three-fifths as high as those obtained from base years in the 1670s, whereas the rates from base years in the 1690s were only about one-half as high as those measured from the 1670s. The possible absolute magnitude of this decline can be illustrated by taking a hypothetical value of the size of the population at risk to appear in the samples; for example, if that population had remained constant at 500 people, these semidecennial mean index values would translate into 10-year persistence rates of 55.5 percent in the early 1670s, 36.5 percent in the second half of the 1670s, and 27.0 percent, 25.5 percent, 22.0 percent, and 20.0 percent, respectively, in the following four semidecennial periods.

In contrast to the pattern found for Barbados, the index calculated for

Table 6.5. *Indexes of persistence of purchasers in Barbados and Jamaica over 10-year intervals, adjusted for terminal-year sample sizes*

Base year	Index of persistence		Base year	Index of persistence	
	Barbados	Jamaica		Barbados	Jamaica
1673	0.321	—	1690	0.049	0.000
1674	0.068	0.159	1691	0.034	0.000
1675	—	0.043	1692	0.072	0.000
1676	0.084	0.105	1693	0.025	—
1677	0.125	0.048	1694	0.020	0.139
1678	0.041	0.134	1695	0.028	0.182
1679	0.075	0.147	1696	0.039	—
1680	0.073	0.038	1697	0.014	—
1681	0.049	0.436	1698	0.051	—
1682	0.044	0.250	1699	0.072	—
1683	0.000	0.178	1700	0.029	—
1684	0.044	0.108			
1685	—	0.287			
1686	0.062	—			
1687	0.054	—			
1688	0.045	—			
1689	0.043	0.142			

Note: See text for method of construction.

Jamaica reveals no clear secular trend. The first observation, for 1674, has a value of 0.159. The weighted means for semidecennial periods then rise from 0.087 in the second half of the 1670s to 0.178 and 0.195, respectively, in the first and second halves of the 1680s. The last two years for which values are available, 1694 and 1695, show index values of 0.139 and 0.182, respectively.

Because the lack of precise information on the relevant population sizes over time makes it impossible to assess the presence or magnitudes of possible biases in the trends shown by the indexes of Table 6.5, inferences can be drawn from them only with considerable caution. The indexes can support only conditional conclusions. If the relevant total population of estate owners and managers resident in Barbados had remained approximately constant in size during the last three decades of the seventeenth century, the estimates of the index would imply that there was a significant early decline in the persistence rate of the members of this group after the 1670s, followed by two decades of moderately declining rates of persistence. If the relevant population had been falling over time, however, these estimates would imply that there was a stronger continuing downward trend in persistence, indicating a larger increase in the rate of geographic turnover among estate owners and managers in Barbados. Charting the magnitude of the trend in persistence rates more precisely would depend on obtaining measurements of the total size of the resident population of planters and estate managers in Barbados over time; what the estimates obtained to this point do suggest is that there was a secular trend toward lower rates of geographic persistence among estate owners and managers resident in the island in the final quarter of the seventeenth century.

The estimates for Jamaica reveal no obvious trend, either upward or downward, in the persistence of the colony's estate owners and managers over time. It is of course possible that if the estimates could be adjusted for the changing size of this population some trend in persistence might appear, but lacking the necessary population data this remains conjectural.

Persistence and wealth

A number of investigators have suggested that in general one might expect to find a positive relationship across individuals between geographic persistence and wealth. Within an occupational group, the wealthier or more successful residents of a place might be expected to be more likely to remain in the same place over time, because a given set of economic opportunities in other locations for members of that occupational group might be more attractive to those doing less well in their current location. This correlation between wealth and persistence might also exist across members of different occupational groups, for the less successful members of a community might generally be giving up less by moving away from it than would wealthier residents. Historical studies of some nineteenth-century communities have found evidence that the poorer residents of a community were more likely to migrate away from it, with a number of other individual characteristics the same, than were wealthier residents.[19] This relationship need not exist in all cases, however, and some factors might lead to an opposite result. Wealthier planters in the early English West Indies might have been more likely to leave the islands to become absentee owners, perhaps because their greater wealth enabled them to hire better managers, or allowed them to bear the risk of economic loss due to possible abuses by a manager in their absence. It is therefore difficult to predict the direction of the relationship between wealth and geographic persistence in this case. The relationship is of obvious interest not only to the economic history of the islands, but also for their political history, for whether the wealthiest members of these societies were more likely than others to remain resident could have important implications for the concentration of the control of political power, and the continuity of this control.

Some evidence on this relationship for the Barbados planters can be obtained by combining information on the length of individuals' residence in the colony from the invoice accounts of slave sales with evidence on some principal components of individual planters' wealth drawn from the census of Barbados taken during 1679. The procedure followed here was to compare the list of all purchasers who appeared in the Royal African Company invoices between 1673 and 1690 with the list of all estate owners recorded in the census of 1679. Using as the sample for analysis all those individuals who were found on both lists, separate regression equations were estimated in which the elapsed time, measured in months, between the first and last appearances of an individual in the auction invoices was expressed in turn as a function of two different components of wealth, total acres owned and total slaves owned.

Before considering the results, several preliminary points should be noted about the characteristics of the sample analyzed. One is that it involves only a subset of the buyers who appear in the Royal African Company's invoices in the period specified. This is true in part because the census of 1679 records only the names of owners of estates, and therefore hired estate managers who purchased slaves from the company will not be linked to the census, and will not appear in the sample analyzed in this section. Planters who bought slaves sometime during the period 1673–90, but who either sold their estates before the census was taken in 1679 or purchased estates after that time, would also not appear in the linked sample.

The linked sample will not include all those who owned estates in Barbados in 1679, for several other reasons. Absentee owners listed in the census would not appear in the slave sale invoices, and will therefore not appear in the linked sample. Planters who bought slaves only from sources other than the Royal African Company similarly would not appear in the company's invoices.

Some quantitative information on differences in the characteristics of those who do and do not appear in the linked sample can be obtained from both the invoices and the census, for the characteristics of these two groups within both sources can be compared. A total of 2,724 property owners appear in the Barbados census of 1679. Of these 491, or just under one-fifth, match the names of purchasers who appear at least once in the Royal African Company slave sale invoices sometime between the beginning of those records in 1673 and 1690. These planters owned estates with a mean total size of 76 acres, and they owned an average of 32 slaves. In contrast, the 2,233 planters listed in the census whose names did not appear in the sale invoices owned an average of only 23 acres and 9 slaves. The evidence of the census therefore indicates that the members of the linked sample – those planters who appeared in both the census and the slave sale invoices – were disproportionately drawn from among Barbados's wealthier planters.

6. Estimating geographic persistence

Turning to the slave sale invoices, a total of 587 different individuals appear as purchasers during 1678–82.[20] Of these purchasers 256, or about 44 percent, can be found in the 1679 census. This group had a mean length of stay in Barbados, as calculated from the invoices, of 155 months, or almost 13 years. The remaining 331 purchasers from the invoices of 1678–82 – those not found in the census – had a mean stay in Barbados of only about 57 months, or less than 5 years. Therefore slave purchasers who were not found in the census had a mean stay in Barbados, as measured from the invoices, only about 37 percent as long as that of those who were found in the census. It seems likely that this large difference is the result of the fact that both estate managers and small planters turned over geographically at rates higher than did large planters, for members of both these groups must have made up significant shares of those who could not be linked from the sale invoices to the census; as noted above, estate managers who were not owners would not appear in the census of 1679, and as the evidence of the census indicated, large planters were more likely to appear in the invoices than were small planters.

A total of 491 individuals could be linked from the Royal African Company invoices of sales held in Barbados during 1673–90 to the Barbados census of 1679 in the manner described earlier. The following results were obtained when the duration of the stay of each of these individuals in Barbados was related in separate linear regressions to the two measures of their wealth mentioned earlier, acres owned and slaves owned, as given by the census of 1679 (standard errors are shown in parentheses):

$$\text{length of stay (months)} = \underset{(7.0)}{105.6} + \underset{(0.048)}{0.193} \text{ acres owned}$$
$$R^2 = 0.032, \quad F = 16.37, \quad n = 491$$

$$\text{length of stay (months)} = \underset{(7.1)}{108.0} + \underset{(0.115)}{0.384} \text{ slaves owned}$$
$$R^2 = 0.022, \quad F = 11.16, \quad n = 491$$

Several features of these results are of interest. One is that there is a positive and statistically significant relationship between length of stay and each of the indexes of wealth: The measured stay of a planter in Barbados increased by nearly one month for every five acres he owned, or by almost two months for every five slaves.[21] These relationships are highly significant statistically, although it should be emphasized that they explain only a very small proportion of the total variance of the dependent variable – only about 3 and 2 percent in the two equations, respectively. This means that there was considerable variation in measured length of stay that is not accounted for in this analysis, and that these measures of wealth alone fall very far short of fully explaining the observed variation of the planters' length of stay in Barbados in the period. Yet among this sample group, planters who owned large plantations did tend to remain longer in the colony than owners of smaller estates, and the magnitude of this effect was considerable, with a big planter by Richard Dunn's definition (60+ slaves) staying on average at least 15 months longer than a small planter (less than 20 slaves).[22]

Geographic persistence in Barbados and Jamaica: comparative perspective and interpretation

The major question that remains to be considered concerns the interpretation of the evidence examined in the preceding sections of this chapter. What do the levels and trends in the persistence rates estimated by this study tell us about the economy and society of the early English West Indies?

One way to approach this question is to begin by obtaining a comparative perspective on the estimates produced here for Barbados and Jamaica. One particularly intriguing opportunity is to compare the West Indies with the towns of early New England, for colonial New England's towns and villages have long been portrayed by historians as in many ways the antithesis of contemporary settlements in the West Indies, with the tranquility, stability, and settlement of the former in sharp contrast to the boisterous, rowdy, unsettled society of the latter.

A number of recent studies of persistence in colonial New England provide a basis for such a comparison. A recent compilation listed 17 estimates of persistence rates over 10-year periods in New England towns and cities in the seventeenth and eighteenth centuries.[23] Even the lowest of these, of 50 percent found for Beverly, Massachusetts, during 1741–51, is higher than any of the 10-year persistence rates for Barbados or Jamaica shown in Tables 6.1 and 6.2, while the highest rate, of 83 percent found for Dedham, Massachusetts, during 1690–1700, is more than twice as high as all but one of the 10-year persistence rates of Tables 6.1 and 6.2.

This comparison strongly confirms that persistence rates were substantially higher among residents of colonial New England towns than among planters in the early English West Indies, just as the traditional accounts would imply. Yet this is hardly surprising, because mortality rates were much higher in the West Indies than in New England. While the comparisons made above provide evidence on rates of population turnover in these regions from all sources, another significant question concerns the relative rates of voluntary population turnover, due to outmigration. To what extent was the observed difference between persistence rates in the West Indies and New England due to differences in mortality rates rather than differences in rates of outmigration?

6. Estimating geographic persistence

A persistence rate can be represented as the result of the decline of an initial population over time due to mortality and outmigration. A 10-year persistence rate can be expressed as

$$r = (1 - d - m)^{10}$$

where

r = 10-year persistence rate
d = average annual mortality rate
m = average annual rate of outmigration

With a known 10-year persistence rate and a known average annual mortality rate, this formula can be used to solve for the implied average annual rate of outmigration from an area:

$$m = 1 - d - r^{1/10}$$

The annual average rate of mortality for adult males in the seventeenth-century West Indies can be estimated as a minimum of 33 per thousand.[24] The annual rate of outmigration implied by this mortality rate and the 10-year persistence rate of 41 percent shown in Table 6.1 for Barbados in 1674 is 0.052, indicating that Barbados's estate owners and managers left the island at an estimated rate of 5.2 percent per year during the 10 years following 1674. Combining the same mortality rate with Jamaica's 27 percent persistence rate shown in Table 6.4 for 1675 implies a rate of outmigration for that island's planters of 9.0 percent per year. In comparison, an upper bound of annual mortality rates for adult males in colonial rural Massachusetts can be placed at 23 per thousand.[25] In conjunction with the 50 percent persistence rate noted above for Beverly, this would imply that the adult males of that town outmigrated at an annual rate of at least 4.4 percent during 1741–51. Furthermore, 8 of the other 16 estimates of 10-year persistence rates for New England found in the survey mentioned earlier were in the range from 53 to 59 percent, implying annual average outmigration rates of 2.8–3.9 percent.

Although Jamaica's rates of outmigration are substantially higher than those found for New England throughout the period considered here, the same is not true for Barbados. The difference between the average annual rates of outmigration of Barbados's planters during the 1670s and those of the residents of New England towns in the seventeenth and eighteenth centuries may have been as small as the eight-tenths of one percentage point found in comparing Barbados with Beverly – a difference of less than one outmigrant per hundred residents annually – while the annual Barbados outmigration rate of the early 1670s is within two and a half percentage points of the rates found

136

for a total of 9 of the 17 New England towns and villages for which 10-year persistence rates have been calculated.[26]

Population turnover and the development of a plantation economy in the English West Indies

This comparative perspective is illuminating. It indicates that during the 1670s Barbados had a low rate of voluntary outmigration, little higher than the rates found in a number of those colonial New England towns and villages that have served historians as models of stability in American history. After the 1670s in Barbados, however, and during the whole period considered in Jamaica, outmigration rates were considerably higher, with average annual rates generally double and often triple those found in the colonial New England towns with the highest turnover rates.[27] It is of intense interest to the economic and social history of the early West Indies to understand why Barbados's population of planters was initially surprisingly stable geographically, and why it later became so much less so, as well as why Jamaica's population was so unstable throughout the late seventeenth century.

The features of life in the colonial West Indies that made the region unattractive to the English are well known from the vivid accounts of contemporaries. First among these were the shockingly high mortality rates suffered by residents of the islands, with consistently high levels of death rates punctuated by occasional increases caused by the outbreak of virulent epidemics, often of unknown cause; in one case Richard Ligon wrote of 1647 that "the Inhabitants of the Ilands . . . were so grieviously visited with the plague, (or as killing a disease), that before a month was expired after our Arivall, the living were hardly able to bury the dead."[28] English settlers found the heat and humidity of the sugar islands' climate oppressive – Ligon reported that he and his companions felt as if they were being "fricased" – and they were appalled by the damage done to both life and property by tropical storms and hurricanes.[29] Many English planters also disliked living among populations made up predominantly of blacks, not only because of their distaste for the customs of the Africans, but increasingly over time from fear of slave insurrections.[30]

In view of the existence of these powerful forces tending to drive away those Englishmen who came to the West Indies in the seventeenth century, perhaps the most surprising result obtained here is that indicating the low rate of voluntary outmigration from Barbados the island's estate owners and managers in the 1670s. Yet the source of this result may lie in a particularly strong connection in this early period of English West Indian history between the

137

profitability of sugar plantations and the presence of an astute and diligent owner in residence.

That enormous profits could be made from sugar cultivation in Barbados in the decades after the introduction of sugar to the island in the 1640s was widely recognized among contemporaries, and is firmly witnessed by the fortunes accumulated by a number of planters on the island during the 1650s, 1660s, and 1670s.[31] What might have been somewhat neglected in public discussion of the West Indies in this period, however, was an appreciation of the difficulties of estate management, resulting from the novelty to English settlers of the seventeenth century of operating large-scale sugar plantations and supervising their large bound labor forces. In his history of Barbados Richard Ligon, who lived on the island during 1647–50, was at pains to stress the accomplishments of the planters:

Now for the Masters, I have yet said but little, nor am able to say halfe of what they deserve. They are men of great abilities and parts, otherwise they could not go through, with such great works as they undertake; the managing of one of their Plantations, being a work of such a latitude, as will require a very good head-peece, to put in order, and continue it so.

Ligon went on to discuss the work of the planters, emphasizing both the variety of jobs required of them and the skill involved in carrying many of these out. In summary, he concluded,

Now let us consider how many things there are to be thought on, that go to the actuating this great work, and how many cares to prevent the mischances, that are incident to the retarding, if not the frustrating of the whole work; and you will finde them wise and provident men, that go on and prosper in a work, that depends upon so many contingents.

Ligon evidently felt that the difficulties of plantation management were not adequately appreciated by absentee plantation owners, for he immediately added: "This I say, to stop those mens mouths, that lie here at home, and expect great profit in their adventures, and never consider, through what difficulty, industry, and paines it is acquired."[32]

Richard Sheridan has recently emphasized the increase in the complexity of plantation management that occurred in the early English West Indies during the region's movement toward monoculture, as the successful operation of a large sugar plantation came to require a diverse combination of agricultural, administrative, and commercial skills. As Sheridan has described, the eventual solution to this problem was to divide these tasks among several members of a hired managerial plantation hierarchy. In the eighteenth century it became common for an absentee plantation owner to employ a resident attorney to superintend the planter's estate; an overseer or manager would be responsible for the agricultural operations of the plantation, while the attorney would handle the plantation's commercial transactions.[33]

This division of responsibility evidently appeared not only as a result of the complexity of managing large sugar plantations, but also as a solution to a severe principal–agent, or monitoring, problem that plagued absentee plantation owners in the seventeenth century. The history of this early period in the sugar islands is marked by a number of stories like that of Chrisopher Jeaffreson, in which a resident planter trained a hired manager to run his plantation and then returned to England, leaving his employee in charge, only to find some time later that the previously conscientious and sober manager, having become corrupt and dissolute, had stolen from him and run down the value of his plantation, abusing his trust and destroying his property in his absence.[34] The occasional and casual supervision of the absentee's plantation by friends who remained in the region could sometimes alert the owner to the existence of this problem, but it could rarely provide a solution to it. In contrast, the employment of not only a manager but also a resident attorney, who was typically compensated in part by a commission calculated as a percentage of the value of the plantation's exported crops, probably did much more to reduce cheating and shirking by the resident manager or overseer.

A set of instructions written by an absentee plantation owner to the manager of his estate provides an early and explicit example of this solution that was to become commonplace in the eighteenth-century West Indies. These were the work of Henry Drax, probably upon the occasion of his departure from Barbados for England around 1680.[35] Drax had inherited the estate of his father James, who had been one of the founders of Barbados's sugar industry and had become the island's wealthiest planter in the first decades of the sugar revolution. The instructions Henry wrote for his manager, which were published as an example to others in the mid eighteenth century, contain 76 numbered items in a total of 36 pages, and constitute an extraordinarily detailed plan of how to operate a great sugar plantation.[36] In the course of these instructions, Drax stressed the importance of the continuous presence of the manager on the plantation, and informed him that in consequence the commercial affairs of the plantation that had to be carried out in Bridgetown, Barbados's port, would be handled by others:

For your greater Ease, and that you may not be taken off from solely minding the Plantation Affairs of planting and making Sugar, and that you may have as little Occasion as possible, of being absent from the Plantation, which I have experimentally found, to be very pernicious to all Proceedings there, every Person being more diligent in his Employ, when the Master is at home, although he stirs not out of his Chamber, than when he is abroad; therefore it must be observed for a Rule, that you never be absent from the Plantation, but in Case of Necessity: I say for your greater Ease, I have engaged proper Persons to act in, and do all my Business in Bridge-Town.

The "persons" Drax referred to were paid attorneys. Drax later specified the obligations of the manager to these men:

6. Estimating geographic persistence

My Attorneys must be invited by you to view the Plantations once a Year, when they must be well entertained, and you must desire them carefully to inspect every Thing, and show them all Accounts relating to Plantation-affairs, and acquaint them with all your Schemes and Intentions for the Management and Improvement of the Estate, and their Directions and Advice I would have you to observe and follow.

Drax's instructions may have been very detailed precisely because of the novelty of his arrangement. In the 1670s the management of large sugar plantations was still a relatively new problem for the English, and this system of dividing managerial responsibilities was apparently not yet widely used. More must be known about the timing of the spread of the use of paid attorneys by absentee planters before firm conclusions can be drawn,[37] but the hypothesis can be offered that in this period the relatively high persistence rates found among the estate owners and managers of Barbados resulted from the demands that the process of organizational development placed on the time and resources of the English West Indies' early entrepreneurs. These early plantation owners might have been grappling simultaneously with the problems of developing techniques of management that would result in the efficient operation of large sugar plantations and of dividing the authority of hired managers so as to make the prosperity of their plantations possible even in their absence. The falling persistence rates observed for Barbados in the decades after the 1670s might testify to their growing success in solving these problems, for they might indicate that the island's plantations were increasingly under the direction of hired managers who changed jobs more frequently than wealthy resident owners bought and sold plantations.

This explanation of the initially high level of persistence rates found in Barbados, and of the subsequent decline, must clearly remain conjectural pending more detailed research on the evolution of plantation management and its effect on population turnover in the English West Indies. It might be noted, however, that some evidence consistent with it was found above, specifically that owners of large estates in Barbados in the 1670s and 1680s were likely to remain on the island longer than poorer planters. Though obviously not conclusive, it is interesting that this is the opposite of what might have been expected if in this period the wealthiest planters had quickly been leaving Barbados to become absentees; this finding instead is consistent with the view that perhaps particularly in this early period the residence of an owner in Barbados was critical to the economic success of a large plantation.

As is the case for Barbados, only tentative hypotheses can be offered to explain the results found here for Jamaica. In part, the lower persistence rates estimated for Jamaica in the 1670s and 1680s could have been the result of higher mortality rates on the island, caused by the presence of some diseases there, including malaria, that were apparently absent from Barbados.[38] It is also possible that the political turbulence often remarked on by contemporaries in the early history of British settlement in Jamaica led to a less stable resident population of planters there. Even the apparent economic opportunity promised by the much greater amounts of land available in Jamaica might have failed to compensate planters for the losses and frustrations caused by the constant struggle for political power on the island during the 1670s and 1680s between the planters and the buccaneers, as well as what the planters perceived as the abuses of a series of English kings who attempted to derive economic advantage from the island's status as a royal colony.[39]

This investigation of the geographic persistence of West Indian planters, using the Royal African Company slave sale invoices, has produced significant results and suggested some intriguing possibilities. The estimates of persistence rates produced here clearly demonstrate the potential value of market observations for the study of population turnover, for comparable results as comprehensive on the geographic persistence of the planters of the early English West Indies cannot be derived from any other known sources. Although the estimates confirm that persistence rates among this group were low, this was apparently caused in large part by the extremely high mortality rates that existed in the region. Decomposing the source of the failure of planters to persist into separate rates of estimated mortality and outmigration yielded the surprising result that during the 1670s, Barbados's estate owners and managers might have left the island at rates little higher than those at which heads of households in the stable and peaceful settlements of colonial New England migrated away from their towns and villages. Matching the names of slave purchasers to a census of property taken in Barbados in 1679 furthermore revealed a positive relationship between the length of a planter's stay on the island and the amount of land and the number of slaves he owned. The persistence estimates also showed that outmigration rates rose substantially in Barbados in the 1680s and 1690s, and that the rates for Jamaica's planters were similarly high throughout the period studied.

These results constitute a substantial addition to our knowledge of the history of population turnover in the early English West Indies, for they represent the first systematic estimates based on the observation of large numbers of individuals over time. They have important implications for many aspects of the history of the region in this period. One particularly interesting possibility for the present investigation concerns the relationship between outmigration and the early development of the system of plantation management. The surprisingly low rates of outmigration found among Barbados's plantation owners in the 1670s, and the subsequent increase in these rates in later decades, may identify this as a key period in the development not only of efficient methods of managing large sugar plantations but also of techniques for monitoring the operation of plantations in the absence of the owner. The latter would eventually make possible the widespread absentee ownership that was to have profound effects on the history of the sugar islands during the

6. Estimating geographic persistence

eighteenth and nineteenth centuries. More important for the immediate concerns of this investigation is the implication that the prospect of economic gains during the 1670s may have been sufficiently strong in many cases to hold planters in the West Indies, doing difficult and complicated work, despite their strong distaste for the conditions of life in the region.

7

The economic structure of the early Atlantic slave trade

The challenge of Adam Smith's analysis

The conduct of the early Atlantic slave trade

This study has provided strong evidence of diligent and systematic behavior aimed at profit maximization by English slave traders and West Indian sugar planters in the late seventeenth and early eighteenth centuries. These traders and planters were hindered by severe handicaps, yet the evidence shows that they responded to these energetically and intelligently. The evidence of rational responses to market stimuli comes from both quantitative evidence on aggregate outcomes in the slave trade and qualitative evidence that affords a rare glimpse into the internal operation of a large company operating in the late seventeenth century. What emerges overall is a picture of a series of closely connected competitive economic markets, in Africa and America, in which large numbers of traders and planters responded promptly and shrewdly to economic incentives.

The primary purpose of the Royal African Company was to earn profits by transporting slaves from West Africa to the English West Indies, and a variety of evidence indicates that the company pursued this goal carefully and intelligently in the presence of severe constraints. Company factors in West Africa selected cargoes of slaves in ways that were dictated by the concern of earning profits. Company agents in London and America kept the factors informed about transatlantic shipping costs and the preferences of West Indian planters, and they paid careful attention to these in determining the age and sex composition of the slaves to be shipped to America. They responded to shifts in freight rates and changing conditions in American markets with a clear understanding of the necessary conditions for the profitability of transporting slaves, so that when shipping charges fell or the American demand for slaves rose, the factors included a larger share of children among their cargoes. They carefully chose the sizes of slave cargoes in order to avoid the overcrowding that might increase mortality rates, and they paid close attention to the amounts and kinds of provisions they bought for company ships. Their success in these efforts is attested to by the absence of any systematic relationship between the mortality rates of slaves on company ships and either the length of a voyage or the ratio of slaves carried to ship size. They scheduled slaving voyages both so as to avoid the hurricane season in the West Indies and in order to avoid collecting cargoes of slaves during the rainy season, when disease levels were higher among West African populations. The absence of any effect of seasonality on passage mortality rates suggests that when they did dispatch cargoes during the rainy season, their care in selecting the slaves was sufficient to eliminate the tendency toward greater mortality.

Similar evidence of the company's careful attention to the pursuit of profit derives from its operations in the West Indies. The company structured the salaries of its agents to give them incentives to maximize the receipts from slave sales. The attempt by the company to institute formal slave auctions in the islands demonstrates its understanding of the potential advantages of auctions in maximizing the revenue from sales, while the company's rapid abandonment of this format when it observed unfavorable outcomes equally demonstrates that it was able to recognize practical problems quickly, and respond to them pragmatically. The company's close scrutiny and supervision of its agents in the West Indies, as well as of its factors in West Africa, are evidenced in the hundreds of detailed letters of inquiry and instruction that were sent out from the central office in London.

The West Indian planters who bought the company's slaves were no less interested in economic profit, and their investments in land and slaves paid off handsomely, making many of them the wealthiest men in English America by the second half of the seventeenth century. They ran their sugar plantations like the businesses they were; the care they devoted to plantation management befitted the position of their great plantations, with hundreds of acres of land and labor forces of a hundred slaves or more, among the largest private economic enterprises of the preindustrial world. Some evidence of the systematic results of their behavior is also reflected in the Royal African Company's records. The relative valuation of slaves by age and sex that emerged from the company's sales appears to have been similar to that found in the slave markets of the nineteenth-century American South, indicating that slaves were valued according to their expected productivity in field work, with primary concern for their physical strength and health. The wealthiest planters bought the most valuable slaves, just as their estates were situated on the most valuable land. The willingness of the wealthiest planters to remain in Barbados in the late seventeenth century for surprisingly long periods in spite of conditions of life they considered unpleasant, and a disease environment they knew to be extremely hazardous to their health, attests to the strength of their desire to capture the economic profits that sugar production offered at the time; the increase in their rates of outmigration over time might further have been the result of their success in developing a system for operating their estates as absentees that allowed them to secure at least part of these profits while living in England.

Adam Smith's analysis and the causes of the failure of the Royal African Company

Recent research has found evidence of rational economic behavior within a context of highly competitive markets elsewhere in the Atlantic economy of the late seventeenth century, and particularly in the commerce of early English America. The results of this study would add another major Atlantic trade to this category, and in this would make a telling contribution to an emerging portrayal of competitive enterprise in the colonial American economy that would have major implications for our understanding of resource allocation in this early period of settlement. Yet it might seem dangerous to accept this conclusion without some further consideration, for it is diametrically opposed to the analysis of the same episode that was presented much closer to the date of its occurrence by the most distinguished economist of the era. The direct challenge his analysis poses to the conclusions drawn here suggests the importance of examining his arguments with some care.

Part of Adam Smith's famous attack on mercantilism in the *Wealth of Nations* was devoted to an exposition of the unfortunate economic consequences that ensued when legal monopolies were granted to groups of merchants to set up joint stock companies to carry on England's foreign trade. Smith contended that these companies were bound to fail because hired directors, managing the money of others, would lack sufficient motivation to succeed in a business as demanding as that of foreign trade:

To buy in one market, in order to sell, with profit, in another, when there are many competitors in both; to watch over, not only the occasional variations in the demand, but the much greater and more frequent variations in the competition,or in the supply which that demand is likely to get from other people, and to suit with dexterity and judgment both the quantity and quality of each assortment of goods to all these circumstances, is a species of warfare of which the operations are continually changing, and which can scarce ever be conducted successfully, without such an unremitting exertion of vigilance and attention, as cannot long be expected from the directors of a joint stock company.[1]

Smith's general conclusion followed directly from this:

Negligence and profusion . . . must always prevail, more or less, in the management of the affairs of such a company. It is upon this account that joint stock companies for foreign trade have seldom been able to maintain the competition against private adventurers. They have, accordingly, very seldom succeeded without an exclusive privilege; and frequently have not succeeded with one. Without an exclusive privilege they have commonly mismanaged the trade. With an exclusive trade they have both mismanaged and confined it.

The first example Smith proceeded to give in support of this proposition was precisely that of the Royal African Company. He offered a capsule summary of the company's history, stressing its inability to compete against the smaller "private adventurers" after it had lost the protection of its royal charter in 1688:

The Royal African Company . . . had an exclusive privilege by charter; but as that charter had not been confirmed by act of parliament, the trade, in consequence of the declaration of rights, was, soon after the revolution, laid open to all his majesty's subjects . . . The Royal African Company soon found that they could not maintain the competition against private adventurers, whom, notwithstanding the declaration of rights, they continued for some time to call interlopers, and to persecute as such. In 1698, however, the private adventurers were subjected to a duty of ten per cent. upon almost all the different branches of their trade, to be employed by the company in the maintenance of their forts and garrisons. But, notwithstanding this heavy tax, the company were still unable to maintain the competition. Their stock and credit gradually dwindled. In 1732, after having been for many years losers by the trade of carrying negroes to the West Indies, they at last resolved to give it up altogether . . . Their affairs continued to go gradually to decline, till at last, being in every respect a bankrupt company, they were dissolved by act of parliament.

Smith's analysis of the failure of the Royal African Company was therefore straightforward. The premise was that the company enjoyed a monopoly of the slave trade to English America as a result of the royal charter it received in 1672. Smith further assumed that the company suffered from the inefficiency due to "negligence and profusion" of management that he believed to be common to all companies in such sheltered positions. Consequently, when the company lost its monopoly upon the flight of James II in 1688, it was unable to compete with the "private adventurers," for the latter operated without the company's inefficiencies and therefore with lower costs. Exposed to competition, the company steadily declined into bankruptcy.

Subsequent research has shown that Smith erred in both premises and conclusions. His first mistake, which has since become a widespread error in the historical literature on the early slave trade, was to equate a charter that granted an exclusive privilege to a trade in law with an effective economic monopoly. As was seen in the first chapter of this book, the clause of the Royal African Company's original charter that excluded all other English subjects from the African trade was never effectively enforced. In consequence, throughout its history the company had to compete with many smaller English traders, and never attained the effective economic monopoly of the slave trade to English America that its charter granted to it in law. The company had of course never expected to hold a monopoly of the purchase of slaves in Africa, for seventeenth-century English traders were well aware of the Dutch, French, and slave shippers of other nationalities who together accounted for the bulk of all purchases in the West African coastal markets, but it was disappointed in its hopes of monopolizing the sale of slaves in English America.

Smith's confidence that the Royal African Company's failure could be traced to the insufficient "vigilance and attention" of its directors also appears misplaced. Careful study of the company's history, accompanied by an inspection of the scores of surviving volumes of internal company memoranda and correspondence between the central office and the company's employees overseas, cannot help but impress the reader with the energy and intelligence that were brought to bear on the company's operations by its directors and staff at African House in London.[2] Indeed, the vigilance and attention to detail evidenced in these documents are the more striking in view of the reports of serious problems and setbacks that flowed regularly into the company's offices, for they suggest a refusal to become discouraged in the face of persistent adversity.

Finally, the timing of the company's economic decline suggested by Smith's summary appears incorrect. The logic of Smith's analysis is that the lack of profitability of the Royal African Company that eventually caused its demise appeared after 1688. In fact, the origins of the company's economic problems have convincingly been traced to the years before this date. While recognizing that both the Glorious Revolution of 1688 and the French wars that began in 1689 were severe blows that hastened the Royal African Company's decline, K. G. Davies's authoritative history of the company concluded that the failure to earn satisfactory profits could be established prior to 1688, and that it was consequently in the initial period of the company's operation, between its founding in 1672 and the beginning of the French wars in 1689, that the causes of its failure had to be found.[3]

Although Smith's analysis did not accurately identify the reason, the Royal African Company did fail. It never produced adequate profits for its shareholders, its debts grew steadily over time, its role in the transatlantic slave trade dwindled rapidly after the 1680s, it became altogether inactive in that trade after 1730, and it finally ceased to exist in 1752.[4] If the source of this failure could not be found in poor management, as Adam Smith contended, where did it lie?

The answer cannot be found in the industry as a whole. The transatlantic slave trade was growing rapidly in size throughout the period of the Royal African Company's activity, and it continued to do so well beyond into the eighteenth century; the same was true in particular of the branch of the trade to English America.[5] Furthermore, as its vigorous expansion would suggest, the trade appears to have been a very profitable business for at least some of those traders who engaged in it.[6]

The Royal African Company's failure appears to have been the result of a

147

combination of problems both within the company and in its external environment. Although it is difficult both to determine whether any enumeration of these is complete and to measure the relative importance of different problems, three appear to stand out as particularly serious sources of the company's economic difficulties.

Technological constraints, including the lack of rapid long-distance communications, constituted a severe handicap to an enterprise that maintained substantial establishments in more than a dozen locations on three continents separated by thousands of miles. That communication between these places could occur only by ship, at no more than the speed at which the company transported its cargoes between locations, meant that responses to changing market conditions could occur only slowly. The inability of factors in West Africa quickly to notify the central office in London about the availability of slaves at particular locations, or of agents in the West Indies to inform ships' captains of developing scarcities or gluts of newly imported slaves in their colonies, often proved very costly to the company. These consequences of poor communications of course affected all who participated in the transatlantic slave trade. Yet another consequence, which did not affect all traders, was perhaps even more damaging to the company's finances. As discussed earlier in this book, the poor communications between London and the overseas agencies made it difficult to direct and monitor the performance of company employees in Africa and the West Indies. This raised the cost to the company of the dishonesty and incompetence of any of its overseas employees, a problem that appears particularly to have plagued the company's establishments on the West African coast.

A second basic difficulty faced by the company resulted from the position it assumed as a result of the charter originally granted to it in 1672. Simply put, the conditions of the charter imposed costs that were accepted by the company throughout its history, but the benefits that were supposed to flow from the charter were never captured by the company. The main costs imposed by the charter were the expenditures the company made to maintain and staff its forts and factories in West Africa. The real justification for these settlements lay in international politics rather than in private economics. Although there could conceivably have been economic benefits, in the form of reduced waiting times for slaving ships, from efficiently operated factories at which slaves were collected on the African coast, in fact these potential benefits never materialized, and these establishments proved to be an expensive liability to the Royal African Company. The factories were not run efficiently by company employees, and high mortality among slaves awaiting the arrival of ships often resulted in considerable losses for the company. The real purpose of the forts, which not only motivated the charter granted to the company by Charles II but also led Parliament to subsidize the company in the decades after the Glorious Revolution, was to maintain an English presence in West

Africa to prevent the military domination of the region, and the possible exclusion of the English, by France or another European power.

The company accepted the economic burden of the West African forts in return for benefits specified by the charter. These were to accrue in consequence of the company's position as the sole supplier of African slaves to the colonies of English America. Yet neither Charles II nor his successor James II was willing to make a significant commitment of resources to the enforcement of this privilege. In fact, neither appears to have been willing even to exert significant pressure on colonial West Indian governors to support company agents in their attempts to apprehend and prosecute the interlopers who infringed the company's monopoly by delivering slaves to the islands. The reason for this, as for the persistent pressure brought to bear on the company by the English Lords of Trade and Plantations to lower slave prices and increase the quantities of slaves delivered to the islands, was the strong political lobby maintained in England by West Indian sugar planters. Although the company's directors recognized relatively early the asymmetry between costs and benefits that resulted from their position, they continued for many years to maintain the African forts in the hope of changing the political balance in their favor and gaining an enforceable monopoly of the English slave trade. This hope was never realized.

The company's third major problem also grew out of the political power of the West Indian planters. The refusal of the English government to allow the West Indian colonies to issue their own currencies caused a chronic shortage of money that complicated all trade in the region. The shortage imposed a particularly heavy burden on the Royal African Company, for the company granted extensive credit to planters for their purchases of slaves, and soon became the planters' major creditor. For much of the company's history it held colonial debts equivalent to, or greater than, the full value of its outstanding equity. What made this such a crippling problem was the great difficulty the company encountered in its attempts to recover debts under colonial legal systems, judicial as well as legislative, that were controlled by those favorable to debtors, and indeed often by the debtors themselves. Here too the English government proved unwilling – or unable – to intervene effectively on the company's behalf.

In sum, the economic failure of the Royal African Company was due not to inefficiency spawned by a sheltered monopoly position, but on the contrary to the very competitiveness of the trade in which it was engaged from the beginning of its career. The legal monopoly of the slave trade to English America granted to the company by royal charter in 1672 never actually gave it the dominant economic position its directors and shareholders had hoped it would attain. Exposed to competitive pressures, the company suffered from a number of disadvantages. The major problems that appear to have caused the company's failure under these circumstances were the poor performance of its overseas employees, the high cost of maintaining its forts in West Africa, and the growing floating debt owed to it by West Indian planters. Both the inefficiency and dishonesty of some of its employees in West Africa and the general expense of maintaining and staffing its forts there raised the company's costs relative to those of its independent competitors, while the difficulty the company's agents in the West Indies met in collecting planters' debts lowered its revenues. Any one of these problems by itself might have been sufficient to cause the company's failure; the presence of all three appears to have ensured it.

Interestingly, the poor economic performance of the Royal African Company may have surprised few of those who invested in the company. K. G. Davies's analysis of the composition of the company's shareholders revealed that throughout its history a substantial majority of these, who never held less than three-quarters of its outstanding stock, were drawn from England's mercantile community. In particular, London investors known to have been actively involved in other branches of overseas trade held more than half the company's equity. So although a visible minority of the company's investors came from the upper reaches of English society, including peers and courtiers who might have invested to gain favor with Charles II or James II, quantitatively the most important group was made up of men who might have been expected to be as well informed about the economic prospects for a joint stock company engaged in overseas trade as any group in England. That their judgments about the Royal African Company's prospects were not entirely wrong, and that they might not have been greatly surprised by the company's failure ever to yield returns higher than they could have earned in investments generally considered to be much safer, are suggested by another of Davies's findings, specifically that their investments in the company were almost without exception small ones.[7] This points to the possibility that these merchants consciously chose to gamble small amounts of capital on a risky investment that they believed to hold a small probability of a large return; when the gamble did not pay off, none appears to have been ruined, and few may have been surprised.

The applicability of economic theory to history

Both the problems encountered by the Royal African Company and the assessments of its prospects made by contemporary investors therefore appear consistent with the results that have emerged from the present investigation, which show the company pursuing profits intelligently, but under severe constraints, within the context of a competitive transatlantic trade in African slaves. The implications of this conclusion would be considerable for our understanding of market behavior in the early modern era. Yet again it must be noted that this conclusion is in potential conflict with the beliefs of some eminent scholars. Their objections arise from a very different kind of skepticism than that of Adam Smith. Smith accepted the existence of markets in the seventeenth century, and believed that participants in these markets were motivated by the pursuit of profits; his skepticism concerned the competitiveness of the particular trade in which the Royal African Company participated. Yet many other scholars have expressed a very different kind of skepticism about modern analyses of past societies, by denying the very existence of economic markets and of profit motivation on the part of economic agents. These objections have therefore directly challenged the value of modern economic analysis in analyzing history.

The question of the applicability of modern economic theory to the past was raised conspicuously in the economics profession at least as early as 1892, when William Cunningham, newly installed as professor of economics in the University of London, contributed a paper entitled "The Perversion of Economic History" to the *Economic Journal,* then in only its second year of publication. Castigating economists for blithely assuming "free competition and the laws of supply and demand," Cunningham stated a desire to recant his own earlier belief that the history even of an economy as close in time and space as that of eighteenth-century England "could be conveniently studied as a series of illustrations of modern economic theory," and proceeded vigorously to attack Alfred Marshall's recently published *Principles of Economics* for what Cunningham argued was its implicit and erroneous assumption that people throughout history had behaved in accordance with the assumptions of modern economic theory. In a sharp reply to his former student, Marshall rejected Cunningham's characterization of his work, and emphasized his belief in the importance of recognizing the influence of custom on economic outcomes when interpreting the history of earlier periods. Marshall did note, however, that "lately some historians of mediaeval times have assigned to custom a rather narrower scope and a rather greater pliability than before," and he cautiously suggested that optimizing approaches to economic problems under competitive circumstances might have appeared earlier, and occurred more often, than historians had often believed.[8]

The exchange between Cunningham and Marshall was an early example of a debate that was to recur in a number of disciplines, including anthropology and history as well as economics, over the question of whether competitive markets, in which large numbers of people, motivated by the pursuit of profit, participated without the control of any central authority, existed at particular times and places in the past. This question is an important one for understanding how effectively a past society used its endowment of resources to meet the material needs of its members. As Adam Smith stressed, producers and traders motivated by the pursuit of profit in competitive markets can be expected to operate more aggressively and efficiently than their counterparts in noncompetitive or regulated markets, for their motivation to earn profits is not vitiated by the protection of monopoly, the dilution of self-interest resulting from command or confiscation, or the rigid adherence to behavior established by custom. The operation of competitive markets results in higher levels of output and generally lower prices than noncompetitive or heavily regulated markets, and their existence therefore tends to raise the welfare of a society's consumers.

The particular focus of the debates concerned with the existence and extent of competitive markets in the past has varied; a few important examples among many, involving characterizations of societies separated in time by as much as 5,000 years, can be mentioned in illustration. The hypothesis that an early Sumerian temple economy was controlled hierarchically by priests, with no market exchange or fluctuating prices, has recently been disputed by researchers who argue that archeological evidence points to the existence of economic markets and fluctuating prices in Mesopotamia as early as the end of the fourth millennium B.C.[9] Among a series of propositions he advanced in characterizing the society of the Near East in the second millennium B.C., the economic historian Karl Polanyi denied the existence of markets in which prices were determined by the interplay of supply and demand, claiming instead that prices were determined in trade between states by treaty, and in trade within states by government fiat. Polanyi also denied that merchants worked for their own profit, and viewed them instead as agents who acted for rulers who monopolized trade.[10] Recent studies have emphatically rejected Polanyi's views of the Babylonian and Assyrian economies, not only for the second but also for the third millennium, arguing that surviving textual evidence attests to both the importance of profits as a motivation for private traders and the existence of commodity prices that fluctuated in response to changes in conditions of supply and demand.[11] A number of prominent classical historians have recently challenged previous scholarship by arguing that ancient Greece had no sizable markets in which the actions of private individuals produced fluctuating prices; debate continues over whether this position is accurate, and if not, when such markets might have emerged in Greek history.[12] Many of the same participants in these debates about ancient Greece have been involved in similar controversies concerning the economy of the Roman Empire. One particular point of contention has been the belief of the historian M. I. Rostovtzeff that professional traders and manufacturers could enjoy high status in Roman society, as M. I. Finley and others have argued that involvement in commerce generally relegated an individual to a position of low status. Those involved in this argument believe that the answer has direct implications for the importance of business and the general sophistication of the imperial Roman economy.[13] And Karl Marx's contention that in England prior to the sixteenth century the role of markets was minimal, because both large estates and peasant households produced for their own use rather than for exchange, has been vigorously contested by a number of later scholars, including the anthropologist Alan Macfarlane, who recently concluded that "the majority of ordinary people in England from at least the thirteenth century were rampant individualists, highly mobile both geographically and socially, economically 'rational,' market-oriented and acquisitive."[14]

Many of these debates, and others like them concerning other times and places, continue today, as scholars attempt to determine whether competitive markets influenced the allocation of resources in particular past societies. The issue is a major one, and much of the recent research in these debates has produced important evidence that competitive markets did exist in the past. In most cases, however, evidence on the operation of these markets has been scanty or fragmentary, and our view of their behavior remains clouded. In contrast, this book has used rich and detailed evidence to study the behavior of a major market of the late seventeenth century. This evidence has permitted us not only to show that a large, competitive market existed at this time, but also to document its behavior in detail. The results are striking, for although some economists and historians have suspected that large competitive markets existed at this time, it has not previously been realized how complicated and sophisticated their behavior was. Although this study obviously cannot settle the issue of when large-scale competitive markets first emerged, or the even more important related issue of how rapidly and widely such markets diffused, it does provide very strong evidence that these existed at an earlier date than has often been believed. This discovery therefore adds an important dimension to our understanding of the development of market economies.

The Atlantic slave trade and early English America

The competitiveness of the transatlantic slave trade of the late seventeenth and early eighteenth centuries had major implications both for the nature of the society that emerged in the English West Indies and for its later history. The availability of slave labor in large quantities was essential to the emergence and rapid development of a new kind of society in the West Indies, based economically on a virtual monoculture in sugar grown on great plantations much larger than the productive units that characterized any industry in seventeenth-century Europe. Growing sugar in the tropics was hard and unpleasant work, and free workers quickly learned to avoid the sugar islands; although a free labor force undoubtedly could have been attracted to the region with the proper economic inducements, its cost would have been very high. A large supply of coerced labor was therefore a key element in the extraordinarily profitable operation of these early sugar plantations. The ability of planters in the West Indies to buy this labor under competitive conditions meant that no barriers other than the actual costs of enslaving Africans and transporting them to America were placed in the planters' way in obtaining the labor that would allow them to realize the value of the region's natural endowments of climate and soil. The natural suitability of the West Indies for sugar cultivation made the region's planters able to afford larger numbers of slaves than their counterparts in the British colonies of the mainland, and by the end of the seventeenth century this not only had made the islands wealthier than any other English American settlements, but had also produced fundamental differences in the racial composition of these regions that would persist and influence their histories to the present day.

The implications of competition in the slave trade for the economic and social development of the early English West Indies were therefore great. Yet another question remains, of whether this tells us anything more generally about resource allocation in the preindustrial Atlantic economy. The slave trade was an exceptional industry in a number of respects, and those who engaged in it might have been drawn from among those contemporaries most interested in economic gain even at the expense of morality, perhaps resulting in economic outcomes that were atypical of their time. Yet this hardly seems likely. As appalling as trading in human beings seems to us today, few investors of the seventeenth century appear to have been deterred from buying shares in the Royal African Company or its predecessors owing to moral objections. Members of England's royal family not only invested in the African companies, but also played an active role in their affairs. Prince Rupert, nephew of Charles I, took an early interest in the African trade, and helped convince his cousin Charles II to grant a charter to the Royal Adventurers into Africa in 1660. Rupert was not alone at court in his enthusiasm; more than half of the original 32 beneficiaries of the first charter granted to the Royal Adventurers were peers or members of the royal family.[15] Charles II himself invested in the Royal Adventurers, and assisted the company on several occasions.[16] When the Royal African Company was chartered in 1672, the Duke of York was named its governor, and he continued in that role when he succeeded to the throne as James II in 1685. James had helped to direct the affairs of the Royal Adventurers, and he appears to have continued to do so with the Royal African Company.[17] Nor was it only the royal family and its immediate entourage that had no objections to the business of slave trading; among the many investors who held shares in the Royal African Company, for example, was the political philosopher John Locke.[18]

Just as investors in the Royal African Company were apparently not unusual among their contemporaries in their attitudes and motivations, so might the competitive structure of the industry in which the company participated, the transatlantic slave trade, have been unexceptional in the Atlantic economy of the late seventeenth century. This is an important possibility. A central question about any past society concerns not only whether competitive markets existed, but more crucially, how much of the society's resources were drawn into the vortex of market activity. Measuring the extent of competitive markets in a society is of course even more difficult than documenting their existence, but it is critical in determining the efficiency of resource allocation in the society. The findings of this study concerning the competitiveness of the early slave trade therefore gain even more significance in the light of recent discoveries about the structure of other industries operating at the same time. Basic characteristics of highly competitive markets have been found in other transatlantic trades of the period, including that in European indentured servants.[19] The rapid expansion of settlement not only in the West Indies, but throughout the colonies of English America, and the concomitant expansion of a wide variety of profitable economic activities together were fostered by the existence of large competitive markets, for both factors of production and final products, that spanned the Atlantic. These markets made an important contribution to the extensive economic growth of the colonial period that made English America one of the world's wealthiest areas in the seventeenth and eighteenth centuries.

Appendix A

The Royal African Company's homeward bound invoice account books

The format of slave sale records

Among the Royal African Company records deposited at the Public Record Office in London are 24 manuscript volumes of homeward bound invoice accounts.[1] These books contain invoices of all goods sent on the "homeward" legs of Royal African Company voyages, including not only goods sent to England by company factors in the West Indies, but also the contents of voyages that departed from West Africa on the company's account. The greater part of the latter was made up of slaves, and these books therefore contain the records of the sales of slaves held by company factors in America.

The earliest sale of slaves recorded in the company's accounts was held in Barbados on March 11, 1673; photographs of the two pages of the record are shown in Figure A.1. This record describes the sale of 220 slaves delivered to the island by the *London Merchant,* under the command of Captain Edmond Sabine. As was often the case in the early years of the company's trading in Barbados, the slaves were recorded as sold both for money and for sugar by the company's factors on the island, Robert Bevin and Edwyn Stede, whose names appear at the close of the account.[2] Slave purchasers are listed individually by name, along with an itemization of the number of men, women, boys, and girls they bought and the amounts they paid; in this early sale the agents also sometimes recorded the duration of the credit given to a purchaser and the price per head he paid for the slaves.

The sale record contains a total of 42 transactions and 39 purchasers; each of two planters appears in two separate transactions, while a sale for "ready Mony" – cash – does not identify the purchaser. The latter omission points up the purpose of these accounts, for their primary function was to serve as a record of debts owed to the Royal African Company by planters who purchased slaves on credit.

This sale displays the declining slave prices discussed in Chapter 4. The initial transactions record the sale of adult slaves for £20–20.5 each, or 4,000 pounds of sugar. Midway through the sale there had been a decline, to 3,200

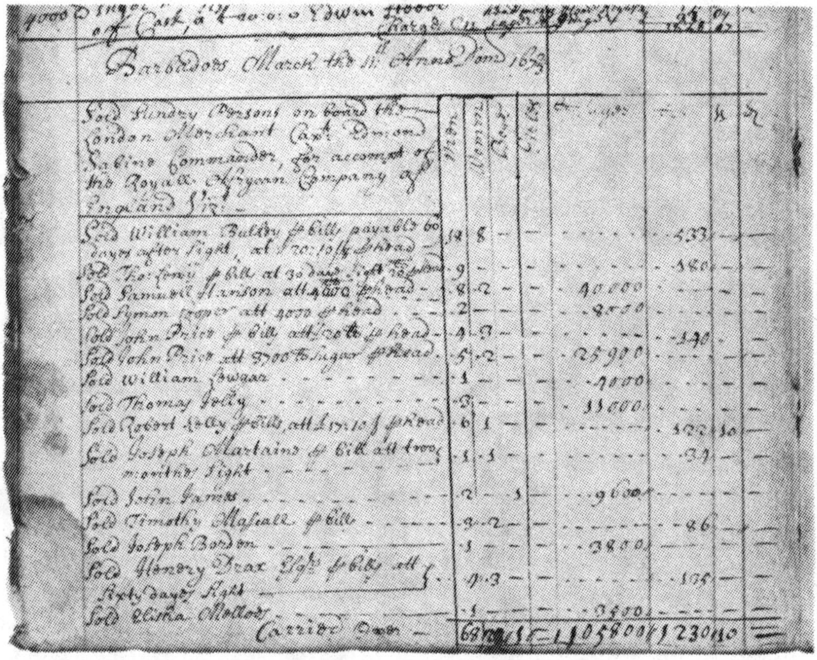
Barbadoes March the 11th Anno Dom 1673

Sold Sundry Persons on board the London Merchant Capt. Edmond Sabine Commander, for account of the Royall African Company of England viz:

Figure A.1. First (above) and second (opposite) pages of the account of the sale of slaves held by the Royal African Company in Barbados, March 11, 1673. *Source:* PRO T70/936, ff. 11v, 12.

pounds of sugar in the twenty-first transaction, and to £17.75 in the twenty-fourth. By the close of the sale prices had fallen more sharply, to less than 2,000 pounds of sugar for adults by the thirty-eighth transaction, while in the forty-first transaction the agents recorded the sale of 10 "refuse and sickly negroes" at 1,500 pounds of sugar each.

This same basic format for sale records was used in the following years and for sales held in other colonies. This can be seen, for example, in Figure A.2, which shows the first page of the record of a sale held in Jamaica in June 1675. This sale clearly illustrates the tendency, described in Chapter 4, for Royal African Company agents to make bargains with influential and wealthy planters early in a sale. The first purchase in this sale was made by John Lord Vaughan, who had been appointed governor of Jamaica three months earlier. The second transaction (as well as the fourth) was a purchase by the buccaneer Henry Morgan, recently knighted and installed as Jamaica's lieutenant governor. The third transaction recorded a sale to Sir Thomas Modyford, former governor of both Barbados and Jamaica, who was probably the wealthiest planter in Jamaica at this time; at his death in 1679 he owned an estate of 20,000 acres with more than 600 slaves and servants.[3] Among other promi-

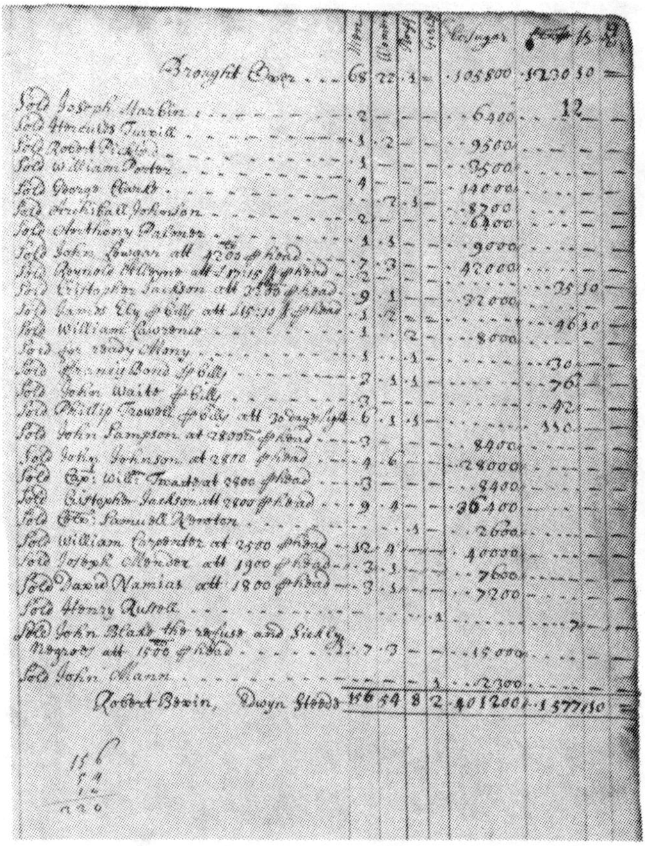

Figure A.1 *(cont.)*

nent planters who made purchases early in this sale was William Beeston, who later served as governor of Jamaica.

The sale record shown in Figure A.2 also demonstrated the tendency for slaves to be sold in lots of fixed sizes that appeared in Royal African Company sales in Jamaica. In this case the lots were made up of four men and two women, but the size and composition could vary from one shipload to the next. Where present, the use of lots was usually concentrated in the early portions of sales.

The coverage of the slave sale records

The homeward bound invoice accounts are known to be incomplete records of the Royal African Company's total deliveries of slaves to the West Indies for two reasons. First, the account books for some periods are missing, and

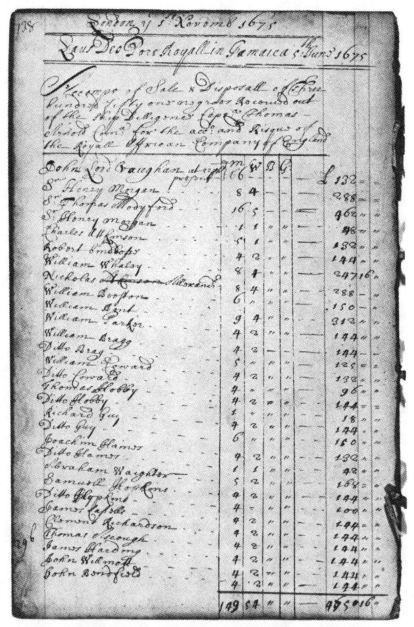

Figure A.2. First page of the account of the sale of slaves held by the Royal African Company in Jamaica, June 5, 1675. *Source:* PRO T70/936, f. 76v.

Table A.1. *Tabulation of annual slave deliveries recorded in Royal African Company accounts compared to Davies's estimates of total company deliveries*

Year	Barbados Accounts	Barbados Davies's estimates	Jamaica Accounts	Jamaica Davies's estimates	Leewards Accounts	Leewards Davies's estimates
1673	220	220	—	—	—	—
1674	1,185	1,066	404	410	447	469
1675	1,480	1,512	1,278	1,269	481	502
1676	1,435	1,836	1,042	1,188	554	571
1677	847	940	1,157	1,156	495	495
1678	1,941	2,392	997	990	491	627
1679	547	676	421	464	705	1,058
1680	1,372	1,673	1,540	1,623	820	1,033
1681	1,503	2,404	1,143	1,150	882	829
1682–3	923	3,676	2,571	3,483	196	765
1684–5	1,454	3,630	2,006	3,841	—	255
1686–7	1,788	3,585	4,061	6,223	352	1,007
1688	1,165	1,516	717	447	410	536
1689	897	1,119	682	682	550	894
1690	398	520	359	359	—	—
1691	607	1,175	579	579	—	—
1692	894	645	583	583	—	—
1693	154	282	977	1,332	86	84
1694	796	2,130	936	369	—	—
1695	706	—	962	1,129	309	296
1696	455	491	113	113	—	—
1697	830	997	—	—	—	—
1698	235	469	—	313	336	312
1699	876	961	127	161	368	125
1700	879	1,123	688	897	509	872
1701	349	—	768	1,071	246	161
1702–3	1,039	1,726	572	558	377	893
1704	836	1,215	801	801	683	536
1705	528	685	1,392	1,384	279	255
1706	904	759	—	—	252	281
1707	442	544	196	196	612	472
1708	900	782	1,576	1,709	161	161
1709	479	578	—	—	630	638
1710	531	439	—	—	—	—
1711	111	345	—	—	—	50
Total	29,706	42,111	28,648	34,480	11,231	14,177

Notes: The columns headed "Accounts" are my tabulations of the numbers of slaves whose sales are recorded in the invoice account books of the Royal African Company. The columns headed "Davies's estimates" are those made by K. G. Davies of total Royal African Company deliveries. Davies obtained these estimates by supplementing the information of the invoice account books with other company records both to remedy the loss of some of these account books and to allow for those slaves delivered by the company on prearranged contracts for whom no records of sale appear in the invoice account books. For further discussion of these estimates, see Davies, *Royal African Company*, pp. 361–2.

Sources: Accounts: Tabulated from Public Record Office, Treasury 70/936–959. Davies's estimates: K. G. Davies, *The Royal African Company* (London: Longmans, 1957), p. 363.

second, the account books contain only the records of those slave cargoes sold publicly by the company in the colonies; they do not include records of those slaves delivered on contract, according to prearranged agreements with individual buyers or groups of buyers. An important question therefore concerns how fully the records of the accounts can be taken to represent the volume of the company's activity in the slave trade over time and space.

K. G. Davies has specifically attempted to estimate the total numbers of slaves delivered by the Royal African Company to the colonies during 1673–1711, including those who did not appear in the account books. It is therefore possible to compare the annual totals of slaves delivered that are obtained from the account books with Davies's estimates of total company deliveries. This comparison is presented in Table A.1.

The account books contain records of the sale of a total of 69,585 slaves delivered by the company to the West Indies during 1673–1711, which is 77 percent of Davies's estimate of a total of 90,768 delivered by the company in these years.[4] The account books cover 71 percent of the estimated total deliveries to Barbados, 83 percent of those to Jamaica, and 79 percent of those to the Leeward Islands. The accounts' coverage furthermore appears reasonably consistent over time. Although the accounts clearly cannot be taken to indicate the absolute level of company deliveries, their degree of coverage is high and appears good both over time and across colonies. There is furthermore no apparent reason for believing that the slave cargoes omitted from the invoice accounts would have differed systematically in any important respects from those covered by them.[5] Overall, the invoice accounts therefore appear to constitute a large and representative sample of the Royal African Company's slave trading activity in the West Indies.

Data used in the analysis of passage mortality, 1720–5

The data used in Chapter 2 to analyze the passage mortality of slaves are drawn principally from a volume entitled "List of Ships and their Voyages in the Service of the Royal African Company of England from November the 4th 1719 To 1733."[1] This volume contains summary records of all voyages made on the Royal African Company's behalf in this period, including a large number of shuttle voyages carrying goods from England to West Africa and back, but it includes records of a total of 38 transatlantic slaving voyages made by the company between 1720 and 1725. Table B.1 presents information for these voyages on some variables used in the analysis of passage mortality. The variables listed for each voyage are the following:

1. Ship's name
2. Whether the ship was hired or owned by the Royal African Company
3. Recorded tonnage of the ship[2]
4. Crew size (This appears to be the number of men hired at the beginning of a voyage in England. The register contains no further information on subsequent changes in crew size or mortality during the voyage.)
5. Number of guns carried
6. Date of departure from Great Britain (This and other dates are given as month/day/last two digits of year.)
7. Date of arrival in Africa
8. Place of arrival in Africa
9. Number of slaves the ship was intended to carry from Africa
10. Number of slaves with which the ship departed from Africa
11. Date of departure from Africa
12. Place of departure from Africa
13. Date of arrival in America
14. Place of arrival in America (This and the preceding variable refer to the ship's final destination in America. Several voyage records indicate stops made in route from Africa to an American destination, usually owing to bad weather. Whenever it is possible to determine,

Table B.1. Summary information of slaving voyages, 1720–5

Ship (1)	Owned/hired (2)	Tons (3)	Crew (4)	Guns (5)	Depart GB (6)	Arrive Africa Date (7)	Arrive Africa Place (8)	Slaves carried Plan (9)	Slaves carried Act. (10)	Depart Africa Date (11)	Depart Africa Place (12)	Arrive America Date (13)	Arrive America Place (14)	Slaves deliv'd (15)	Depart America (16)	Arrive GB (17)
1. Generous Jenny	Hired	230	27	10	11/20/19	3/18/20	CCC	260	260	6/12/20	CCC	9/16/20	Virginia	218	—	3/15/21
2. King Solomon	Owned	200	33	12	8/19/20	10/17/20	CCC	350	311	1/26/21	CCC	3/16/21	St. C.	296	6/ 4/21	7/16/21
3. Dispatch	Owned	80	15	4	8/19/20	10/28/20	CCC	150	110	6/18/21	CCC	8/ 4/21	Antigua	104	9/18/21	10/26/21
4. Sarah	Owned	120	23	8	10/ 2/20	12/ 9/20	—	240	250	4/ 9/21	CCC	6/25/21	Virginia	233	9/17/21	11/ 1/21
5. Otter	Owned	170	26	9	12/25/20	2/ 4/21	Gambia	240	211	6/25/21	Gambia	8/14/21	Virginia	193	9/13/21	10/19/21
6. Martha	Owned	250	39	6	2/ 4/21	4/ 2/21	Gambia	400	200	1/12/22	Gambia	2/11/22	Jamaica	185	5/18/22	7/30/22
7. Cape Coast Frigate	Owned	120	23	8	2/ 4/21	4/28/21	CCC	250	240	10/ 6/21	CCC	3/ 3/22	Barbados	192	8/10/22	10/12/22
8. Whydah Frigate	Owned	300	48	18	2/ 4/21	4/28/21	CCC	550	500	9/ 9/21	Whydah	11/18/21	Barbados	371	5/11/22	6/27/22
9. Sherbro Gally	Owned	170	28	8	2/27/21	3/29/21	SL	260	229	9/24/21	SL	11/12/21	Jamaica	184	1/18/22	3/29/22
10. Prince George	Hired	210	30	14	4/26/21	8/15/21	Cabenda	350	350	9/17/21	Cabenda	10/25/21	Barbados	335	1/ 4/22	2/ 8/22
11. Royal African Packet	Owned	97	20	6	4/15/22	9/ 8/22	Cabenda	200	201	12/24/22	Cabenda	3/ 3/22	Jamaica	198	4/19/23	8/ 1/23
12. Greyhound Sloop	Owned	75	12	4	2/ 4/21	4/30/21	CCC	—	120	11/20/21	CCC	1/ 8/22	Barbados	107	5/ 1/22	12/ 3/22
13. Lady Rachel	Hired	170	25	10	8/ 3/21	9/29/21	CCC	280	280	12/23/21	CCC	3/ 8/22	Antigua	241	5/30/22	7/13/22
14. Carlton	Hired	280	40	16	9/24/21	11/19/21	CCC	450	500	1/23/22	Whydah	3/38/22	Jamaica	398	7/12/22	9/26/22
15. Chandos	Owned	240	42	14	1/ 2/22	2/ 6/22	SL	500	417	10/20/22	Jaquin	1/22/23	Jamaica	349	3/ 5/23	5/ 1/23
16. Hamilton	Owned	120	22	4	1/ 1/22	4/ 7/22	CCC	250	212	9/ 4/22	CCC	12/ 8/22	Jamaica	198	3/ 5/23	1/ 1/23
17. Neptune	Hired	200	34	10	12/ 2/21	3/ 1/22	Cabenda	400	—	5/28/22	Cabenda	8/23/22	Jamaica	395	2/ 7/23	4/ 9/23
18. Unity	Hired	150	25	8	12/ 2/21	3/ 5/22	CCC	280	278	5/24/22	CCC	7/18/22	Barbados	253	—	—
19. King Solomon	Owned	200	33	12	11/ 2/21	1/ 9/22	CCC	300	300	6/12/22	CCC	9/12/22	Jamaica	251	2/ 7/23	4/13/23

No.	Ship		Tons														
20.	*Margaret*	Hired	120	23	4	10/23/21	1/ 6/22	CCC	250	265	3/27/22	Benin	6/11/22	Antigua	204	7/—/22	9/14/22
21.	*Dove*[a]	Owned	150	24	6	3/13/22	4/27/22	Gambia	250	253	6/18/22	Gambia	8/ 3/22	Jamaica	244	12/13/22	3/12/24
22.	*Dove*	Owned	150	24	6	—	2/21/23	Gambia	—	138	9/ 2/23	Gambia	11/20/23	Jamaica	113	1/ 2/24	—
23.	*Helden Frigate*	Hired	202	35	12	4/23/22	8/10/22	CCC	450	457	10/20/22	Cabenda	1/28/23	Jamaica	356	—	—
24.	*Sarah Galley*	Hired	150	26	8	4/23/22	—	CCC	300	300	8/24/22	CCC	12/10/22	Jamaica	284	—	—
25.	*Expedition Galley*	Owned	110	20	2	5/ 5/22	7/ 2/22	Gambia	—	—	9/19/22	Gambia	11/28/22	Jamaica	141	1/28/23	—
26.	*Diligence Galley*	Owned	110	20	2	5/29/22	7/13/22	SL	—	200	12/18/22	CCC	2/28/23	Barbados	182	5/ 5/23	7/22/23
27.	*Essex Galley*	Hired	300	46	16	5/30/22	7/27/22	CCC	500	384	10/31/22	Whydah	1/ 4/23	Jamaica	316	—	5/10/23
28.	*Sherbro Galley*	Owned	170	28	8	8/ 9/22	11/ 4/22	Cabenda	350	350	1/23/23	Cabenda	3/22/23	Jamaica	269	6/19/23	9/ 1/23
29.	*Bladen*	Owned	180	35	10	7/21/22	9/26/22	CCC	500	250	2/12/23	CCC	5/ 3/23	Jamaica	229	7/26/23	9/10/23
30.	*Squirrel Galley*	Hired	270	40	14	10/12/22	1/ 4/23	Whydah	450	400	3/30/23	Whydah	4/26/23	Jamaica	366	8/ 1/23	10/25/23
31.	*Francis Galley*	Hired	160	27	10	10/14/22	12/18/22	CCC	300	300	3/ 6/23	CCC	5/ 2/23	Jamaica	283	7/25/23	10/ 5/23
32.	*Sloper Galley*	Hired	140	27	6	9/29/22	12/18/22	CCC	300	264	3/28/22	CCC	—	Barbados	202	—	—
33.	*Lady Rachel*	Hired	170	29	10	1/ 7/23	2/ 8/23	Gambia	300	217	5/ 7/23	Gambia	7/11/23	SC	190	—	—
34.	*Advice*	Owned	80	14	2	1/29/23	4/19/23	Gambia	—	150	12/22/23	Gambia	1/23/24	Jamaica	147	3/ 5/24	5/ 2/24
35.	*Carlton*	Hired	280	42	16	7/ 9/23	9/ 1/23	CCC	500	414	5/21/24	CCC	5/21/24	Jamaica	396	—	9/22/24
36.	*Chandos*	Hired	310	42	24	8/10/23	9/29/23	CCC	500	520	1/ 8/24	Whydah	3/ 4/24	Jamaica	437	7/10/24	9/13/24
37.	*Cape Coast Frigate*	Owned	120	16	8	3/ 5/24	4/13/24	Gambia	300	205	7/15/24	Gambia	9/ 7/24	SC	—	11/24/24	1/14/25
38.	*Chandos*	Owned	240	30	14	1/22/25	3/14/25	CCC	500	500	6/17/25	CCC	8/22/25	Jamaica	465	11/10/25	2/ 3/26

Abbreviations: GB, Great Britain; CCC, Cape Coast Castle; St. C., St. Christopher; SL, Sierra Leone; SC, South Carolina.

[a] The *Dove* is the only one of the ships for which records were kept in PRO, T70/1225, that made two consecutive slaving voyages without returning to England. After leaving Jamaica in December 1722 (entry 21), it returned directly to Africa, arriving in Gambia in February 1723 to make a second voyage (entry 22).

the place recorded here is that in which the ship's cargo of slaves was sold.)

15. Number of slaves delivered (This appears to refer to slaves accepted by the company's agents for sale – that is, those healthy enough to "go over the side" of the ship.)
16. Date of departure from America
17. Date of arrival in Great Britain

Although the "List of Ships . . ." is the principal source for the data in Table B.1, in several instances the evidence of that volume has been supplemented or corrected by using information drawn from other volumes of Royal African Company records and correspondence.

The variables for which data are presented in the table are the main ones systematically recorded in the "List of Ships . . ." For a number of voyages, however, supplementary notes provide additional information about the journeys. Among the most interesting of these are notes concerning the deaths of ships' captains. These were apparently made in order to explain and record the transfer of command from the captain to the first mate, and are therefore likely to constitute systematic records of all captains' deaths. Although some of these notes are ambiguous about the precise date at which a death occurred, it appears that four ships suffered the death of their captains while in passage from Africa to America, while another captain died immediately prior to the arrival of his ship in Africa on the voyage from England, and two more died during the stays of their ships on the West African coast.[3] With a total of 38 records of transatlantic slaving voyages, these figures indicate that about 10.5 percent of the ships' captains died during the Middle Passage, and that in sum 18.4 percent of the captains who left England to make slaving voyages for the Royal African Company during 1720–5 died before the arrival of their ships in America. Although the 10.5 percent of ships' captains who died on the transatlantic crossing is lower than the 13 percent of the slaves who died in the passage, together with the 5.3 percent of the captains who died on the African coast it confirms that the slave trade was one of high mortality for the crews as well as the slaves.[4]

Measuring persistence rates and the problem of common names

The problem posed by common names, in which the presence in a sample of different individuals with the same names can result in false linkages and thereby cause estimates of persistence rates to be biased upward, has of course been encountered by previous persistence studies. One solution, used by Stephan Thernstrom in his study of Boston, was to omit from his base-year samples any individual with a common name, with the latter defined as any name (first and last) that appeared two or more times in the Boston city directory for the base year from which the sample was drawn.[1]

Lacking complete listings of the population of Barbados for the appropriate period, a different procedure was followed here. After obtaining the persistence estimates of Table C.1, which use all the names of purchasers that appear in the Royal African Company invoices, all the names of purchasers in the sample were compared to the listing of names obtained by the first federal census of South Carolina in 1790.[2] Two groups of common names from the Barbados sample were then identified on the basis of comparison with the South Carolina listings. One group was the most common names, defined as those names (first and last) that appeared two or more times in the South Carolina census. Of the total of 2,886 names in the Barbados sample of purchasers, there were found to be 234 of these most common names. These were then removed from the Barbados sample, and a second set of persistence rates was calculated; these are presented in Table C.2. The second group identified was an additional set of common names, defined as those names from the Barbados sample that appeared only a single time in the South Carolina listings. There were 186 such names. These were then also removed from the sample, and, still excluding the first group of most common names, a third set of persistence rates was calculated; these were presented in Table 6.1.

Like many of the procedures followed to deal with the problem of common names in nominal record linkage in earlier persistence studied, the procedure followed here is a provisional one. Its primary justification lies not in the early connection of the populations of Barbados and South Carolina,[3] but rather in

167

Table C.1. *Persistence of purchasers in Barbados (all names)*

Base year	N:	1	2	3	4	5	10	15	20	No. of buyers in base year
					Percent present sometime after N years					
1673		77	74	74	69	64	49	36	31	39
1674		66	60	57	57	51	42	29	22	192
1675		65	62	60	52	51	34	26	19	212
1676		63	61	54	53	52	43	28	16	193
1677		67	59	57	51	49	39	26	17	111
1678		53	51	46	44	43	33	24	16	265
1679		66	62	58	53	53	41	25	18	76
1680		65	60	56	56	52	39	29	21	181
1681		61	56	56	46	46	32	26	20	149
1682		56	55	48	48	43	30	22	15	112
1683		56	44	44	40	40	20	16	12	25
1684		45	45	40	38	36	25	18	11	185
1686		57	54	49	44	41	29	21	15	209
1687		58	52	47	44	40	27	17	10	104
1688		58	52	48	45	41	30	24	12	203
1689		51	48	42	37	37	24	15	5	227
1690		42	39	32	31	29	23	16	8	117
1691		49	39	38	36	34	22	12	2	174
1692		46	46	41	38	36	26	11	2	222
1693		50	39	36	31	19	14	11	0	36
1694		44	39	36	29	28	16	4	1	178
1695		57	51	45	44	37	26	6	2	127
1696		52	41	39	32	30	20	4	2	92
1697		42	40	33	31	30	19	5	4	138
1698		43	34	32	30	27	11	2	2	44
1699		38	37	36	34	31	13	4	3	138
1700		50	45	39	34	31	8	2	0	64

Note: For source and method of calculation for this and Tables C.2–C.4, see text.

the large size of the population of South Carolina in 1790 relative to that of Barbados during the late seventeenth century. This relationship should tend to make the procedure relatively inclusive in searching for names in the Barbados sample that occurred commonly. The census of South Carolina taken in 1790 listed the names of more than 26,000 heads of families. This number is larger than the total white population of Barbados in the period under study, which declined from about 22,000 in 1670 to 15,000 in 1700;[4] the number of heads of households was of course much smaller, on the order of 4,000 in 1684.[5] Clearly the larger the list of names used to define what constitutes a common name, the larger is the number of names that will tend to fall into that category. The use of the South Carolina listing, which is much larger than the Barbados population to which it is compared, is intended to eliminate a large

Table C.2. *Persistence of selected purchasers in Barbados (commonest names eliminated)[a]*

Base year		Percent present sometime after N years								No. of buyers in base year
	N: 1	2	3	4	5	10	15	20	
1673	77	74	74	69	63	46	31	26	35
1674	65	60	56	56	50	40	27	20	179
1675	64	61	59	50	50	31	22	16	195
1676	61	58	51	51	49	39	25	13	175
1677	68	59	57	52	49	39	26	17	108
1678	51	50	44	41	40	30	21	13	244
1679	61	56	53	47	47	33	21	14	66
1680	64	58	54	54	49	37	27	19	170
1681	59	53	53	43	43	28	22	15	134
1682	53	52	44	44	39	27	19	12	104
1683	55	41	41	36	36	14	9	9	22
1684	44	44	38	35	33	23	16	10	168
1686	54	52	46	42	39	28	20	14	198
1687	53	47	45	41	38	25	16	8	92
1688	56	50	48	44	41	29	23	11	181
1689	50	47	41	36	35	22	12	3	210
1690	38	34	29	28	26	18	13	6	98
1691	47	37	36	34	33	21	11	2	160
1692	46	46	40	38	35	27	11	3	204
1693	49	37	34	29	17	11	9	0	35
1694	43	39	35	28	27	15	4	1	167
1695	57	50	43	43	36	25	4	1	113
1696	52	40	38	31	29	18	5	2	85
1697	40	37	31	29	28	17	4	2	123
1698	43	33	31	29	26	12	2	2	42
1699	37	36	34	33	30	12	3	2	126
1700	48	45	38	32	30	9	2	0	56

[a]Purchasers whose names appear at least twice in the 1790 census of South Carolina are eliminated from the sample.

number of names, in an attempt to overestimate the true size of the group of individuals falsely linked in calculating persistence among the Barbados population. Then if the initial measured persistence rates have been inflated by false linkages of different individuals who shared common names, the true persistence rates for the island should lie somewhere between the (high) estimates of Table C.1 and the (low) estimates of Table 6.1. The use of two stages in eliminating common names, with an initial group of most common names eliminated before a second group of less common names, is intended to indicate how sensitive the results are to the particular definition of common names used.

The results for Barbados indicate quite clearly that neither stage in this

Table C.3. *Persistence of purchasers in Jamaica (all names)*

Base year	N: 1	2	3	4	5	10	15	20	No. of buyers in base year
			Percent present sometime after N years						
1674	77	67	62	56	51	38	25	18	61
1675	64	57	49	47	46	29	14	9	177
1676	66	57	54	53	49	31	16	11	142
1677	63	58	58	52	49	17	13	9	167
1678	57	56	51	49	41	20	15	10	157
1679	65	55	54	44	42	26	17	15	69
1680	58	57	42	40	35	19	13	12	209
1681	69	49	49	45	43	21	8	7	75
1682	47	45	39	38	24	15	10	5	240
1683	65	54	52	35	35	20	19	6	54
1684	46	45	24	23	20	11	9	6	123
1685	61	42	39	39	29	15	10	5	41
1686	35	32	28	23	22	11	10	4	250
1687	51	40	37	34	31	20	6	0	35
1688	31	29	27	24	24	14	7	3	59
1689	37	34	30	30	26	17	7	3	70
1690	42	26	21	5	5	5	5	0	19
1691	48	48	28	21	17	10	7	0	29
1692	70	60	40	40	40	30	10	0	10
1693	45	33	31	31	31	18	10	4	51
1694	40	37	37	37	37	25	6	6	73
1695	44	44	44	44	39	31	8	8	36
1699	57	43	36	29	29	7	7	7	14
1700	39	32	28	28	26	5	5	5	92

elimination of the common names has a large effect on the measured persistence rates. For example, considering the 10-year persistence rates, the mean size across years of the change from the rates of Table C.1 to those of Table C.2 for rates for base years of the 1670s is a decline of less than 4 percentage points, whereas the mean size of the change for the same period in comparing Table C.2 and Table 6.1 is less than 1 percentage point; for the 1680s, the respective mean changes in these two stages are declines of less than 3 and less than 2 percentage points, and for the 1690s they are less than 2 and less than 1 point, respectively.

This stability of the results obtained when common names are eliminated according to the criteria described above might indicate that the measured persistence rates have not been significantly inflated from false linkages over time of different individuals sharing common names. Alternatively, it could be argued that the procedure used does not adequately deal with the problem of common names. This could be the case, for example, if names of residents of late seventeenth-century Barbados were drawn to a significant extent from

Table C.4. *Persistence of selected purchasers in Jamaica (commonest names eliminated)*[a]

Base year		Percent present sometime after N years								No. of buyers in base year
	N: 1	2	3	4	5	10	15	20	
1674	76	66	62	55	50	36	22	16	58
1675	63	56	47	45	44	28	14	8	155
1676	64	55	52	50	46	29	15	10	126
1677	62	57	57	52	49	18	13	9	148
1678	56	55	49	47	39	17	12	7	138
1679	63	53	53	42	40	27	18	15	62
1680	58	57	41	39	34	17	12	10	184
1681	69	52	52	47	44	24	9	7	68
1682	45	43	37	36	23	14	9	5	224
1683	60	51	51	34	34	19	17	6	47
1684	47	47	26	25	22	12	10	6	114
1685	63	42	40	40	29	16	11	5	38
1686	35	32	28	23	21	10	8	2	222
1687	50	38	34	31	28	16	6	0	32
1688	30	28	26	23	23	11	6	4	53
1689	36	33	29	29	24	15	5	2	66
1690	44	28	22	6	6	6	6	0	18
1691	48	48	26	19	15	7	4	0	27
1692	70	60	40	40	40	30	10	0	10
1693	46	35	33	33	33	17	9	4	46
1694	40	37	37	37	37	25	6	6	67
1695	41	41	41	41	34	31	9	9	32
1699	50	42	33	25	25	8	8	8	12
1700	37	29	26	26	23	6	6	6	82

[a]Purchasers whose names appear at least twice in the 1790 census of South Carolina are eliminated from the sample.

a different pool of names than the names of residents of South Carolina in 1790. Although this might seem unlikely, a test could be performed by repeating the elimination of common names using a different list of names believed to reflect more closely the universe of names present in Barbados in the appropriate period, and then once more to recompute the persistence rates. This procedure can of course in general be performed any number of times using different lists in order to test the sensitivity of particular sets of persistence estimates to the problem of common names.

The problem of common names in measuring persistence in Jamaica was treated the same way as for Barbados. The persistence rates in Table C.3 were obtained by using all the names of slave purchasers from the Jamaica invoice accounts. The names of the purchasers were then compared to the listing of names from the South Carolina census of 1790. Of the total of 1,587 names in the Jamaica sample, 156 were found listed two or more times in the South Carolina census. These most common names were removed from the Jamaica sample, and the persistence rates were recomputed; the results are shown in Table C.4. An additional 96 names of slave purchasers from the Jamaica invoices were found to appear a single time in the South Carolina census. These were then also removed from the Jamaica sample, and still excluding the common names removed earlier, a third set of persistence rates was calculated. These rates were presented in Table 6.2.

As was the case for Barbados, the elimination of the common names has no significant effect on the measured persistence rates. The mean reduction in the 10-year persistence rates of Tables C.3 and C.4, for example, is one percentage point for base years from the 1670s and less than one percentage point for those in the 1680s and 1690s. The mean difference between the annual 10-year persistence rates of Tables C.4 and Table 6.2 is less than two percentage points for the 1680s and less than one percentage point in each of the following decades.

Tables 6.3 and 6.4 were also constructed after removing all the common names identified for both Barbados and Jamaica.

Notes

Preface

1 Paul E. Lovejoy, *Transformations in Slavery: A History of Slavery in Africa* (Cambridge: Cambridge University Press, 1983), p. 46.

2 For a description of the format of the Royal African Company's slave sale records and an assessment of their coverage, see Appendix A.

3 The full references to these papers are: "The Slave Trade to the English West Indies, 1673–1724," *Economic History Review,* Second Series, Vol. XXXII, No. 2 (May 1979), pp. 241–9; "The Atlantic Slave Trade and the Barbados Market, 1673–1723," *Journal of Economic History,* Vol. XLII, No. 3 (September 1982), pp. 491–511; "Population Turnover in the English West Indies in the Late Seventeenth Century: A Comparative Perspective," *Journal of Economic History,* Vol. XLV, No. 2 (June 1985), pp. 227–35.

1. The Atlantic slave trade and the early development of the English West Indies

1 On the population of Barbados, see John J. McCusker, "The Rum Trade and the Balance of Payments of the Thirteen Continental Colonies, 1650–1775" (unpublished Ph.D. dissertation, University of Pittsburgh, 1970), p. 699; and Richard S. Dunn, *Sugar and Slaves: The Rise of the Planter Class in the English West Indies, 1624–1713* (Chapel Hill: University of North Carolina Press, 1972), pp. 74–6. For the populations of the mainland colonies, see U.S. Bureau of the Census, *Historical Statistics of the United States, Colonial Times to 1970* (Washington, D.C.: U.S. Government Printing Office, 1975), Part 2, Series Z1–19, p. 1168.

2 The data, which cover English and Welsh ports, are drawn from the compilation of Sir Charles Whitworth, *State of the Trade of Great Britain in Its Imports and Exports, Progressively from the Year 1697* (London: G. Robinson et al., 1776), pp. 1–9. The years chosen for discussion here are those for which these customs data appear to have valued imports and exports at current English prices; see McCusker, "The Rum Trade and the Balance of Payments," pp. 1189–96. Similar figures are given by Phyllis Deane and W. A. Cole in *British Economic Growth, 1688–1959,* second edition (Cambridge: Cambridge University Press,

1967), p. 87. Eric Williams based a comparison of the Caribbean and North American colonies on Whitworth's figures in *Capitalism and Slavery* (Chapel Hill: University of North Carolina Press, 1944), pp. 53–5.

3 Ralph Davis, *The Rise of the English Shipping Industry in the Seventeenth and Eighteenth Centuries* (London: Macmillan, 1962), p. 398.

4 Dunn, *Sugar and Slaves*, pp. 48, 205.

5 Richard B. Sheridan, *Sugar and Slavery: An Economic History of the British West Indies, 1623–1775* (Barbados: Caribbean Universities Press, 1974), pp. 26, 29.

6 The calculations are based on estimates of total sugar consumption in *ibid.*, pp. 21–2, and estimates of population from E. A. Wrigley and R. S. Schofield, *The Population History of England, 1541–1871: A Reconstruction* (Cambridge, Mass.: Harvard University, 1981), p. 528.

7 Dunn, *Sugar and Slaves*, p. 203.

8 Sheridan, *Sugar and Slavery*, pp. 487–8.

9 Carl and Roberta Bridenbaugh, *No Peace Beyond the Line: The English in the Caribbean, 1624–1690* (New York: Oxford University Press, 1972), p. 32.

10 Dunn, *Sugar and Slaves*, p. 228.

11 Dunn, *Sugar and Slaves*, pp. 55–74; Bridenbaugh, *No Peace Beyond the Line*, p. 33.

12 F. C. Innes, "The Pre-Sugar Era of European Settlement in Barbados," *Journal of Caribbean History*, Vol. 1 (November 1970), pp. 1–22.

13 On service in husbandry, see Ann Kussmaul, *Servants in Husbandry in Early Modern England* (Cambridge: Cambridge University Press, 1981); also see Peter Laslett, *Family Life and Illicit Love in Earlier Generations* (Cambridge: Cambridge University Press, 1977), Chapter 1.

14 On the development of indentured servitude, see Abbot Emerson Smith, *Colonists in Bondage: White Servitude and Convict Labor In America, 1607–1776* (Chapel Hill: University of North Carolina Press, 1947), Chapter 1; also David W. Galenson, "The Rise and Fall of Indentured Servitude in the Americas: An Economic Analysis," *Journal of Economic History*, Vol. XLIV, No. 1 (March 1984), pp. 1–6.

15 On the use of Irish servants, see Richard Pares, *Merchants and Planters*, Economic History Review Supplement No. 4 (Cambridge: Cambridge University Press, 1960), p. 15; Bridenbaugh, *No Peace Beyond the Line*, pp. 14–15.

16 William Hay to Archibald Hay, Barbados, September 10, 1645; Scottish Record Office, Edinburgh, Hay of Haystoun Papers, GD 34/945.

17 The region's reputation further suffered from the fact that during the late 1640s transportation to the West Indies began to be used as a punishment for political prisoners and convicted felons. This was considered a severe form of punishment. When Oliver Cromwell had suppressed the Irish rebellion in 1649, he wrote of the captured army: "When they submitted, these officers were knocked on the head, and every tenth man of the soldiers killed, and the rest shipped for Barbados"; quoted in Vincent T. Harlow, *A History of Barbados, 1625–1685* (Oxford: Clarendon Press, 1926), p. 295.

18 Richard Dunn commented of Barbados: "The island planters continued to employ plenty of indentured servants, but the striking thing is how eagerly they plunged into the slaveholding business"; *Sugar and Slaves*, pp. 67–8. On the Chesapeake's

slower transition from servants to slaves, see Russell Menard, "From Servants to Slaves: The Transformation of the Chesapeake Labor System," *Southern Studies,* Vol. XVI, No. 4 (Winter 1977), pp. 355–90; and David W. Galenson, *White Servitude in Colonial America: An Economic Analysis* (Cambridge: Cambridge University Press, 1981), pp. 151–4.

19 Pares, *Merchants and Planters,* pp. 15–16.

20 Henry Whistler, "Voyage to the West Indies, 1654''; British Museum, London, Sloane MSS 3926, f. 9, Barbados, February 9, 1654.

21 Dunn, *Sugar and Slaves,* pp. 312–13; Alfred D. Chandler, "The Expansion of Barbados," *Journal of the Barbados Museum and Historical Society,* Vol. XIII, Nos. 3 and 4 (1945–6), pp. 106–36.

22 Dunn, *Sugar and Slaves,* pp. 68–9.

23 Galenson, *White Servitude in Colonial America,* pp. 128–39; also J. Harry Bennett, "Cary Helyar, Merchant and Planter of Seventeenth-Century Jamaica," *William and Mary Quarterly,* Third Series, Vol. XXI, No. 1 (January 1964), p. 70.

24 J. Harry Bennett, "William Whaley, Planter of Seventeenth-Century Jamaica," *Agricultural History,* Vol. XL, No. 2 (April 1966), p. 121.

25 Galenson, *White Servitude in Colonial America,* pp. 158–9.

26 Public Record Office (PRO), London, CO 1/50, f. 303, "To the Kings most Excellent Matie.: The Humble Petition of the Persons Who Have Estates in Your Maties. Plantations in America," November 3, 1682.

27 PRO, CO 29/3, p. 92, Governor Sir Jonathan Atkins to Lords of Trade and Plantations, Barbados, October 26, 1680.

28 On the role of indentured servants in the eighteenth century, see Galenson, *White Servitude in Colonial America,* pp. 126–39.

29 The quotation is from Bryan Edwards, *The History, Civil and Commercial, of the British West Indies,* fifth edition (London: G. and W. B. Whittaker et al., 1819), Vol. II, p. 287. On the capital required for a sugar plantation in the seventeenth century, see Sheridan, *Sugar and Slavery,* pp. 264–6, and Dunn, *Sugar and Slaves,* p. 197.

30 This and the following two sentences are based on Dunn, *Sugar and Slaves,* pp. 88–9, 96.

31 *Ibid.,* pp. 128–9, 142–3, 170–1.

32 This figure is based on probate inventories of estates on Maryland's lower western shore during 1658–1710. See Russell R. Menard, "The Maryland Slave Population, 1658 to 1730: A Demographic Profile of Blacks in Four Counties," *William and Mary Quarterly,* Vol. XXXII, No. 1 (January 1975), p. 35.

33 Adam Smith, *An Inquiry into the Nature and Causes of the Wealth of Nations* (New York: Modern Library, 1937), p. 158; Dunn, *Sugar and Slaves,* p. 85.

34 The distributions of land and slaves in Barbados in 1680 appear to serve as good proxies for the distribution of total wealth both because land and slaves were the principal forms of wealth on the island and because both were highly correlated with the ownership of other forms of wealth. Additionally, as Richard Dunn has noted, the intense cultivation of all the arable land on the island eliminates the problem of comparing developed and undeveloped land that would be encountered elsewhere; *Sugar and Slaves,* pp. 90–1. Dunn finds that 175, or 6.9 percent, of the

island's 2,592 property holders (excluding residents of Bridgetown) owned 53.4 percent of the island's acreage and 54.3 percent of its slaves; *ibid.*, p. 96. In contrast, 10 seventeenth-century wealth distributions compiled for rural areas in Massachusetts, Connecticut, and Maryland appear to show less inequality among wealth holders; in 8 of these 10 studies the top 10 percent of wealth holders owned less than 53 percent of the total wealth; see Alice Hanson Jones, *Wealth of a Nation to Be: The American Colonies on the Eve of the Revolution* (New York: Columbia University Press, 1980), Table 8.4, p. 266. Also see similar evidence collected in Jeffrey G. Williamson and Peter H. Lindert, "Long-Term Trends in American Wealth Inequality," in James D. Smith, ed., *Modeling the Distribution and Intergenerational Transmission of Wealth* (Chicago: University of Chicago Press, 1980), Appendix 1, pp. 75–9. This comparison cannot be conclusive, because many differences of method and evidence interfere with comparisons of these wealth distributions, but the contrast between Barbados and the mainland colonies does appear suggestive.

35 This and the following two sentences are based on Dunn, *Sugar and Slaves,* p. 99.

36 K. G. Davies, *The Royal African Company* (London: Longmans, 1957), pp. 21–3; Harlow, *History of Barbados,* p. 310.

37 George Frederick Zook, *The Company of Royal Adventurers Trading Into Africa* (Lancaster, Pa.: New Era Printing Company, 1919), pp. 8–14.

38 *Ibid.,* p. 82.

39 PRO, CO 1/22, No. 21, Ellis Leighton, "By order of the Royall Company," London, January 23, 1668. For discussion, see A. P. Thornton, "The Organization of the Slave Trade in the English West Indies, 1660–1685," *William and Mary Quarterly,* Third Series, Vol. XII, No. 3 (July 1955), pp. 399–409.

40 Zook, *Company of Royal Adventurers,* pp. 23–7; Davies, *Royal African Company,* pp. 44, 57–8.

41 Like its predecessor, the Royal African Company was a joint stock company. For a discussion of the financial organization of the company, see Davies, *Royal African Company,* Chapter 2. The company's charter is printed in Elizabeth Donnan, *Documents Illustrative of the History of the Slave Trade to America* (New York: Octagon Books, 1969), Vol. 1, pp. 177–92.

42 For example, Wesley Frank Craven, *The Colonies in Transition, 1660–1713* (New York: Harper and Row, 1968), p. 290; Clarence L. Ver Steeg, *The Formative Years, 1607–1763* (New York: Hill and Wang, 1964), p. 192; Maldwyn Allen Jones, *American Immigration* (Chicago: University of Chicago Press, 1960), p. 32.

43 Davies, *Royal African Company,* p. 100. For an example of a report by Royal African Company factors in Barbados of the delivery of slaves from Madagascar to the island in 1681, see Donnan, *Documents Illustrative of the History of the Slave Trade,* Vol. 1, p. 274.

44 On the absence of sustained trading monopolies on the African coast, see Paul E. Lovejoy, *Transformations in Slavery: A History of Slavery in Africa* (Cambridge: Cambridge University Press, 1983), p. 101.

45 PRO T70/16, f. 78, Stede and Gascoigne, Barbados, March 15, 1684.

46 Davies, *Royal African Company,* pp. 199–200.

47 *Ibid.*, p. 110.
48 PRO T70/57, f. 9v, Royal African Company to Clement Tudway and Edward Parsons at Antigua; London, August 23, 1687. For some examples of theft by ships' captains, and of the difficulty of discovering and proving it, see the following letters from Edwyn Stede and Stephen Gascoigne in Barbados to the Royal African Company: T70/1, p. 1, October 30, 1678; T70/1, pp. 19–21, May 21, 1679; and T70/1, p. 23, June 10, 1679.
49 Davies, *Royal African Company*, p. 113.
50 *Ibid.*, pp. 308–10.
51 *Ibid.*, p. 117; C. S. S. Higham, *The Development of the Leeward Islands Under the Restoration, 1660–1688* (Cambridge: Cambridge University Press, 1921), pp. 162–5.
52 Davies, *Royal African Company*, pp. 120–1; also see the comments of James A. Rawley, *The Transatlantic Slave Trade: A History* (New York: W. W. Norton, 1981), p. 159.

In an attempt to test for the presence of Royal African Company monopoly power in the West Indies, Richard Bean constructed three related indexes of monopoly power, based on comparisons of the cost of slaves in the West Indies and Africa. Each of the indexes fell after 1690, and Bean concluded that this implied the presence of monopoly power before that date: "Thus the period 1689–98 marks the end of the Royal African Company monopoly . . . Since our empirical tests all indicate that a change did occur at the same period, one must conclude that the Royal African Company had been acting as a monopolist in limiting the supply of slaves to British America"; *The British Trans-Atlantic Slave Trade, 1650–1775* (New York: Arno Press, 1975), p. 93. Yet it is odd that each of the three indexes takes on its highest value, indicating the highest degree of monopoly power, for the five-year period centered on 1675, while each index then declines during the 1680s; *ibid.*, p. 89. As shown in Table 1.5, the Royal African Company accounted for approximately 33 percent of total slaves delivered to the British West Indies during the 1670s, compared to 68 percent during the 1680s. The company of course traded for only seven years during the 1670s, and therefore might have delivered a larger share of total slave arrivals during 1673–9. If independent traders had operated at a constant rate during the decade, the company would have accounted for 47 percent of total deliveries during the latter seven-year period. Yet it would nonetheless seem unlikely that this smaller market share would have conferred greater monopoly power on the company during the 1670s than a larger one did during the following decade. Bean's analysis may be severely hampered by poor information on West African slave prices during this period.
53 Davies, *Royal African Company*, p. 122.
54 *Ibid.*, p. 123.
55 K. G. Davies concluded that the Royal African Company was actually forced to pay more in compensation to interlopers after the Revolution than it had gained from the original seizures, and he noted that this was a serious blow to the company at a time when its finances were already shaky; *ibid.*, p. 124.
56 *Ibid.*, p. 148.
57 For 1680–5 and 1700–9, *ibid.*, p. 195; for 1719–25, PRO T70/1225.

58 These agreements are discussed by Davies in *Royal African Company*, pp. 187, 197–9, who describes their method of payment as "unique . . . in the shipping industry."

59 In addition, the captain's commission for the voyage was normally based on the number of slaves he delivered alive to the West Indies. K. G. Davies observed that the captain's resulting incentive to maximize the absolute number of slaves delivered alive to the West Indies might actually have promoted overcrowding of the ships and consequent mortality; *ibid.*, p. 198. Yet although this could have occurred in some cases, this argument neglects the fact that the number of slaves to be carried was normally determined jointly by the Royal African Company and ships' owners, so that the company was generally in a position to place an upper limit on the total number of slaves carried. The captain's incentive to maximize the number of slaves delivered alive, given this constraint of a maximum cargo size agreed to by the company, would therefore have served the company's interest.

60 Davies, *Royal African Company*, p. 186. For 36 ships dispatched on slaving voyages by the Royal African Company during 1719–25, the mean time between departure from England and first arrival in Africa was 70 days, with a standard deviation of 26; the shortest voyage was 30 days, the longest 146; compiled from PRO T70/1225.

61 For a detailed discussion of these regions and the Royal African Company's activities in each, see Davies, *Royal African Company*, Chapter 6.

62 *Ibid.*, pp. 245–52. The large forts and small factories generally served somewhat different purposes. The forts were used as trading centers, where company ships could call to pick up supplies of stored slaves, as described later, whereas most of the smaller factories were used primarily as tributary trading posts, to supply slaves to the larger forts, rather than as direct suppliers of slaves to ships.

63 *Ibid.*, p. 230.

64 *Ibid.*, pp. 262–4.

65 PRO T70/8, f. 30, Jamaica, January 16, 1708.

66 The Barbados agents' motivation for pointing out the abuse to the company was of course clear, as they continued: "which wee the Rather mention, that the Compa. may be informed of the truth of things and ourselves excused from blame"; PRO T70/1, pp. 67–8, Edwyn Stede and Stephen Gascoigne, Barbados, October 26, 1680.

67 At one point the company attempted to use a device in Africa that it employed in the West Indies: making a number of factors jointly responsible for its trade at a fort, in the hope that each would monitor the work of the others to protect himself from bearing the financial penalty for misconduct and inefficiency in the company's business. In January 1688 the company wrote to its three factors at Cape Coast Castle that it expected to hear of an improvement in their trade.

but must mind you that we do not direct any of you Three Cheife Merchants to act in any Single Station for all of you are Equallie Intrusted & we have placed you as we have our Joynt Factors in Barbados Jamaica & other forreinge parts.

The new system was evidently not an immediate success; in June 1689 the company had occasion to remind the same three factors that

Yor. neglect of our Establishment requires us to give you notice againe that as wee have formerly advised you, . . . you are joyntly & severally oblidged to us for the ballance of our Gold Accott. for the Ballance of our Warehouse Accott. & for all Omissions & Errors in all our Accotts. and wee shall not understand nor allow any Objections that you shall make hereafter, that this or that Person did not doe his duty, but if you Can charge each other with any Imbezellment or neglect you are Immediately to doe it soe soon as you shall discover the same, that wee may take satisfaction out of the party's Sallary or Securitty;

> PRO T70/50, ff. 55v, 97; Royal African Company to Samuell Humfreys, Richard Wight, and John Boylston at Cape Coast Castle, London, January 24, 1688, and June 18, 1689.
> In spite of this stern warning, the system apparently remained a failure, and in later years the company reverted to employing a single factor in charge at Cape Coast Castle.

68 Davies, *Royal African Company*, pp. 238–9, 256. In a more recent investigation, Davies has provided additional evidence on the extraordinarily high mortality rates suffered by company employees in Africa. His findings include the observations that one man in three died within his first four months in Africa, and that more than three in five died in the first year after arrival; K. G. Davies, "The Living and the Dead: White Mortality in West Africa, 1684–1732," in Stanley L. Engerman and Eugene D. Genovese, eds., *Race and Slavery in the Western Hemisphere: Quantitative Studies* (Princeton, N.J.: Princeton University Press, 1975), pp. 83–98. The company of course realized that not only were the high morbidity and mortality rates in West Africa demoralizing to its employees there, but also that knowledge of these conditions among potential employees in England meant that most of those the company was able to hire for African service were desperate or dishonest men who went out with the intention of stealing from the company to augment their salaries. In 1686 the company wrote from London to its chief factor at Cape Coast Castle:

Wee are sorry to heare that Negroes are soe Scarce on the Coast whereby all our Ships are compelled to goe downe to Arda in wch. place Mr. Carter instead of doing his duty as a Factor hath done us very great Prejudice by Inhauncing the Prices of Negroes [i.e., falsifying the accounts of purchase prices for slaves]. Wee are of yor. Opinion that it is Needfull to Keepe a Factory there but find it very Difficult to gett any that have their health so as to be Encouraged to Continue there that are worthy to be Trusted;

> PRO T70/50, f. 9, Royal African Company to Agent General Nurse at Cape Coast; London, May 18, 1686.

69 PRO T70/1225.

70 Using the data from the Royal African Company voyages of 1720–5 (see Appendix B), the following regressions were estimated (standard errors in parentheses):

$$\text{Ratio of slaves loaded to slaves intended} \qquad (1)$$
$$= 1.081 - 0.0015 \quad \text{duration of stay in Africa (days)}$$
$$(0.523) \quad (0.0004)$$
$$R^2 = 0.327, \quad F = 13.59, \quad n = 30$$

Ratio of slaves loaded to slaves intended (2)
$$= 0.916 - 0.000054 \quad \text{ship tonnage}$$
$$(0.085) \quad (0.000426)$$

$$R^2 = 0.0005, \quad F = 0.016, \quad n = 32$$

71 For example, in 1720 the company's factors at Cape Coast Castle informed the company of an episode in which they had become suspicious that a captain intended to change the slaves they had loaded on his ship with interlopers lying off Anomabu:

in consequence thereof, & to prevent your being abused by such practices, we sent an express on board to Mr. Young, with a marking Iron, directing him to mark all the slaves . . . & for that purpose a lettr. was sent Capt. Lamberth requiring his compliance therewith: but . . . the Officers on board refused to let Mr. Young mark the Slaves, tho' the Capt. seemingly consented, but withall gave him to understand that as he had received his dispatches, & sailed from Cape Coast he was no longer under the Generals [i.e., the factor's] directions; which we hope your honours will take proper notice, and make him liable for the ill consequence that may attend, if any complaint should be made of the Slaves, not answering to the qualifications of the Masters & Surgeons Certificate; as we assure your honours not to know of any unqualified Slave being on board;

PRO T70/4, p. 6, Cape Coast Castle, July 1, 1720, Messrs. Phipps et al. to Royal African Company.

72 The considerable powers of ships' captains over all those aboard their ships must have deterred crew members from reporting captains' abuses against the company in most cases. In one instance in which a mate "took notice" of a captain's thefts from the company, the captain dealt summarily and harshly with him:

Mr. William Holland late Mate of the Elizabeth Captn. Thorne, complains of said Captn. Thorne, that he was not quallified for his Imploy, that he went to Bermuda by Neglect or Rather design, that he acted not as a Servt. to the Compa. but independant, That he converted the Compa.'s Rum to his own use, tho' he had a large Cargo on his own Accot., That he put aboard of a Sloop in his homeward bound passage 13 of the Compa.'s Slaves, besides two sent to his Own house on his arrivall and one sent from the Coast, And that because Mr. Holland took notice of his proceedings he put him in Irons on the Coast, brought him home before the Mast, having thrown over board his Chest, Instrumts., books and Papers that he might not keep a Journall, and on arrivall at Barbadoes, has had him Imprest aboard the Newcastle Man of War, as was also the Boatswain, but he deposing in his favour, is cleared, but Mr. Holland is Confin'd aboard;

PRO T70/8, f. 55v, William Holland to Royal African Company, Barbados, November 1, 1710.

73 The mean length of 36 company voyages made during 1719–25 was 67 days, with a standard deviation of 25. The median voyage length was 65 days. The shortest voyage was 27 days; the longest, nearly five months, was that of a ship bound from Cape Coast Castle to Barbados whose captain died during the voyage; PRO T70/1225.

74 On the local negotiation of freight rates in the West Indies, see Davis, *The Rise of the English Shipping Industry in the Seventeenth and Eighteenth Centuries*, pp. 276–80.

75 Davies, *Royal African Company*, p. 296.

76 PRO, CO 1/18, No. 39, Thomas Modyford, Barbados, March 20, 1664.

77 For examples of the company's complaints about the growing West Indian debt, see PRO T70/57, ff. 64, 67v. The company might have hoped that division of the agencies would increase collection by making it more difficult for particular agents to favor their friends in collecting debts, as well as making theft by the agents more difficult. Yet the company also recognized that dividing the agencies could dilute the agents' incentives to collect planters' debts, if in consequence the agents' commissions were reduced. In one case when the company added an agent, it also raised the aggregate commission paid to the agency; Davies, *Royal African Company*, p. 296. In another case the company tried a different approach to this problem. Noting that interest charges owed to the company had not been recorded or collected, the company remarked in a letter to its Barbados agents that

we have often made complaint, & written very earnestly to have that Accott. stated, but have not had our Orders answeared to expectacion. The neglect whereof we can not attribute to anything soe much, as that our orders being to our ffactors in Generall none has heartily espoused ye business to bring it aboute.

Consequently, the company decided to place the responsibility with one individual:

We therefore hereby Order that you Mr. Nicho. Prideaux doe take this affaire perticulerly upon yor. selfe, from whom we expect a speedy compliance & answeare hereto, & doe hereby direct & order our other ffactors in noe wise to obstruct or hinder your proceedings therein, but from time to time to give you such assistance as the business will need or require.

Yet the company betrayed its lack of true authority by closing with a pleading postscript: "And we hope you will Looke back into all the former Accotts. of yor. predecessors soe farr as is possible"; PRO T70/57, f. 102v, London, May 8, 1694. The results of this particular instruction are not known, but it is unlikely that they were more successful than more drastic measures to motivate the agents to collect the planters' debts, which included attempts to make the agents personally responsible to the company for all credit given to planters, and which came to little; Davies, *Royal African Company*, p. 296.

2. Shipping and mortality

1 Some comparisons of the company's mean cargo size with that of other branches of the transatlantic slave trade in the eighteenth century are possible. The Royal African Company's average cargo was larger than that of the British transatlantic trade to Virginia in the eighteenth century (199 slaves per vessel), and smaller than those of the Portuguese trade of the eighteenth century (371), the French trade of the eighteenth century (345), and the British trade to Jamaica in the 1780s (396). For a discussion of this and other aspects of these trades, see Herbert S. Klein, *The Middle Passage: Comparative Studies in the Atlantic Slave Trade* (Princeton, N.J.: Princeton University Press, 1978), pp. 28, 124, 145, 187.

2 The mean cargo size of company shipments to Virginia was also relatively low, 157 slaves, but this is based on only four voyages for which records are available in the company's invoice accounts.

3 PRO T70/51, f. 69v, Royal African Company to Joseph Baggs at Cape Coast Castle; London, September 10, 1700.

4 During 1720–5 the mean size of four ships that carried slaves to the Leewards for the Royal African Company was 163 tons. Although this was little different from the mean of 158 tons of seven ships sent by the company to Barbados in this period, it was considerably below the mean of 196 tons of 22 ships sent to Jamaica. This evidence is drawn from PRO T70/1225; for a discussion of the source, see later in this chapter and Appendix B.

5 K. G. Davies, *The Royal African Company* (London: Longmans, 1957), pp. 192–3.

6 The use of evidence on numbers of slaves per cargo to draw inferences about ship sizes obviously assumes a strong correlation between the two variables. The two do appear generally to have been closely related. During 1720–5 the simple correlation between slaves loaded and ship tonnage for 36 company voyages was 0.824; the evidence for this is drawn from PRO T70/1225.

7 The measurements recorded by the company are likely to have been the ships' registered tonnages. On the interpretation of these, see Christopher J. French, "Eighteenth-Century Tonnage Measurements," *Journal of Economic History*, Vol. XXXIII, No. 2 (June 1973), pp. 434–43.

8 The tendency noted here is not due to a comparison between wartime and peacetime, for although war conditions prevailed during most of the period 1691–1713, 1680–8 was a time of peace, as was 1720–5.
Klein has argued that this concentration of ships in the medium range of sizes was a general trend in the British slave trade, with increasing use of ships between 100 and 200 tons over the course of the eighteenth century; *Middle Passage*, pp. 158–9.

9 Ralph Davis, *The Rise of the English Shipping Industry in the Seventeenth and Eighteenth Centuries* (London: Macmillan, 1962), p. 280.

10 This mean is not weighted by the size of ship or numbers of slaves carried. The number of slaves carried per ton in the British transatlantic trade appears to have risen later in the eighteenth century; in the 1780s the mean level in the trade to Jamaica was 2.6 slaves per ton. French slave traders had higher ratios than the Royal African Company, with mean levels of 2.0–2.3 slaves per ton in the first half of the eighteenth century; Klein, *Middle Passage*, pp. 147, 186.

11 The same problem apparently existed in the Royal African Company's earlier trade; see Davies, *Royal African Company*, p. 194.

12 Davies also found this relationship to hold for the company's trade in earlier periods; *Royal African Company*, p. 194. Similarly, Klein found it to exist elsewhere in the transatlantic slave trade; *Middle Passage*, p. 146.

13 For a discussion of the length of sales, and of the delay between a ship's arrival in port and the sale of its cargo, see Chapter 4.

14 Colin Palmer, *Human Cargoes: The British Slave Trade to Spanish America, 1700–1739* (Urbana: University of Illinois Press, 1981), p. 45.

15 On seasonality in shipping to and from the West Indies, see Davis, *Rise of the English Shipping Industry*, pp. 279–82.

16 PRO T70/8, f. 97v, James Gohier, Barbados, August 30, 1715. The demand for slaves also tended to be lively in late winter and spring because planters could use additional workers to harvest the canes.

17 The correlation between Barbados's monthly percentage distribution of Table 2.4

and the contemporaneous distribution for the Leewards is 0.212, whereas that between the Barbados distribution and the contemporaneous distribution for Jamaica is −0.698. In contrast, the correlation between the Barbados distribution and the Leewards distribution lagged two months is 0.472, and that between the Barbados distribution and the Jamaica distribution lagged two months is 0.556.

18 On the problems of coordinating slave deliveries and the purchases of sugar cargoes in the islands, see Davis, *Rise of the English Shipping Industry,* pp. 279–85. Within Jamaica, in the early nineteenth century the sugar harvest on the island's south side ran from January through June, like that of Barbados, whereas on the north side the harvest ran from March to November. The greater importance of the south than the north side during the early 1720s suggests that harvest seasonality is not likely to have been the principal factor underlying the differences in seasonality of slave deliveries across islands. (I am grateful to Barry Higman for supplying this information on the seasonality of sugar harvests in a letter of January 11, 1984.)

19 An example of this behavior was reported by the company's agent in Barbados in 1714, who wrote that "Captn. Neal in a Bristol ship arrived there ye 2d Instant wth. 300 Gold Coast Negroes, but not liking ye Market proceeded to Jamaica;" PRO T70/8, f. 8v, Patrick Thomson, Barbados, July 7, 1714.

It might be thought that the captains of ships rented by the Royal African Company had no incentive to follow this procedure in order to maximize the prices received for slaves, because the revenue from slave sales accrued to the company. However the company invariably paid the owners of hired ships (of whom the captain was usually one) part of their earnings in the form of slaves; see Davies, *Royal African Company,* pp. 198–200. The captain would therefore have been interested in finding the best market in which to sell these commission slaves in order to maximize his own earnings.

20 PRO T70/8, f. 34, Bate and Stewart, Barbados, May 18, 1708.

21 The commissions of Royal African Company agents in the West Indies were determined as a fixed percentage of the proceeds from the slave sales they conducted in the colony where they held an agency. On the timing of slave sales and the order of slave purchases by quality at sales, see Chapter 4.

22 An example of a ship stopping in Barbados for provisions is the *Unity.* A company shipping register noted that after a voyage from Cape Coast Castle in 1722 that had begun on May 24, the ship "Putt into Barbados for refreshment July 18th having lost in the Voyage 25 slaves. Sailed thence for Jamaica July 19th 1722"; PRO T70/1225. (The unfortunate captain had his ship taken by a Spanish sloop nine days later near the coast of Jamaica, and although he was later sent ashore, his cargo and ship were lost.)

23 C. S. S. Higham, *The Development of the Leeward Islands Under the Restoration, 1660–1688* (Cambridge: Cambridge University Press, 1921), pp. 159–60. The Royal African Company's agents at Barbados informed the company in 1708 that they had sent on 51 slaves from one cargo to Nevis, explaining that "ye Gambia Negroes not being Saleable at Barbados"; PRO T70/8, f. 40v, Bate and Stewart, Barbados, October 12, 1708. At times it appears to have been routine for the agents to send on to the Leewards portions of cargoes that sold poorly in Barbados. In 1709 they reported that "having but a Dull Markett [in Barbados] do Ship 57 [remaining of a cargo of 380] for Nevis," and in 1712 wrote of a cargo of 292

slaves that "they go off but Slowly, so they are about sending One hundred of them to Nevis"; PRO T70/8, f. 45, Bate and Stewart, Barbados, May 9, 1709; T70/8, f. 62v, Bate and Stewart, Barbados, September 18, 1712. For an interesting parallel comment by a governor of Jamaica later in the eighteenth century, noting that previously it had been common for slavers bound for Jamaica first to try the market of the "Windward Islands" instead of coming directly to Jamaica from Africa, see Richard B. Sheridan, "The Slave Trade to Jamaica, 1702–1808," in B. W. Higman, ed., *Trade, Government and Society in Caribbean History, 1700–1920* (Kingston, Jamaica: Heinemann Educational Books Caribbean Ltd., 1983), p. 9.

24 Higham, *Development of the Leeward Islands,* pp. 154, 160.

25 For example, see Johannes Postma, "Mortality in the Dutch Slave Trade, 1675–1795," in Henry A. Gemery and Jan S. Hogendorn, eds., *The Uncommon Market: Essays in the Economic History of the Atlantic Slave Trade* (New York: Academic Press, 1979), pp. 239–60.

26 In an article published in 1981, Joseph Miller stated that there were then only six such known bodies of evidence; "Mortality in the Atlantic Slave Trade: Statistical Evidence on Causality," *Journal of Interdisciplinary History,* Vol. XI, No. 3 (Winter 1981), p. 391. Recent interest in the quantitative analysis of mortality has stimulated subsequent investigations that have brought additional evidence to light; for example, see David Eltis, "Mortality and Voyage Length in the Middle Passage: New Evidence from the Nineteenth Century," *Journal of Economic History,* Vol. XLIV, No. 2 (June 1984), pp. 301–8.

27 PRO T70/1225, "List of Ships, and their Voyages in the Service of the Royal African Company of England From November the 4th 1719 To [1733]."

28 Of the 38 voyages covered by the register, two have no record of the number of slaves carried away from Africa, and a third has no record of the number delivered alive in America.

29 Sheila Lambert, ed., *House of Commons Sessional Papers of the Eighteenth Century* (Wilmington, Del.: Scholarly Resources, 1975), Vol. 70, Part 4, p. 198. The annual figures on mortality given there show a decline in the percentages of deaths during the decade, from 21–29% during 1680–5 to 15–19% during 1686–8.

30 Johannes Postma, "Mortality in the Dutch Slave Trade," p. 253; Herbert S. Klein and Stanley L. Engerman, "A Note on Mortality in the French Slave Trade in the Eighteenth Century," in Gemery and Hogendorn, eds., *The Uncommon Market,* p. 269; Robert Louis Stein, *The French Slave Trade in the Eighteenth Century: An Old Regime Business* (Madison: University of Wisconsin Press, 1979), p. 99; and Klein, *The Middle Passage,* p. 161. There was apparently a sizable decline in mortality rates at the end of the eighteenth century; studies of the English and Portuguese trades during the 1790s found lower mean mortality rates for the Middle Passage of 6–8% per voyage; *ibid.,* p. 161.

31 Farley Grubb, "Immigration and Servitude in the Colony and Commonwealth of Pennsylvania: A Quantitative and Economic Analysis" (unpublished Ph.D. dissertation, University of Chicago, 1984). Also see James C. Riley, "Mortality on Long-Distance Voyages in the Eighteenth Century," *Journal of Economic History,* Vol. XLI, No. 3 (September 1981), pp. 651–6.

32 That the percentage of all slaves in the sample who died in passage was greater

than the mean of the individual ships' percentage losses is the result of a tendency for the larger ships in the sample to suffer higher percentage losses than smaller ships. The four ships in the sample of under 100 tons had a mean loss of only 4.9% of their cargoes, compared with 12.7% for the 17 of 100–99 tons, 11.6% for the 11 of 200–99 tons, and 19.8% for the three of 300 tons and over.

33 This measure was suggested by Miller, "Mortality in the Atlantic Slave Trade," p. 394.

34 The average daily mortality rate M is calculated in this study as

$$M = 1 - \left(\frac{s_a - s_b}{s_a} \right)^{1/d}$$

where

d = days between departure from Africa and arrival at an American destination

s_a = slaves on board at the ship's departure from Africa

s_b = slaves delivered alive in America

35 The sample includes one voyage that was clearly atypically long: The *Cape Coast Frigate* is recorded as having left Cape Coast Castle on October 6, 1721, and did not reach Barbados until March 3, 1722, nearly five months later. It lost 48 (20%) of its 240 slaves on the voyage. Omitting this observation from the sample has virtually no effect on the results presented in Table 2.6 (or on those of Tables 2.7– 2.11). It might also be noted that omitting the duration variable from the equations for which results are reported in Tables 2.7–2.10 has no significant impact on the estimated coefficients of other variables.

36 The equation estimated in Table 2.6 can be written as

$$\frac{m/t}{d} = a + b_1 d$$

where

m = slaves dead in passage

t = total slaves carried from Africa

d = duration of voyage

This equation can be transformed by multiplying both sides by d; the resulting equation is then

$$m/t = b_1' d + b_2' d^2$$

The test discussed in the text, of whether $b_1 = 0$, is therefore equivalent to testing $b_2' = 0$; that is, the absence of a significant and positive effect of voyage duration on average daily mortality rates implies the absence of a significant effect of the square of duration on the simple mortality rate per voyage.

37 For example, see Klein and Engerman, "A Note on Mortality in the French Slave Trade in the Eighteenth Century," pp. 261–72.

38 *Ibid.;* Raymond L. Cohn and Richard A. Jensen, "The Determinants of Slave Mortality Rates on the Middle Passage," *Explorations in Economic History,* Vol. 19, No. 3 (July 1982), pp. 269–82.

39 The decision of a shipowner in provisioning his ship for a slaving voyage can be stated more precisely. In principle, the owner would wish to provision his ship up to the point at which the cost of adding increments of food and water to his stores – the sum of both the direct cost of the provisions and the opportunity cost of its space in the ship, for example in slaves not loaded – was just equal to the expected benefit to the captain of carrying the additional food, in the value of additional slaves surviving the voyage. The trader's calculation of the optimal amount of provisions to load, and the optimal number of slaves to carry, would therefore depend on a number of variables, including the size of his ship, African and American slave prices, the rental value of space on his ship, the trade-off between food supplies and slave mortality, and the distribution of past voyage lengths on the route he planned to follow. It would also depend on the trader's judgment of his ability to make a faster, or slower, voyage than other traders: The maximum length of voyage anticipated – and consequently the location of the kink in the mortality schedule of Figure 2.1 – could therefore vary across ships.

Adequate quantities of supplies were of course not always sufficient to prevent mortality rates from rising on long voyages, because some diseases were related closely to the particular kinds of food available and to food quality. For example, long voyages tended to make slaves susceptible to scurvy if no antiscorbutics were provided.

It should be clear that a voyage longer than d in Figure 2.1 would show a higher average daily mortality rate than one shorter than d because each day beyond d would involve higher marginal mortality levels than those up to d.

Within the sample analyzed here there is no indication whatever of an increase in mortality rates with voyage duration. To test for the presence of a kink in the relationship, 10 separate regressions were estimated of the form:

$$\text{average daily mortality rate} = a + b_1 \text{ voyage duration (days)} + b_2 \text{ long voyages}$$

where "long voyages" was a binary variable that took the value of 1 for the single longest voyage in the sample in the first equation, the two longest voyages in the second equation, and so on up to the longest 10 voyages in the tenth equation, and 0 for other voyages. Only in one equation – that in which "long voyages" included the 10 longest voyages – did the variable's estimated coefficient approach statistical significance, and in that case the coefficient was actually negative.

40 Some authors have suggested that there would be a positive relationship between daily mortality rates and voyage time in the initial stages of a voyage (e.g., Cohn and Jensen, "Determinants of Slave Mortality Rates," p. 275), whereas others have argued for a negative relationship (Miller, "Mortality in the Atlantic Slave Trade"). These arguments might be seen as pointing out factors tending to produce rising, and others tending to produce falling rates, respectively, early in a voyage, without any clear prediction of the net outcome.

Miller's recent suggestions that daily mortality fell in the early stages of slaving voyages, and that longer voyages would consequently show lower average daily mortality rates than shorter ones, suggests that a closer examination of the relationship between voyage duration and mortality rates might be useful. Instead of using a single continuous independent variable for duration, as in Table 2.6, the voyages in the present sample were divided by duration into three groups of roughly equal numbers. The following regression was estimated with separate dichotomous variables for the shortest voyages (50 days or less) and the longest (75 days or more), with the omitted category being voyages of 51 to 74 days (standard errors in parentheses):

$$\begin{array}{l} \text{average daily mortality} = \quad 2.394 \quad - \quad 0.472 \quad \text{short} \quad - \quad 0.727 \quad \text{long} \\ \text{rate per thousand slaves} \quad\;\; (0.340) \quad\;\; (0.504) \quad\qquad\qquad (0.492) \\ \qquad\qquad\qquad\quad R^2 = 0.070, \quad F = 1.133, \quad n = 33 \end{array}$$

In this equation no statistically significant difference in mortality rates appears between short and medium-length voyages, or between medium-length and long voyages. This analysis therefore does not support any pattern other than a constant relationship between the average daily mortality rate and voyage length.

41 For example, see Klein, *The Middle Passage*, pp. 229, 234.

42 It was long ago noted, in eighteenth-century parliamentary hearings, that the available space for slaves did not increase in the same proportion as a ship's tonnage. Herbert Klein has suggested the following index of area for slaving ships:

$$A = T^{2/3}$$

where A is the index of area and T is the ship's tonnage; *Middle Passage*, p. 195. Reestimating the equation reported in Table 2.7 after substituting this index of area for tonnage yields the following results (standard errors are given in parentheses):

$$\begin{array}{l} \text{average daily mortality} = \quad 1.861 \quad - \quad 0.0096 \quad \text{duration of voyage (days)} \\ \text{rate per thousand slaves} \quad\;\;\; (1.005) \quad\;\; (0.0087) \\ \qquad\qquad\qquad\qquad\quad + \; 0.0869 \quad \text{slaves per unit of area} \\ \qquad\qquad\qquad\qquad\quad (0.1067) \\ \qquad\qquad\quad R^2 = 0.047, \quad F = 0.741, \quad n = 33 \end{array}$$

The measure of slaves per unit of area has no statistically significant effect on mortality rates in this equation.

43 For example, see Cohn and Jensen, "Determinants of Slave Mortality Rates," p. 281.

44 PRO T70/51, f. 69v, Royal African Company to Agent Joseph Baggs at Cape Coast Castle; London, September 10, 1700. For an example of a factor reducing the cargo a ship would carry, see T70/14, f. 67, Thomas Weaver, James Island, June 10, 1704.

45 Quoted in Palmer, *Human Cargoes*, p. 48.

46 Quoted in *ibid.*, p. 49. Similar examples of this problem can be found with the captains of hired ships, whose freight charges and commissions depended on the total number of slaves they delivered alive in America. In one case, the company's factors in Africa advised the company to agree to pay higher fares per slave in order to induce captains to agree to carry smaller slave cargoes:

wee find the Covetusnesse of Commanders crowding in their Slaves above their proportion for the advantage of Freight is the only reason of the great Loss [in mortality] to the Compa., If yr. Honours would be pleased to beate them downe in the number though you gave them five shillings per head exterordinary Your Honours would be considerable gainers at ye yeares end;

PRO T70/1, f. 112, Henry Greenhill et al., Cape Coast Castle, April 6, 1681.

47 PRO T70/2, f. 66, Edward Chester, Antigua, May 29, 1713.
48 Similarly, when tonnage is controlled, variation in the number of slaves per ton has
no significant effect on mortality rates:

average daily mortality $=$ 0.994 $-$ 0.0049 voyage duration (days)
rate per thousand slaves (1.204) (0.0080)
$+$ 0.0084 ship tonnage $-$ 0.100 slaves per ton
(0.0029) (0.578)
$R^2 = 0.255,$ $F = 3.308,$ $n = 33$

49 Indeed, Klein has reported the opposite result, a negative relationship; *Middle
Passage,* p. 66. Robert Louis Stein found slightly higher mortality on large than on
small slaving ships in the French trade of the eighteenth century; *The French Slave
Trade in the Eighteenth Century,* pp. 100, 226.
50 This is consistent with the arguments of Philip D. Curtin, "Epidemiology and the
Slave Trade," *Political Science Quarterly,* Vol. LXXXIII, No. 2 (June 1968), pp.
190–216.
51 The estimated effect on mortality from equation 2 of Table 2.8 of increasing a
ship's tonnage by two standard deviations (134 tons) is an increase of 1.17 deaths
per day per thousand slaves, whereas the analogous effect from equation 3 of Table
2.8 of increasing the size of a ship's crew by two standard deviations (18 men) is
an increase of 1.15 deaths per day per thousand slaves. (The mean crew size across
ships within the sample is 29 men, for a mean ratio of one man to 6.2 tons. On the
generally large crews of slaving ships, see Davies, *Royal African Company,* pp.
193–4.) Tonnage and crew size are highly correlated within the sample (the simple
correlation is 0.94) and their inclusion in a single regression produces statistically
insignificant estimated coefficients for both:

average daily mortality $=$ 0.680 $-$ 0.0066 voyage duration (days)
rate per thousand slaves (0.815) (0.0078)
$+$ 0.0033 ship tonnage $+$ 0.041 crew size
(0.0089) (0.066)
$R^2 = 0.264,$ $F = 3.468,$ $n = 33$

52 For a discussion of diseases that were endemic among African populations and
caused significant mortality in the transatlantic voyages, see Richard B. Sheridan,
"The Guinea Surgeons on the Middle Passage: The Provision of Medical Services
in the British Slave Trade," *International Journal of African Historical Studies,*
Vol. 14, No. 4, (1981), pp. 601–25.
53 The correlation between cargo size and ship tonnage within the sample was 0.82. It
is therefore not surprising that the effect of cargo size on the mortality rate is highly
significant in a regression equation from which tonnage is omitted:

average daily mortality $=$ 1.231 $-$ 0.0072 voyage duration (days)
rate per thousand slaves (0.716) (0.0075)
$+$ 0.0044 number of slaves
(0.0017)
$R^2 = 0.203,$ $F = 3.826,$ $n = 33$

The high correlations among the sizes of ships, crews, and cargoes appear to make it dangerous to attempt to conclude from this sample which might have been more important in determining variations in mortality rates across voyages, and therefore what the specific causal mechanisms involved might have been. The positive association observed in this sample between these variables and passage mortality rates might suggest that this is an interesting issue to examine using other data sets on the slave trade.

54 There do appear to have been significant fixed costs in slave shipping that gave rise to some economies of scale. A merchant testifying before Parliament in 1788, when asked about the economic effects on the trade of limiting slave cargoes to a maximum of two slaves per ton of a ship's burden, replied as follows:

In a small Ship of Two hundred Tons or under, it would certainly be a Loss, because there is One certain Expence of Outfits, Wages, and Duty that would attend her, whether she takes more or less, and which could not be diminished if she takes a less Number. – The certain Expence will arise, whether she goes for 400, 300, or 200 – Any Number she takes less is a certain loss to her;

Lambert, ed., *House of Commons Sessional Papers of the Eighteenth Century*, Vol. 68, p. 44. Klein has suggested that the size of a slave ship's crew did not decline proportionally with the size of a slave cargo because of the concern of captains with the safety of the voyage; *Middle Passage*, p. 166.

There were similarly some fixed costs in the sale of slave cargoes by Royal African Company agents in the West Indies, because the agents spent several days notifying planters throughout their island of the date of the sale before actually making any sales. Company agents in Barbados noted in 1684 that "wee are forced to stay 3, 4, or 5, daies from selling [after the arrival of a cargo] that soe wee may give due notice of the time of our sales & invite Customers to come," and that this process involved "our Labour & Cost in sending upp & downe the Countrey to Invite Customers to our day of Sale"; PRO T70/16, f. 78, Stede and Gascoigne, Barbados, March 15, 1684. These costs of alerting planters did not vary with the size of a cargo, and would therefore have given rise to some economies of scale. It remains to be determined whether the sum of the economies of scale in shipping and selling the slaves would have compensated for the large ships' greater losses from high mortality.

It might be argued that the Royal African Company could benefit from economies of scale in the actual shipping of slaves only for ships they owned, since they paid flat rates per slave delivered alive on rented ships. The following regression, which includes as an independent variable an interaction term between a ship's tonnage and its status of rented or owned by the company, indicates that the company's ownership of a ship did not significantly affect the relationship between mortality rates and ship size:

average daily mortality = 0.826 − 0.0053 voyage duration (days)
rate per thousand slaves (0.787) (0.0076)
+ 0.0084 ship tonnage + 0.00017 tonnage
(0.0030) (0.00199)
· hire/own

$R^2 = 0.254, \quad F = 3.298, \quad n = 33$

where hire = 0 and own = 1. This could imply that economies of scale in shipping did not compensate the company for the higher mortality rates on larger hired ships, as long as freight rates for slaves did not differ by ship size.

55 The place of origin used here is the African port from which the ship ultimately departed. This is of course an imperfect variable for a number of purposes, because many ships called at several ports along the African coast, taking in some slaves at each.

56 A related variable that could have influenced passage mortality is the length of time a ship spent collecting a cargo in Africa. There are several possible effects. If a ship spent a long time collecting a cargo, some of its slaves might already have been on board for a substantial period prior to its departure from Africa and might therefore have been at risk longer to contract a disease due to exposure to unhealthy slaves, some of whom might have died before the ship sailed. This could then have raised mortality rates during the actual period of the voyage. A different effect could have been caused by measurement error. If a ship had reported to the company the number of slaves it had purchased, rather than the number it actually carried upon departure from Africa, deaths that occurred while the ship was on the African coast might incorrectly be attributed to the period of the transatlantic voyage. Long stays in Africa could then have produced a significant difference between the number of those purchased and those carried away. This effect should not be present in the data analyzed here, because the register typically records that a ship left Africa with a given number of slaves, but ships' captains might have reported inaccurately to the company, or total purchases could sometimes have been recorded owing to a misunderstanding.

The time elapsed between a ship's first arrival on the African coast and its departure for America can be calculated from the shipping register from which the data analyzed here are drawn. When this variable is included in an equation together with voyage duration, the following results are obtained:

$$
\begin{array}{ll}
\text{average daily mortality} = & 2.543 \;-\; 0.0050 \;\; \text{voyage duration (days)} \\
\text{rate per thousand slaves} & (0.771) \quad\;\; (0.0088) \\
& -\; 0.0012 \;\; \text{days in Africa} \\
& (0.0034)
\end{array}
$$

$$ R^2 = 0.015, \quad F = 0.218, \quad n = 32 $$

These results show that the length of time a ship spent in Africa had no statistically significant effect on the mortality rate of its cargo on the subsequent passage to America.

57 Seasonal variation in slave prices – whether lower prices in West Africa or higher prices in the West Indies – could have compensated traders for higher passage mortality rates in some seasons, as could lower freight charges. Neither freight charges nor West Indian slave prices appear to have displayed significant seasonal variation; it is not known whether African slave prices did.

58 Traders would of course have been willing to accept higher mortality rates among the slaves purchased from a particular region if the prices they paid there for slaves had been lower than elsewhere by an amount sufficient to compensate them for the greater numbers lost in transit.

59 PRO T70/4, p. 20, Thomas Harper, Barbados, November 8, 1721.

60 PRO T70/4, p. 6, Messrs. Phipps et al., Cape Coast Castle, July 1, 1720.

61 PRO T70/4, p. 1, Captain Lamberth, Maryland, September 16, 1720; *ibid.*, p. 1, Mr. Bowles, Maryland, December 10, 1720. Bowles's reference to the loss occasioned by Lamberth's long voyage might include both the unfavorable effects on the condition of the slaves delivered and the problems caused by the ship's arrival in September, after the peak demand for slaves to work on the season's tobacco crop. On seasonal variation in the price of newly imported slaves in Virginia, see the statement of Governor Jenings in 1709, quoted in Gerald W. Mullin, *Flight and Rebellion* (London: Oxford University Press, 1972), p. 15.

62 PRO T70/26, ff. 4v, 5v, Dalby Thomas, Cape Coast Castle, September 1706.

63 PRO T70/50, f. 8, Royal African Company to Agent General Nurse at Cape Coast Castle; London, May 16, 1686.

3. Slave prices in the Barbados market, 1673–1723

1 Public Record Office (PRO), Treasury 70/936–59.

2 The one exception to this statement involves a number of slaves sold during 1673–86 whose prices were recorded in pounds of sugar rather than in currency. Lacking a farm price series for sugar in this period, these transactions were excluded from the sample when estimating prices.

3 On credit in slave sales in the English West Indies, see K. G. Davies, *The Royal African Company* (London: Longmans, 1957), pp. 316–25. That the slave prices recorded in the invoice accounts were the actual amounts to be collected at the agreed future date is consistent with a statement made in a letter of 1694 from the company to its agent in Barbados, Nicholas Prideaux, which indicates that further interest charges were to be added to the recorded amounts only if payment was not made at the agreed time:

We have alwayes understood that for what debts our ffactors made upon Sale of Negroes they tooke bonds for the payment at a certaine time perfixed, & if payment was not made as agreed, that then the buyers were to pay intrest according to the rules in that Country.

Yet that these charges were often not collected is indicated by the letter's continuation:

And though greate sumes have been continually due to us yett there hath been but very inconsiderable sumes brought to our Credditt for Intrest, of wch. we have often made complaint, & written very earnestly to have that Accott. stated, but have not had our Orders answeared to expectacion. The neglect whereof we can not attribute to anything soe much, as that our orders being to our ffactors in Generall none has heartily espoused ye business to bring it aboute.

In recognition of this problem, the company ordered Prideaux to "take this affaire perticulerly upon yor. selfe," and gave him authority to require the company's other factors to assist him in seeking payment of these unpaid sums; PRO T70/57, f. 102v, May 8, 1694. The effect of the planters' failure to pay the interest charges would of course be to make the prices recorded in the account books overstatements of the true cost of slaves to purchasers, though once again by amounts that cannot generally be determined.

4 The estimating equation was

$$P_i = b_1 M_i + b_2 W_i + b_3 B_i + b_4 G_i + e_i$$

where

i = index of transaction number
P = amount paid per transaction
M = number of men
W = number of women
B = number of boys
G = number of girls

The regression line is constrained to pass through the origin.

Throughout this chapter, price estimates have been treated as missing information in reporting results when estimated coefficients failed to be significant for two-tailed t-tests at the 0.10 level.

In all tables that report estimated prices, the figures reported for sample sizes (n) represent the total number of individual slaves on which the reported price estimate is based. In Table 3.4, n excludes slaves in dummied transactions. (See n. 8 for a discussion of this specification.)

5 The estimating equation was:

$$P_i = b_1 M_i + b_2 W_i + b_3 B_i + b_4 t_i M_i + b_5 t_i W_i + b_6 t_i B_i + e_i$$

where

t = transaction number within each auction expressed as a percent of total transactions (i.e., the estimates of Table 3.2 were obtained for $0 < t \leq 50$).

For definitions of other variables, see n. 4.

6 All three correlations are significant at the 0.01 level.

7 The estimating equation was the same as that given in n. 5, except for the omission of the two variables involving B. The sample was defined as $50 < t \leq 100$.

8 The estimating equation was:

$$P_i = b_1 M_i + b_2 W_i + b_3 t_i M_i + b_4 t_i W_i + b_5 d M_i + b_6 d W_i + e_i$$

where

$d = 1$ if $(M_i + W_i + B_i + G_i) \geq 10$ and $d = 0$ otherwise

For definitions of other variables, see n.4.

9 Both correlations are significant at the 0.01 level.

10 Some comments are in order here concerning the difference between the current estimates and two previous uses of the Royal African Company invoice account records to produce price series for slaves. K. G. Davies's Barbados price series, presented in *Royal African Company*, p. 364, represents the mean price of all slaves sold in the colony in each year, without regard to age and sex; his series was obtained by dividing total receipts in a given year by the total number of slaves sold. The series therefore does not permit the separation of price changes within a demographic category from changes in the shares of categories over time. (I am grateful to K. G. Davies for a description of his procedure in a letter of October 18, 1976.)

My own previously published series for adult men and women in Barbados, given in David Galenson, "The Slave Trade to the English West Indies, 1673–1724," *Economic History Review*, Second Series, Vol. XXXII, No. 2 (May 1979), p. 242, were constructed using those transactions from the Royal African Company's sales in which either only a single category of slaves appears or, although more than one category appears, the price of each is separately marked. Those series were therefore based on only a small subset of the accounts' information, unlike the current estimates, which use the information of virtually all public slave sales made by the company in Barbados during this period.

A third slave price series that includes the period considered here is that of Richard Nelson Bean, *The British Trans-Atlantic Slave Trade, 1650–1775* (New York: Arno Press, 1975), pp. 132–6, reprinted with some changes in U.S. Bureau of the Census, *Historical Statistics of the United States, Colonial Times to 1970* (Washington, D.C.: U.S. Government Printing Office, 1975), Part 2, Series Z-166, p. 1174. This series is based on a variety of sources, most of which fail to provide information about the demographic composition of the slaves purchased. As a result, the series does not allow distinctions between price changes due to changes in the prices of slaves within demographic categories and those due to shifts in the shares of demographic categories in the trade.

11 PRO T70/123, "Minute Book of the Bye-Committee of the Committee of Trade and Correspondence," p. 2, June 14, 1720; also quoted in Elizabeth Donnan, *Documents Illustrative of the History of the Slave Trade to America* (New York: Octagon Books, 1969), Vol. II, p. 244. For a similar specification see Davies, *Royal African Company*, p. 300. Determination of the slaves' ages must of course have been subject to some error, for it was based largely on such physical evidence as height and weight, condition of teeth, and presence of body hair. For some descriptions of the process, see George Francis Dow, *Slave Ships and Slaving* (Salem, Mass.: Maritime Research Society, 1927), p. 61; Douglas Grant, *The Fortunate Slave: An Illustration of African Slavery in the Early Eighteenth Century* (Oxford: Oxford University Press, 1968), pp. 54–5; and Walter Rodney, *A History of the Upper Guinea Coast, 1545–1800* (New York: Monthly Review Press, 1980), pp. 190–1.

12 This mean ratio is lower than either of the mean ratios calculated from Tables 3.1 and 3.3 because the lower, second-half women's prices of Table 3.3 receive a much larger weight than those of Table 3.1 in calculating the prices in Table 3.5. In contrast, the men's prices of Table 3.1 and 3.3 receive approximately equal weight in calculating the prices of Table 3.5.

13 Robert William Fogel and Stanley L. Engerman, *Time on the Cross: The Economics of American Negro Slavery* (Boston: Little, Brown, 1974), Figure 18, p. 76. I am grateful to Robert Fogel and Stanley Engerman for supplying me with the prices by age upon which this figure is based. For additional discussion of the relative prices of male and female slaves in a number of societies, see Manuel Moreno Fraginals, Herbert S. Klein, and Stanley L. Engerman, "The Level and Structure of Slave Prices on Cuban Plantations in the Mid-Nineteenth Century: Some Comparative Perspectives," *American Historical Review*, Vol. 88, No. 5 (December 1983), pp. 1209–13.

14 Fogel and Engerman, *Time on the Cross*, p. 76.

15 *Ibid.* Analysis of the length of indentures signed by English servants traveling to the American colonies in the mid eighteenth century suggests that the productivity of females was rising less rapidly than that of males between the early teen ages and 21, thus yielding the same result of higher valuations of teen-aged relative to adult females than for males; see David W. Galenson, *White Servitude in Colonial America: An Economic Analysis* (Cambridge: Cambridge University Press, 1981), pp. 103–7. The appearance of this result in diverse circumstances – for slaves in seventeenth-century Barbados, for indentured servants in the eighteenth-century colonies, and for slaves in the nineteenth-century United States – suggests that the earlier physical maturation of females caused this outcome.

16 The full listing of the numbers of slaves in each category carried annually by the company to Barbados is given in Table 5.1.

17 Richard Ligon, *A True & Exact History of the Island of Barbados* (London: Humphrey Moseley, 1657), p. 46.

18 John J. McCusker, *Money and Exchange in Europe and America, 1600–1775* (Chapel Hill: University of North Carolina Press, 1978), p. 240.

19 Ligon's quotation of slave prices has been cited by a number of recent historians – for example, Carl and Roberta Bridenbaugh, *No Peace Beyond the Line: The English in the Caribbean, 1624–1690* (New York: Oxford University Press, 1972), p. 34; Richard B. Sheridan, *Sugar and Slavery: An Economic History of the British West Indies, 1623–1775* (Barbados: Caribbean Universities Press, 1974), p. 253; and Richard S. Dunn, *Sugar and Slaves: The Rise of the Planter Class in the English West Indies, 1624–1713* (Chapel Hill: University of North Carolina Press, 1972), p. 72.

20 The volume is held in the PRO T70/646. The estimates of Table 3.7 were made using equations of the form described in n. 4, except for the omission of the independent variable $G;$ no estimates are given for girls because of the lack of sufficient numbers of observations. Transactions given in the source in which slaves were sold for sugar rather than currency were excluded from the sample analyzed here, because of the lack of farm prices for sugar during 1663–4. No account was taken of transaction order in the empirical analysis of this source, for the order of sale is not known.

21 The exchange rate used is that suggested by McCusker, *Money and Exchange in Europe and America 1600–1775,* p. 240.

22 Richard Bean's investigation found very few slave price quotations for years prior to 1660, and no consistent trend appears in their erratic behavior. Like the historians cited in n. 19, Bean accepted Ligon's price quotation, and he incorporated it into his price series; Bean, *The British Trans-Atlantic Slave Trade, 1650–1775,* pp. 77, 185.

23 Noel Deerr, *The History of Sugar* (London: Chapman and Hall, 1950), Vol. 2, p. 530.

24 PRO T70/57, f. 4, London, May 31, 1687.

25 Not surprisingly, in view of their economic stake in following slave price movements, the company's sophistication in analyzing these records appears to have been considerable, as they used them frequently over the years to refute the complaints of West Indian planters of high slave prices and inadequate supplies; for example, see Davies, *Royal African Company,* pp. 308–14. Interestingly, in an

entry dated 1729 in a book of company advices, there appears a table entitled "The Prices of Negroes in Jamaica and Barbados in average from 1672 to 1700"; (PRO T70/168, f. 70, September 18, 1729). The two series are shown in the accompanying table.

Year	Barbados £	s	d	Jamaica £	s	d	Year	Barbados £	s	d	Jamaica £	s	d
1672	16	5	6				1688	14	1	0	16	2	11
1674	14	16	4	21	16	4	1689	16	11	9	20	11	4
1675	15	13	4	24	6	0	1690	16	7	3	24	11	6
1676	14	8	3	19	6	6	1691	17	13	6	23	4	3
1677	15	3	9	18	5	9	1692	17	18	0	17	17	6
1678	16	5	6	18	3	9	1693	19	19	0	19	5	6
1679	13	5	0	15	19	7	1694		—		21	19	3
1680	13	14	9	17	17	1	1695	23	14	0	16	0	0
1681	13	7	6	14	1	9	1696	26	2	0	16	0	0
1682	13	18	0	15	17	3	1697	19	17	3	—	—	—
1683	13	10	0	15	17	6	1698	16	10	0	23	0	0
1684	13	2	6	16	14	7	1699	19	17	0	21	5	3
1685	13	3	0	18	1	9	1700	21	15	3	22	4	0
1686	13	14	9	18	4	0							
1687	13	7	3	16	2	6							

The company's price series for Barbados is quite highly correlated with the price index presented in Table 3.6; the correlation with the currency index of Table 3.6 is 0.82. An even stronger correlation appears between the company's price series and that constructed by K. G. Davies (*Royal African Company*, p. 364), with a simple correlation of 0.97. Although no indication is given in the source of how the company's price series were constructed, the high correlation between the company's Barbados prices and Davies's series suggests that the company might have calculated the mean value of all slaves sold in each colony in each year, as did Davies (see n. 10).

The company's series given for Barbados shows a decline of 11 percent from the mean of the values of the 1670s to those of the first half of the 1680s, with a larger decline for Jamaica during the same period of 18 percent.

26 Russell Menard, "From Servants to Slaves: The Transformation of the Chesapeake Labor System," *Southern Studies*, Vol. XVI, No. 4 (Winter 1977), p. 367.

27 The absence of records of cargoes bound for the Chesapeake from the Royal African Company's invoice account books in this period is not surprising, for as discussed above these do not contain the records of shipments of slaves made on contracts – that is, cargoes in which buyers agreed in advance to purchase specified numbers of slaves at stated prices. In view of the substantially longer voyage to the Chesapeake than to the West Indies and the absence of other markets nearby, the company was probably reluctant to send its ships to the region without the guarantee of advance contracts. There is indirect evidence that this had earlier been

the attitude of the Company of Royal Adventurers. Thus in 1664 Charles Calvert, the governor of Maryland, wrote to his father, Lord Baltimore, in England:

I have endeavoured to see if I could find as many responsable men that would engage to take a 100 or 200 neigros every yeare from the Royall Company at that rate mentiond in yr. Lopps letter but I find wee are nott men of estates good enough to undertake such a buisnesse, but could wish wee were for wee are naturally inclin'd to love neigros if our purses would endure it;

Maryland Historical Society, *The Calvert Papers*, Number One (Baltimore: Maryland Historical Society, Peabody Publication Fund No. 28, 1889), p. 249. The implication seems clear that the company was willing to ship cargoes of at least 100 slaves to Maryland as long as advance contracts were guaranteed by the planters at agreed rates.

For estimates of the net migration of blacks to the Chesapeake by decade, see Galenson, *White Servitude in Colonial America*, p. 217.

28 PRO T70/1, f. 19, Nathaniel Bacon and Edward Jones, Virginia, June 25, 1679.
29 Menard, "From Servants to Slaves," p. 372. Converting the men's price series of Table 3.5 to sterling yields Barbados prices for adult men generally £6–8 less than those given by Menard for the Chesapeake during the 1670s and 1680s. In part, the higher Chesapeake prices were the result of the higher transportation costs from Africa to the mainland than to the West Indies; in 1672 the Royal African Company declared its willingness to sell slaves for £3 per head more in Virginia than in Barbados (Davies, *Royal African Company*, p. 295). Menard's series is drawn from valuations of slaves in probate inventories, and this probably explains the additional premium in their prices: Most of these slaves would already have been in the region for some time, and their survival of the dangerous initial period of "seasoning" made them more valuable than newly arrived slaves like those sold by the Royal African Company. On this price effect in Virginia, see Edmund S. Morgan, *American Slavery, American Freedom: The Ordeal of Colonial Virginia* (New York: W. W. Norton, 1975), pp. 175–6.
30 Davies, *Royal African Company*, pp. 198–9, 313.
31 PRO T70/57, f. 46, London, December 17, 1689.
32 Davies, *Royal African Company*, pp. 198–9, 366; Deerr, *The History of Sugar*, Vol. II, p. 530.
33 Sheridan, *Sugar and Slavery*, pp. 420–1, 425.

4. On the order of purchases by characteristics at slave sales

1 The figures quoted bound the means of the respective variables calculated by decade from the Royal African Company invoices. The mean number of slaves sold per transaction, calculated by decade, ranged from 4.0 to 5.5.
2 Quoted in K. G. Davies, *The Royal African Company* (London: Longmans, 1957), p. 307.
3 PRO T70/1211, ff. 79–80, "A Journall of my Intended voyage for ye gold Coast kept by mee Peter Blake Commaunder of ye Royall Companys Ship James in ye searvis of ye royall Affrican Company of England," March 1675.
4 Evidence that the transactions were listed in the order the sales were made is afforded by running notations of the specific days of particular transactions, which

sometimes appear in the margins of the accounts. Whenever these appear, the dates invariably run chronologically down the pages listing the transactions; the implication appears straightforward that the transactions were recorded in the order in which the bargains were agreed on. No other consistent arrangement of the transactions can be inferred from the records; for example, they are not arranged alphabetically by purchaser's surname or in order by the amount of the transaction or the numbers of slaves purchased.

5 One minor exception to this is noted later, involving notations of "refuse" slaves. Although this information is useful, it is not sufficient to eliminate the basic problem alluded to here.

6 One obvious positive association between quality and price is supported by Richard Ligon's comment on the Barbados slave market that the planters "choose them as they do Horses in a Market; the strongest, youthfullest, and most beautiful, yield the greatest prices"; *A True & Exact History of the Island of Barbados* (London: Humphrey Moseley, 1657), p. 46.

It has been proved that under conditions in which bidders know the value of a good to them, the expected value of the winning bid for the good in an auction is the same under both English and Dutch rules – that is, whether the sale price is approached from below or above; see William Vickery, "Counterspeculation, Auctions, and Competitive Sealed Tenders," *Journal of Finance*, Vol. 16, No. 1 (March 1961), pp. 8–37; and Gerard R. Butters, "Equilibrium Price Distributions and the Economics of Information" (unpublished Ph.D. dissertation, University of Chicago, 1975), Chapter II. An implication of this result is that the most efficient way to sell homogeneous goods under conditions of good information is to set a single price. That the accounts of Royal African Company sales in Barbados indicate that slaves were not sold in this way implies the existence of considerable heterogeneity in their quality.

Tables 4.1–4.3 clearly show that decreasing price per slave was a phenomenon common to both demographic categories examined, adult men and women. It might be noted, however, that the distribution of the numbers of slaves in each of these categories was quite different over the course of sales in the aggregate. Thus aggregating over all sales held in Barbados, about 49 percent of the adult men sold appeared in transactions within the first halves of sales by transaction number, compared with only about 28 percent of the adult women. According to the interpretation of declining prices suggested in the text, this might be taken to indicate that the adult women sold in Barbados were disproportionately of poor "quality" in comparison with the adult men sold there. This could have been the case, for example, if the incidence of disease had been higher among women than among men on the transatlantic voyage, or if the average quality of the women purchased in Africa was worse than that of the men. These possible explanations remain speculative, however, for no evidence has been found either in the invoice records or in Royal African Company correspondence that bears on this problem. It might furthermore be noted that Farley Grubb has found a negative relationship between the sale price of indenture contracts in eighteenth-century Philadelphia and the length of the interval between the indentured servant's arrival in port and the sale of his contract, after controlling a number of personal and contract characteristics; Farley Grubb, "Immigration and Servitude in the Colony and Commonwealth of Pennsylvania: A Quantitative and Economic Analysis'' (unpublished Ph.D. dissertation, University of Chicago, 1984), pp. 231, 242.

7 PRO T70/17, f. 52, Edwin Stede et al., Barbados, December 15, 1691.
8 PRO T70/15, f. 43, Edwin Stede et al., Barbados, October 26, 1680.
9 PRO T70/8, f. 26, Gavin Corbin, Virginia, September 15, 1707.
10 PRO T70/8, f. 62, Bate and Stewart, Barbados, September 18, 1712.
11 PRO T70/3, f. 19v, John Hussam, Nevis, April 2, 1714.
12 PRO T70/15, f. 49v, Jamaica, January 28, 1681.
13 PRO T70/1211, ff. 79–80.
14 Davies, *Royal African Company*, p. 292.
15 PRO T70/57, f. 50, London, November 11, 1690. Also see the accompanying letter to James Kendall, governor of Barbados, *ibid.*, f. 51.
16 PRO T70/57, f. 50, Royal African Company to Barbados agents, London, November 11, 1690; also T70/57, f. 51v, Royal African Company to Jamaica agents, London, November 11, 1690. Later the company explained to its agents in Jamaica that it had actually agreed to the introduction of the formal auctions as part of a settlement ordered by the Lords of Trade and Plantations:

Upon the Planters complaints against the method our former ffactors used in Sale of our Negroes wee gave order that they should sell them at the candle every Negroe apart or at most not above two together which method if duely put in practice wee apprehend would please the Planters though at first it may appear Strange. This designe was proposed before the Lords of the Comttee. of Trade and Plantations when the Company was summoned before them upon complaint of the Planters and was soe well liked by the Planters that the Comttee. made an order for putting the same in practice;

PRO T70/57, f. 80, London, October 13, 1692.
17 PRO T70/57, f. 64, London, August 25, 1691.
18 PRO T70/57, f. 81, London, November 1, 1692.
19 PRO T70/57, f. 67v, London, August 25, 1691.
20 PRO T70/57, f. 82v, London, December 10, 1692.
21 PRO T70/57, f. 83, Royal African Company to James Kendall, governor of Barbados, London, December 29, 1692. Writing to its agents in Barbados the same day, the company noted that in comparing the prices of slaves sold by formal auction with those sold by the normal method, ''we find not the great difference in their prices you seem to intimate, due Consideration being had to the goodness of the Slaves, the Mony received for the Ones, and the large time given for the Others.'' Yet they stressed that they would nonetheless trust the agents' judgment and diligence:

upon due consideration of yor. Argumts. [concerning the method of sale] . . . we thought proper in confidence of yor. Skill and Integrity to leave for the future to the dictates of yor. own reason & judgmts . . . Our buisness is to sell our Negroes by such Methods, as may be most to our Advantage but still with an Eye to the Lessening, and not further Enlargeing our Debts than is absolutely necessary. Since therefore . . . We have wholly left this important Affaire to yor. Conduct;

PRO T70/57, f. 84, London, December 29, 1692.
22 Davies, *Royal African Company*, p. 317.
23 It might be noted here that descriptions of a different form of slave sale appear at a

later date. A number of witnesses before a British parliamentary committee investigating the operation of the Atlantic slave trade in 1790 described what was known as a "scramble." George Baillie, who stated that he had lived in Georgia and South Carolina as a merchant and planter for 25 years, was asked to describe "the ordinary mode of conducting the sales of the African [slave] cargoes of your time," and responded as follows:

The common mode of conducting them was by giving public notice of the day appointed for the public sale, some days before its commencement, which generally brought together a considerable number of buyers; the Slaves were then placed in a close yard, ranged in order for sale; the gates being shut immediately before the sale commenced, a great gun was fired, and the purchasers with their adherents and assistants, rushed into the yard with great violence, and laid hold of the most healthy and good looking Slaves, which parcels they afterwards picked and culled to their mind; they were immediately purchased, and hurried out of the yard; so that in a few hours afterwards there remained none but those who were called the refuse Slaves; whose health had been injured in the voyage, generally, as I conceived, proceeding from too cramped a situation and confined air on board of the ships; those Slaves were afterwards sold at a very great under price;

Sheila Lambert, ed., *House of Commons Sessional Papers of the Eighteenth Century* (Wilmington, Del.: Scholarly Resources, 1975), Vol. 73, p. 184.

Similar descriptions of scrambles were given by other witnesses; one referred to the scramble as the common method of selling slave cargoes in Jamaica, and another reported having seen scrambles in Jamaica and at Grenada; *ibid.*, Vol. 73, p. 120; Vol. 72, pp. 307–8.

The extreme haste of the buyers to select their slaves, which was so basic a characteristic of the scramble that it was the source of its name, might appear puzzling from the description given by Baillie. Yet a critical feature of the scramble, which Baillie did not mention, provides a ready explanation. This feature was mentioned in a separate account of the slave trade published by Alexander Falconbridge, who served as a ship's surgeon for four slaving voyages during the 1780s, and who also testified before the parliamentary committee in 1790. In describing sales of slave cargoes in the West Indies, Falconbridge stated: "The mode of selling them by *scramble* is most common. Here, all the negroes scrambled for bear an equal price; which is agreed upon between the captains and the purchasers before the sale begins"; George Francis Dow, ed., *Slave Ships and Slaving* (Salem, Mass.: Marine Research Society, 1927), p. 152. In view of this uniform pricing, it is obvious why planters rushed to get the best slaves, and the consequences described by Falconbridge are understandable:

It is scarcely possible to describe the confusion of which this mode of selling is productive. It likewise causes much animosity among the purchasers who not unfrequently fall out and quarrel with each other. The poor astonished negroes are so much terrified by these proceedings.

Those slaves judged not to be worth the uniform price would be left unpurchased. They might be sold off individually or perhaps, if a large number remained, the scramble might be repeated at a lower uniform price.

That the Royal African Company did not use the scramble in its Barbados sales is clear, for whereas scrambles would yield large numbers of sales at uniform prices – perhaps only one, or possibly several, in descending order – as mentioned earlier, the company sale invoices from Barbados show clearly that slave prices varied across transactions from the very outset of sales.

24 Ligon, *A True & Exact History of the Island of Barbados,* p. 46.
25 There appear to have been special marketplaces in the ports normally served by the Royal African Company. The market in Bridgetown was referred to as "African house" by the company's agent in Barbados in his explanation for incurring unusual expenses for holding a sale elsewhere in 1715:

At this time the Island especially the Town is very Sickly being Infected with Small Pox & Malignant & Spotted fever of which Distemper many Dyes, and Cuased me to dispatch the Sale of your Negroes finding many of them began to Droope 'tho no more than two Dyed between the Ship Anchoring and last day of Sale but feared many of Them would have fallen down wth. Feavers having Violent Ship Colds upon them. And did indeed Compell me to put your Honors to the Charge of Getting a Convenient house a Quarter of a Mile in the Country to Windward of ye Town to Preserve ye Negroes from Infection and Encourage Country Gentlemen to Come to the Sale, for many of them would not have gone to the African house for the Vallue of the Negroes;

PRO T70/3, ff. 72–72v, James Gohier, Barbados, August 30, 1715.
26 PRO T70/15, f. 13, Edwin Stede and Stephen Gascoigne, Barbados, May 6, 1679.
27 PRO T70/13, f. 56, Phillip Broome, Nevis, February 14, 1704. It is clear from the actions of company agents that purchasers assumed the risk of slave mortality in these transactions. Some evidence suggests that the same was normally true of the slave trade to the mainland colonies in the eighteenth century. William Vernon of Newport, Rhode Island, wrote in 1756 to Austin Laurent of South Carolina:

You observe to us that the Girl sold Benjamin Yarnold is since dead, that you had prevailed upon him to submit the Matter to Arbitration, that is, whether he should pay for her or not. We don't imagine . . . that you warrented her to be perfectly sound and well which is not customary for new slaves . . . We conceive it in this Light, if you (which we don't suppose) contrary to all Custom of the Sale of New Slaves Warrented the girl to be sound & well and she proved to be otherwise in Justice he ought not to pay for her;

Newport Historical Society, Letterbook of William Vernon, No. 3, p. 62, Vernon to Laurent, June 18, 1756. I am grateful to Ronald Michener for this reference.
28 PRO T70/8, f. 32v, Virginia, February 12, 1708.
29 Davies, *Royal African Company,* p. 296.
30 PRO T70/13, f. 56.
31 PRO T70/3, f. 72, James Gohier, Barbados, August 30, 1715.
32 The objection might be raised that Royal African Company agents would not know the wealth of purchasers, and that the ordering of bargains could therefore not have been done as described here. Yet even beyond such outward signs of wealth as clothing, agents could be expected to be well informed as to the approximate wealth of most purchasers. In a market in which large sums were promised by buyers for future payment, a critical part of the sellers' job was the evaluation of buyers' creditworthiness. In a colony like Barbados, with a total of only about 3,000 property owners in 1680, the agents could have quite accurate knowledge of the wealth of most planters. Determining the approximate wealth of a planter was relatively easy, for most wealth was held in the visible form of land and slaves. Moreover, the ordering described here would really require agents to be able to identify only the relatively wealthy buyers, an even easier task in an economy with

such highly concentrated wealth holding as early Barbados; thus for example in 1680 only 365 planters owned 20 or more slaves.

33 For some recent evidence that wealthier firms generally tend to use higher-quality inputs, and a theoretical treatment, see Walter Y. Oi, "Heterogeneous Firms and the Organization of Production," *Economic Inquiry*, Vol. XXI, No. 2 (April 1983), pp. 147–71. Oi's stress on the importance of monitoring costs might be particularly relevant to the case considered here, in which slaves were placed in gangs and supervised as a group in sugar production. Wealthier planters, with higher-quality supervisory labor (whether their own or that of employees), might have preferred one expensive slave of high productivity to two cheaper slaves of lower productivity because of the greater costs involved in supervising larger numbers of workers.

34 Richard S. Dunn, *Sugar and Slaves: The Rise of the Planter Class in the English West Indies, 1624–1713* (Chapel Hill: University of North Carolina, 1972), p. 95.

35 The slaves delivered to ships' captains in payment of freight ceased to be the company's property. They were sold separately by the captains, and records of their sales do not appear in the company's accounts. As a result, information on the prices of these slaves is not available.

36 PRO T70/16, f. 78, Stede and Gascoigne, Barbados, March 15, 1684.

37 PRO CO 1/44, pp. 142–379. For discussion of this census, see Dunn, *Sugar and Slaves,* Chapter 3.

38 That the agents dealt first with the wealthiest planters is not surprising, because they would generally have been interested in maintaining good relations with their wealthiest customers to ensure their repeat business. Serving the wealthiest planters first might also have contributed to the maximization of the agents' own expected income from a given sale. The agents' commissions were determined as a fixed percentage of all returns from slave sales that were actually sent to the main office in England (Davies, *Royal African Company*, p. 296), and the agents' income therefore depended not only on the prices they negotiated with planters, but also multiplicatively on the probability that the planter would actually pay at the end of the time agreed on. It is possible that the prices negotiated for slaves were fully adjusted to take into account individual planters' default risks; if they were not, however, the agent would maximize his expected income by selling the highest-priced slaves to the buyers with the lowest default risk. Because default risk would normally have varied inversely with wealth, this would imply that the agent would have desired to order sales by matching slaves in descending order of quality with planters in descending order of wealth. Income maximization could therefore have led the agent to allocate his time to planters in order from wealthiest to poorest. (That default risk and wealth were inversely related is consistent with the fact that the length of a planter's stay in Barbados in this period has been found to have been positively related to wealth; see Chapter 6.)

Available evidence is not adequate to determine the extent to which slave prices were adjusted to allow for the differential default risks of planters. It might be noted, however, that to the extent that the recorded prices were so adjusted and the default risk of planters increased as sales progressed, the observed decline in slave prices within demographic categories would tend to understate the true decline in the present values of the slaves – and hence in their quality – that occurred over the course of sales, for the smallest credit premiums would have been added to the prices of the most valuable slaves, and the size of the credit premiums would have risen, as slave prices fell, thereafter as the sales progressed.

It might be thought that the wealthiest planters would send agents to the sales in their places, and that as a result the ordering described here might in some way be weakened. Although this delegation might have occurred in some cases, it is unlikely to have been common. The selection of slaves involved judgments of quality that planters might generally have been reluctant to trust to others, particularly since the expenditures for slaves were one of the largest costs involved in operating a sugar plantation. (Some quantitative perspective on the sums involved in purchasing slaves can be gained by noting that in 1688, when Table 3.2 shows the price of a prime adult male slave to have been £19 – or about £17.2 sterling – Gregory King estimated per capita income in England to have been about £8, or less than half this price. It is consequently not difficult to understand why the purchase of slaves was taken very seriously by planters.) When planters did send agents, however, or when plantation managers bought slaves on behalf of absentee plantation owners, it would be expected that these agents would make purchases in nearly the same ordering as the planters would if they had been present. The motivation of the agents to buy slaves of a quality consistent with that of the plantations' other inputs would lead them to bid for slaves at the same time as the owners of plantations of similar size and input quality.

39 Under some sale formats sellers might still have economic incentives to present their goods in order of descending quality for other reasons. Thus for example just as a seller known to deal in only high-quality goods might be expected to obtain a higher price for a given item than another seller known to carry some goods of very poor quality, buyers at an auction who have not inspected all the goods to be sold but who have seen a series of high-quality items opening the auction might be less wary in judging the quality of a particular good than if they had seen a number of low-quality items.

5. The demographic composition of the slave trade

1 Richard B. Sheridan, *Sugar and Slavery: An Economic History of the British West Indies, 1623–1775* (Barbados: Caribbean Universities Press, 1974), pp. 242–3; J. D. Fage, *A History of West Africa* (Cambridge: Cambridge University Press, 1969), pp. 84–9; Herbert S. Klein, *The Middle Passage: Comparative Studies in the Atlantic Slave Trade* (Princeton, N.J.: Princeton University Press, 1978), pp. 242–7.

2 Whether the transatlantic slave trade was a competitive industry has long been a controversial issue. As discussed in Chapter 1, however, there is reason to doubt that the Royal African Company exercised any significant monopoly power, and the derivation of the relationship between African and American slave prices that is done here therefore assumes competition. The precise forms of equations (5.1) and (5.2) depend on this assumption. It should be noted, however, that the implications of the analysis that are examined empirically later in this chapter do not depend on perfect competition, but can equally be derived from models in which traders exercise monopoly power, although the precise quantitative magnitudes of the

predicted effects may change. The prediction of a positive relationship between American slave prices and the share of children among slaves traded, for example, follows from a positive correlation between American and African slave prices, and therefore depends only on profit maximization by slave traders, regardless of the structure of the industry.

3 This formulation of total cost assumes that transportation charges were paid only on slaves who survived the voyage to the West Indies. This is based on K. G. Davies's discussion of the typical method of payment in rental agreements made by the Royal African Company with shipowners, and the rates used in the empirical analysis here are those given by Davies: *The Royal African Company* (London: Longmans, 1957), p. 198. However Colin Palmer has cited examples of contracts in which partial payment of a quoted passage charge was made for slaves who died during the voyage; *Human Cargoes: The British Slave Trade to Spanish America, 1700–1739* (Urbana: University of Illinois Press, 1981), p. 12. Because slaves carried for any part of the trip would clearly impose some costs on the shipper, it would seem likely that in the case of contracts of the kind described by Davies, the charge per slave delivered alive would have been set at a level sufficiently high to cover the total transportation costs of all slaves carried in view of expected losses in passage. The expression for total shipping costs in equation (5.1) would then yield the true mean value for actual total cost if a contract was of the type described by Davies as long as the appropriate values of t were used.

4 The amount the Royal African Company paid the owners of hired ships for slave transportation from Africa to particular West Indian destinations did not vary with the age or sex of the slaves, but was a flat sum per slave levied on live deliveries; Davies, *Royal African Company*, p. 198. A qualification of this analysis for the case of company-owned ships is examined later.

5 Klein, *The Middle Passage*, p. 242. If mortality did vary significantly by age, it can be seen from equation (5.2) that this would have tended to lower the implied African relative price of the group with the higher mortality rates; this is because the higher probability of death in transit would raise the full cost of transportation for that category of slaves relative to others. Higher mortality rates for a particular demographic group would therefore have tended to lower that group's share in the transatlantic trade. Although the effect of this on changes in particular groups' relative shares in the trade due to American slave price changes cannot be determined precisely without additional empirical evidence, if (as seems likely) children had had higher average passage mortality rates than adults, this would probably have tended to weaken the relationship predicted below of a positive correlation between American slave prices and the share of children among total slaves transported.

6 This analysis could equally be done under the assumption of any given positive minimum price for slaves in Africa, whether constant or variable by age.

7 The case shown in Figure 5.1 might not be considered obviously to be the general one. For example P_B could be sufficiently high and/or transportation costs sufficiently low that the derived African price profile P_A would be everywhere positive. This does not appear relevant to the period considered here, however. It would imply that slaves of all ages would be eligible for shipment to America on economic grounds, which conflicts with evidence such as that presented later in this

chapter, of the Royal African Company's West Indian agents criticizing African factors for sending some slaves both too young and too old to reimburse their freight costs.

8 In every year for which evidence is available in the account books, the Royal African Company carried some children to the West Indies. This implies that the range of ages of slaves eligible for the trade always included the age – A^* in Figure 5.1 – that was used to divide boys from men.

9 The assumption in this analysis is that, as shown in Figure 5.2, increases in West Indian prices that derived from sources other than changes in freight costs changed the prices of slaves of all ages in the same proportion, and therefore left the relative prices of slaves at all ages unchanged. It is furthermore assumed that the elasticity of substitution for slaves of different ages in production on West Indian plantations was infinite, and therefore that at the appropriate relative prices planters would be indifferent among slaves of different ages.

10 The best detailed evidence on the demographic structure of African populations for a period close to that under consideration here is derived from a census of the population of Angola in 1777, presented in John Thornton, "The Slave Trade in Eighteenth Century Angola: Effects on Demographic Structures," *Canadian Journal of African Studies*, Vol. 14, No. 3 (1980), Table 1, p. 421. The age structure of male slaves given by Thornton is used as the basis for the diagram in the lower quadrant of Figure 5.2.

11 This would have been the case, for example, if traders had purchased randomly with respect to age from the economically eligible population, either in selecting from a larger available pool or in buying from African sellers who had preselected from that pool. According to this analysis, traders would have had no economic reason for not selecting randomly from that pool with respect to age – that is, for preferring any particular age groups within the eligible range of ages. This is not necessarily contradicted by evidence that traders might, for example, express a willingness to carry slaves aged 12 but indicate a preference for those 13 or 14. In practice, not only would there normally be some uncertainty about the precise ages bounding the profitable range, but, as discussed below, physical considerations other than age – such as size and health – were obviously also taken into account in determining the potential profitability of shipping slaves. The predictions of the analysis presented here in terms of age should nonetheless be valid on average.

12 The discussion in the text concentrates on the relationship between slave prices and the relative, rather than absolute, quantities of the various demographic categories in the trade because evidence on the total annual volume of slaves delivered to the West Indies by all suppliers is not available. The Royal African Company deliveries are deficient as a measure of this because, although as discussed in Chapter 1 the company's share of the total slave trade to the West Indies clearly changed over time, the precise annual share of the total trade made up by the company's deliveries is not known, and no other evidence is available that would allow accurate estimation of the demographic composition of deliveries to the West Indies from sources other than the company in this period. The predicted sign of the relationship between West Indian slave prices and the total volume of slaves delivered to the region would of course be positive for price increases due to rising American

demand for labor, and negative for price increases due to falling African slave supply.

The analysis presented here of age composition properly applies to the transatlantic slave trade as a whole; it is applied here to shipments of slaves by one company to a single region under the assumption that, lacking evidence for the whole trade, these can be taken as a representative sample with respect to the overall trade's age composition.

13 This argument assumes that the traders who supplied slaves to the British West Indies were price takers in the African slave market, and therefore that changes in freight rates to the islands alone would have tended to change slave prices there without affecting African slave prices, that is, that changes in t specific to the region could have changed P_B – here the price in the West Indies – by the same amount, while leaving P_A unchanged. Some evidence on the relationship between changes in freight costs and changes in slave prices can be derived from the case in which freight costs from Africa to Barbados rose from about £5 per slave in 1688 to about £10 two years later, following the outbreak of war between England and France in 1689; Davies, *Royal African Company*, pp. 198–9. Table 3.1 shows that the Barbados price of prime adult men rose by £4.52 between 1688 and 1690, the price of women increased by £4.68, the price of boys by £2.71, and the price of girls by £4.69. Three of the four categories therefore showed estimated increases in price very close to the £5 increase in freight costs.

It is also assumed in the analysis of this chapter that changes in West Indian slave prices in this period that occurred when transportation costs were stable were caused by market forces that affected wider areas – whether changes in African supply conditions or changes in the general demand for labor in the Americas due to changes in the world market for sugar – that would have affected African slave prices.

14 Davies, *Royal African Company*, pp. 198–9.

15 *Ibid.*, p. 195.

16 *Ibid.* During 1720–5, 22 of 38 ships that undertook slaving voyages for the company were owned by it; see Appendix B.

17 In 1708 Dalby Thomas wrote to the company urging it to negotiate with the owners of hired ships for reduced fares for slaves under the age of 15, arguing that "they Lying in less Room & stand better usually than Men or Women"; PRO T70/26, f. 28.

18 The analysis of the demographic composition of the trade in this chapter is based insofar as possible on all slaves carried by the Royal African Company from Africa intended for the West Indies; the data used are those of Table 5.1. Unlike the analysis of prices in Chapter 3, this analysis therefore includes the numbers of slaves listed in the invoice accounts without positive prices.

19 The price variable of the male equation is the annual mean of the prices for adult males and females from Tables 3.1 and 3.3, converted to sterling. Missing annual values for women's prices were interpolated as 0.85 of the appropriate men's price.

The price variable of the female equation is the price series for women from Table 3.5, converted to sterling.

The binary variable used here to represent the higher wartime freight rates was coded as 0 for the years 1673–88 and 1 for 1689–1723.

The time-trend variable was entered as a number ranging from 73 (for 1673) to 123 (for 1723).

20 For the development of this method, see A. Zellner, "An Efficient Method of Estimating Seemingly Unrelated Regressions and Tests for Aggregation Bias," *Journal of the American Statistical Association*, Vol. 57 (1962), pp. 348–68.

The results obtained from estimating the two equations separately are quite similar to those presented in the text. The ordinary least-squares estimates are as follows, with standard errors in parentheses:

$$\text{share of boys} = -0.2677 + 0.00381 \text{ slave prices}$$
$$(0.0934) \quad (0.00246)$$
$$-0.08550 \text{ wartime} + 0.00437 \text{ time}$$
$$(0.03133) \quad (0.00113)$$
$$R^2 = 0.378, \quad F = 7.50, \quad n = 41, \quad \text{D-W} = 1.41$$

$$\text{share of girls} = -0.3166 + 0.00051 \text{ slave prices}$$
$$(0.0740) \quad (0.00150)$$
$$-0.07813 \text{ wartime} + 0.00502 \text{ time}$$
$$(0.02441) \quad (0.00089)$$
$$R^2 = 0.509, \quad F = 12.80, \quad n = 41, \quad \text{D-W} = 1.28$$

21 Both coefficients are significant at better than the 0.01 level.

22 Both coefficients are significant at better than the 0.001 level.

23 Palmer, *Human Cargoes*, pp. 52–4; Davies, *Royal African Company*, p. 292. The assumption here is that the declining passage mortality rates were not exclusive to shipments to the British West Indies, but rather would have extended to other parts of the transatlantic slave trade as well.

Effects on the supply side could also have contributed to the rising share of children in the slave trade, but knowledge of African demography in this early period is not sufficient to identify these with any precision. It is possible, for example, that an increase in the share of children in the trade could have resulted from the earlier removal of adult males from the African population for shipment to America. John Thornton has argued that in spite of the export of slaves to the Americas the African population might have maintained its total size through an increase in the incidence of polygamy, but that the age structure of the population shifted markedly toward the younger ages; Thornton, "The Slave Trade in Eighteenth Century Angola," and Thornton, "Sexual Demography: The Impact of the Slave Trade on Family Structure," in Claire C. Robertson and Martin A. Klein, eds., *Women and Slavery in Africa* (Madison: University of Wisconsin Press, 1983), pp. 39–48. This could then have resulted in progressively larger proportions of young Africans being offered to European traders over time.

24 This coefficient is significant at the 0.05 level.

25 Robertson and Klein, *Women and Slavery in Africa*, p. 4; Paul E. Lovejoy, *Transformations in Slavery: A History of Slavery in Africa* (Cambridge: Cambridge University Press, 1983), p. 46.

26 Robertson and Klein, *Women and Slavery in Africa*, p. 4.

27 Philip D. Curtin, *Economic Change in Precolonial Africa: Senegambia in the Era*

of the Slave Trade (Madison: University of Wisconsin Press, 1975), pp. 175–6. Also see the discussion of Klein, *The Middle Passage,* p. 151.

28 PRO T70/17, f. 35, "Letter from Cor. Hodges," James Island, September 16, 1690.

29 Robertson and Klein, *Women and Slavery in Africa,* pp. 4–5, 67.

30 David C. Tambo, "The Sokoto Caliphate Slave Trade in the Nineteenth Century," *International Journal of African Historical Studies,* Vol. 9, No. 2 (1976), p. 196.

31 Frederick Cooper, *Plantation Slavery on the East Coast of Africa* (New Haven, Conn.: Yale University Press, 1977), pp. 195–6.

32 Quoted in R. W. Beachey, ed., *A Collection of Documents on the Slave Trade of Eastern Africa* (New York: Harper & Row, 1976), pp. 46–7. For other examples of the high valuation of young female slaves in nineteenth-century Africa, see *ibid.,* pp. 45, 60–1; and Allan G. B. Fisher and Humphrey J. Fisher, *Slavery and Muslim Society in Africa* (London: C. Hurst, 1970), pp. 161–5.

33 See, for example, the essays by Robertson and Klein and by Claude Meillassoux, and references cited by these authors, in Robertson and Klein, *Women and Slavery in Africa.*

34 PRO T70/16, f. 49v, Edwin Stede and Stephen Gascoigne, Barbados, April 1683.

35 PRO T70/51, f. 135v, Royal African Company to John Colebeck, London, August 6, 1702.

36 PRO T70/52, f. 16v, London, May 4, 1704.

37 PRO T70/28, f. 60v, Cape Coast Castle, April 22, 1705.

38 PRO T70/51, f. 103v, London, August 12, 1701.

39 PRO T70/51, f. 150, Royal African Company to Great King of Bandie, London, September 15, 1702.

40 PRO T70/16, f. 48v, Barbados, March 19, 1683.

41 PRO T70/13, f. 16v, Barbados, May 4, 1703.

42 PRO T70/51, f. 186v, London, July 29, 1703.

43 PRO T70/52, f. 35, London, September 28, 1704.

44 For typical examples of the company's general instructions to its factors in Africa on the selection of slaves, see Davies, *Royal African Company,* p. 300.

6. Estimating geographic persistence from market observations

1 James C. Malin, "The Turnover of Farm Population in Kansas," *Kansas Historical Quarterly,* Vol. IV (1935), pp. 339–72; Merle Curti, *The Making of an American Community: A Case Study of Democracy in a Frontier Community* (Stanford, Cal.: Stanford University Press, 1959); Stephan Thernstrom, *Poverty and Progress: Social Mobility in a Nineteenth Century City* (Cambridge, Mass.: Harvard University Press, 1964). For a survey of the results of a number of other persistence studies, see Thernstrom, *The Other Bostonians: Poverty and Progress in the American Metropolis, 1880–1970* (Cambridge, Mass.: Harvard University Press, 1973), Chapter 9.

2 For a survey of the results of some colonial persistence studies, see Douglas Lamar Jones, *Village and Seaport: Migration and Society in Eighteenth-Century Massachusetts* (Hanover, N.H.: University Press of New England, 1981), Chapter 7. Thernstrom surveys the results of some studies of persistence in the twentieth-century United States in *The Other Bostonians,* Chapter 9.

3 This discussion might be summarized by noting that the "loyalty" of a consumer to a particular marketplace will be determined jointly by the costs and benefits of shopping there as opposed to other markets. A consumer might shop repeatedly at a single marketplace even if others are located nearby, for although the cost of going elsewhere might be low, the benefits might be even smaller if the markets are very similar. (This might be an important element, for example, in the loyalty of many consumers to a particular neighborhood grocery store.) To the extent that consumers are not loyal to a single marketplace, and purchase a commodity at a number of different locations over time even though they continue to reside in a single place, market records from any single marketplace might fail to indicate their presence in that location, and this will tend to give a downward bias to persistence rates calculated from these records.

4 On the commissions paid to the agents of the Royal African Company in the West Indies, see K. G. Davies, *The Royal African Company* (London: Longman, 1957), p. 296. Davies remarks that "an agency for the Royal African Company must . . . have been among the best remunerated private employments in the English colonies" and notes that as a result "competition for the posts . . . was keen"; *iid.*, pp. 296–7. On disputes between the company and agents over the accuracy of agents' accounts, see *ibid.*, pp. 298–9.

5 In most cases the registrations served to provide a record of credit transactions. K. G. Davies commented that "the selling of slaves in the English West Indies had everywhere one common characteristic: virtually all buyers, whatever form their eventual payment might take, demanded and got credit"; *Royal African Company*, p. 317. For obvious reasons, markets that operated largely through credit transactions are more likely to have produced written records than markets based on spot payments at the time of exchange of the traded commodity.

6 Richard S. Dunn, *Sugar and Slaves: The Rise of the Planter Class in the English West Indies, 1624–1713* (Chapel Hill: University of North Carolina Press, 1972), p. 7.

7 See n. 5.

8 On the history of Bybrook, see Dunn, *Sugar and Slaves*, pp. 212–22; also J. Harry Bennett, "Cary Helyar, Merchant and Planter of Seventeenth-Century Jamaica," *William and Mary Quarterly*, Third Series, Vol. 21, No. 1 (January 1964), pp. 53–76; and Bennett, "William Whaley, Planter of Seventeenth-Century Jamaica," *Agricultural History*, Vol. 40, No. 2 (April 1966), pp. 113–23.

9 John Cordy Jeaffreson, ed., *A Young Squire of the Seventeenth Century, from the Papers (A.D. 1676–1686) of Christopher Jeaffreson* (London: Hurst and Blackett, 1878), 2 volumes.

10 The high prices of slaves, and the necessary judgment involved in selecting them, meant that the job of purchasing them would rarely have been delegated to lesser employees.

11 This and later statements about the Barbados census of 1679 are based on a quantitative analysis of the census, which is at the Public Record Office, London, Colonial Office 1/44/142–379. For an account of the preparation and scope of the census, see Dunn, *Sugar and Slaves*, Chapter 3.

12 The evidence for this statement is detailed below, in the section of this chapter titled "Persistence and wealth."

13 Persistence studies can establish only that an individual was present in a location on the dates at which he is recorded as present there; they cannot establish that he was continuously present at that location during the interval between those dates. Throughout this study, therefore, as in other persistence studies, an individual will be defined as having persisted in a location during an interval between his first and last appearances there, whether or not he spent that entire interval in residence there.

14 It might be emphasized that the persistence rates of this study are based on measurements between calendar years; an individual traced from 1673 to 1674 is assumed to have been present for at least one year, one traced from 1673 to 1675 for at least two years, and so on. These inferences will be valid on average as long as the distribution of transactions over the course of the year remained stable. This condition appears basically to have been satisfied because the seasonality of the slave trade, which was primarily determined by considerations of climate in both the Caribbean and West Africa, did not change significantly in the period under study.

The length of stay variable used in the regression results reported in the section of this chapter titled "Persistence and wealth" is measured as the actual number of months that elapsed between an individual's first and last appearances in the auction invoices.

15 The rates shown in Tables 6.3 and 6.4 were estimated from the samples after eliminating all purchasers whose names appeared one or more times in the 1790 census of South Carolina, as described in Appendix C.

16 This assumes that the sample s is randomly drawn from the population.

17 For example, see Thernstrom, *The Other Bostonians*, pp. 283–8.

18 As will be noted, it will not normally be possible to convert measured persistence rates into true ones with certainty, because s/p is usually not known for lack of accurate population estimates. In many situations, however, likely bounds of true persistence rates can be obtained by estimating ranges for r_t based on assumptions concerning plausible values of s/p. Therefore if a census is believed to have captured at least 90 percent of a community's population, with an obvious upper-bound coverage of 100 percent, the true persistence rate will lie between the measured persistence rate and a figure 11 percent larger than that rate.

19 Thernstrom, *The Other Bostonians*, pp. 38–41; J. R. Kearl, Clayne L. Pope, and Larry T. Wimmer, "Household Wealth in a Settlement Economy: Utah, 1850–1870," *Journal of Economic History*, Vol. XL, No. 3 (September 1980), p. 491.

20 The sample period is restricted in this comparison to minimize the proportion of slave purchasers who could not be linked to the census because of geographic turnover – that is, departure before or arrival after its preparation in late 1679.

21 That the estimated coefficient of slaves is almost exactly twice as large as that of acres is a reflection of the fact that in this period Barbados planters tended to own one slave for every two acres they planted; Dunn, *Sugar and Slaves*, p. 89.

22 *Ibid.*, p. 91.

23 Jones, *Village and Seaport*, p. 106. The population at risk in these persistence studies was generally all heads of households of a town rather than the whole population.

24 This is the mortality rate obtained as a weighted average of the age-specific rates for males aged 21 and older given by the Model West Level 1 life table of Ansley

J. Coale and Paul Demeny, *Regional Model Life Tables and Stable Populations* (Princeton, N.J.: Princeton University Press, 1966). The weights used are the relative numbers of adult men present in the stable population produced by this mortality regime with an intrinsic rate of growth of zero ($r = 0$). It should be stressed that little precise evidence is available on the demography of the seventeenth-century West Indies. Choice of this model life table is based on available knowledge of crude death rates in the region of this period [e.g., see the discussion of Henry A. Gemery, "Emigration from the British Isles to the New World, 1630–1700: Inferences from Colonial Populations," *Research in Economic History,* Vol. 5 (1980), pp. 190–3] and the more detailed demographic analysis of the Trinidad slave population in the nineteenth century by A. Meredith John, "The Plight of the Slaves in Trinidad: Demographic Analysis of Nineteenth Century Slave Registration Records" (unpublished Ph.D. dissertation, Princeton University, 1984). The mortality rate used here should be considered a tentative estimate; more knowledge is necessary about possible racial differences in mortality and about trends over time in mortality rates before more confidence can be placed in such an estimate. The use of a lower-bound mortality rate in the calculations done here, however, will bias upward the estimates of outmigration rates from the West Indian colonies.

It is possible that the outmigration that occurred from Barbados could have tended to lower the average mortality rate for the colony's population of planters, for older men might have been disproportionately represented among the migrants. Any impact of this on mortality was probably minor, however. If all men above the age of 60 are excluded from the population before calculating the weighted average mortality rate in the manner described in this note, the annual rate falls only to 31 per thousand; if all men above the age of 50 are excluded, it falls only to 29 per thousand.

25 An annual rate of 23 per thousand is the mortality rate obtained as a weighted average of the age-specific mortality rates for males aged 21 and above given by the Model West Level 10 life table of Coale and Demeny, *Regional Model Life Tables and Stable Populations.* The weights used are the relative numbers of adult men present in the stable population produced by this mortality regime with an intrinsic rate of growth of zero ($r = 0$).

This mortality rate appears to be a generous upper bound of the one that would apply to rural colonial New England adult males, because of the assumed age structure of the population and perhaps also the level of the mortality schedule used. Instead using Model West Level 10 with a gross reproduction rate of 3.0 (GRR = 3.0), as suggested by Daniel Scott Smith ["The Demographic History of Colonial New England," *Journal of Economic History,* Vol. XXII, No. 1 (March 1972), pp. 171–2], would result in a mortality rate of 18 per thousand. This lower mortality rate would of course raise the estimated rate of outmigration implied by a given persistence rate; for example, using the mortality rate of 18 per thousand with the 50 percent persistence rate cited in the text for Beverly would yield an average annual outmigration rate of 4.9 percent. Using Model West Level 15 with GRR = 3.0 (see *ibid.,* p. 172) would yield an even lower mortality rate of 13 per thousand for adult males, implying an annual average outmigration rate for Beverly of 5.4 percent. (It might furthermore be noted that using Model North life tables has little impact on the mortality rates estimated. For Model North Level 10 with GRR = 3.0, the procedure described would yield an annual average mortality rate for adult males of 18 per thousand, whereas for Model North Level 15, GRR = 3.0, it would produce a rate of 13 per thousand.)

Actual evidence from some rural colonial New England towns summarized by Jones, *Village and Seaport*, p. 126, shows decennial death rates for adult males of 15.6–19.0 percent. These again support the view that the use of a mortality rate of 23 per thousand is a generous upper bound of the true annual mortality rate. For additional discussion of mortality rates in colonial Massachusetts, see Maris A. Vinovskis, "Mortality Rates and Trends in Massachusetts Before 1860," *Journal of Economic History*, Vol. 32, No. 1 (March 1972), pp. 184–213, and Vinovskis, *Fertility in Massachusetts from the Revolution to the Civil War* (New York: Academic Press, 1981), pp. 26–31.

26 Several possible sources of bias should be kept in mind in evaluating the comparisons given in the text. One concerns the nature of the sources for the persistence estimates. The New England studies have in most cases been based on evidence that would tend to constitute more complete population enumerations (e.g., tax lists, often supplemented by genealogical sources) than the slave sale invoices used here for the West Indies. For reasons discussed earlier in this chapter, this would tend to result in a relative downward bias in the measurement of West Indian persistence rates.

A second possible source of inaccuracy in comparison concerns a form of selection bias. The persistence rates obtained here for the West Indies might tend to overstate the persistence rates of the islands' white populations because of the disproportionate representation of the wealthier, and apparently more geographically stable, planters in the Royal African Company sale invoices. A similar bias could of course be present to some extent in the New England studies as well if the poorer members of the towns' populations were missed by the tax and other enumerations used to define the population to be traced over time. The net effect of these biases on the comparisons between the West Indies and New England cannot be determined, but significant biases could be present.

27 Once again using the annual mortality rate of 33 per thousand, the range of implied annual average rates of outmigration for Barbados and Jamaica in each decade can be obtained from the minimum and maximum values of the 10-year persistence rates in Tables 6.1 and 6.2; these are tabulated here. Also presented are the annual outmigration rates implied by the decennial mean persistence rates for each colony, weighted by the number of purchasers in each base year.

	Outmigration rate					
	Barbados			Jamaica		
Decade	Minimum	"Mean"	Maximum	Minimum	"Mean"	Maximum
1670s	3.6%	6.6%	8.9%	6.7%	10.4%	14.0%
1680s	6.7	9.5	13.4	10.4	14.7	18.1
1690s	9.0	12.1	17.3	7.2	11.2	21.2

The clear increase in outmigration rates that appears for Barbados during the 1680s in the minimum and maximum as well as the decennial mean estimates is consistent with the observations of Richard Dunn, who wrote of Barbados that "absenteeism was not yet a controlling factor in the 1670s and early 1680s . . . During the 1680s, however, the homeward drift picked up"; *Sugar and Slaves,* p. 102.

28 Richard Ligon, *A True & Exact History of the Island of Barbados* (London: Humphrey Moseley 1657), p. 21.

29 On English attitudes toward the climate of the colonial West Indies, see Karen Ordahl Kupperman, "Fear of Hot Climates in the Anglo-American Colonial Experience," *William and Mary Quarterly,* Third Series, Vol. XLI, No. 2 (April 1984), pp. 213–40.

30 In a transatlantic labor market operating at this time, the distaste of Europeans for conditions in the West Indies meant that English indentured servants had to be compensated for migrating there instead of to the American mainland colonies through the use of shorter contracts, or implicitly higher wage rates; see David W. Galenson, *White Servitude in Colonial America: An Economic Analysis* (Cambridge: Cambridge University Press, 1981), Chapter 7.

31 See the analysis of the wealth (land and slaves) of the planters in 1680 in Dunn, *Sugar and Slaves,* Chapter 3. On the early profitability of sugar planting in Barbados, also see J. R. Ward, "The Profitability of Sugar Planting in the British West Indies, 1650–1834," *Economic History Review,* Second Series, Vol. XXXI, No. 2 (May 1978), p. 208.

32 Ligon, *A True & Exact History of the Island of Barbados,* pp. 55–7.

33 Richard B. Sheridan, *Sugar and Slavery: An Economic History of the British West Indies, 1623–1775* (Barbados: Caribbean Universities Press, 1974), Chapter 16.

34 Jeaffreson's story is detailed in Jeaffreson, ed., *A Young Squire of the Seventeenth Century.* Also see Dunn, *Sugar and Slaves,* pp. 200–1, and Carl and Roberta Bridenbaugh, *No Peace Beyond the Line: The English in the Caribbean, 1624–1690* (New York: Oxford University Press, 1972), pp. 304–5.

35 Drax was apparently resident in Barbados in the mid-1670s; Dunn, *Sugar and Slaves,* p. 95. He died in England in 1682; James C. Brandow, ed., *Genealogies of Barbados Families* (Baltimore: Geneological Publishing Co., 1983), pp. 224–5.

36 Henry Drax, "Instructions for the Management of Drax-Hall and the Irish-hope Plantations: To Archibald Johnson," in William Belgrove, *A Treatise Upon Husbandry or Planting* (Boston, 1755). The passages quoted below are items nos. 3 and 8, pp. 52, 54.

37 Richard Sheridan has pointed out that "attorneys are known to have acted for absentee Barbadian planters as early as the 1720s, and it is possible that they were quite numerous before 1700"; "Comments on Papers Presented at the S.S.H.A. Annual Meeting, 1982" (unpublished manuscript). I am grateful to Richard Sheridan for a copy of these comments.

38 Sheridan, *Sugar and Slavery,* pp. 125–6; Dunn, *Sugar and Slaves,* p. 303.

39 For example, see Richard Dunn's discussion of Jamaica's history in the early period of British settlement in *Sugar and Slaves,* Chapter 5.

7. The economic structure of the early Atlantic slave trade

1 Adam Smith, *An Inquiry into the Nature and Causes of the Wealth of Nations* (New York: Modern Library, 1937), pp. 712–3. The passages quoted in the text that follows are from *ibid.*, pp. 700–1.

2 See also the comments of K. G. Davies, *The Royal African Company* (London: Longmans, 1957), pp. 165–84.

3 *Ibid.*, pp. 346–7.

4 From a study of the dividends paid by the Royal African Company to its share-holders, K. G. Davies estimated that in the first 20 years of its existence the company paid an annual average return of 7% on its initial investments, while the rate fell to an annual average of about 4% during the following 20 years; *The Royal African Company*, pp. 72–95. In comparison, at the time investments considered to be very safe, including those in land, earned an annual return of about 5%; for example, see H. J. Habakkuk, "The Long-Term Rate of Interest and the Price of Land in the Seventeenth Century," *Economic History Review*, Second Series, Vol. V, No. 1 (1952), pp. 26–45. Thus at its best the company did only slightly better for its shareholders than investments considered more secure, and after the early 1690s it earned them less than these safe investments.

5 See Philip D. Curtin, *The Atlantic Slave Trade: A Census* (Madison: University of Wisconsin Press, 1969); and Paul E. Lovejoy, *Transformations in Slavery: A History of Slavery in Africa* (Cambridge: Cambridge University Press, 1983), pp. 44–65.

6 For example, see the recent estimates of J. E. Inikori, "Market Structure and the Profits of the British African Trade in the Late Eighteenth Century," *Journal of Economic History*, Vol. XLI, No. 4 (December 1981), pp. 745–76.

7 Davies, *Royal African Company*, pp. 63–74. It is striking to compare the size distribution of holdings in the Royal African Company with those of other joint stock companies at the same time. Whereas in 1693, 72% of all the stock in the East India Company was held by shareholders with investments of £2,000 and more, and in 1694, 48% of the stock of the Bank of England was held by such investors, in 1691 investments of £2,000 and more accounted for only 14% of the stock of the Royal African Company. The share of such investors in the Royal African Company's total stock had furthermore been rising over time, from 8% in 1675 and 9% in 1688; K. G. Davies, "Joint-Stock Investment in the Later Seventeenth Century," *Economic History Review*, Second Series, Vol. IV, No. 3 (1952), pp. 295–300. Davies notes that the East India Company enjoyed a reputation for greater security than the African Company, and it is clear that large investors shared this view; it would also appear that large investors believed the Bank of England to be a safer investment than the African Company from the beginning of the former's career.

8 W. Cunningham, "The Perversion of Economic History," *Economic Journal*, Vol. 2 (1892), pp. 491–506; Alfred Marshall, "A Reply," *ibid.*, pp. 507–19.

9 For references to contributions to this debate, see Philip D. Curtin, *Cross-Cultural Trade in World History* (Cambridge: Cambridge University Press, 1984), pp. 63–4. One recent article that presents evidence of market activity is C. C. Lamberg-

Karlovsky, "Third Millennium Modes of Exchange and Modes of Production," in Jeremy Sabloff and C. C. Lamberg-Karlovsky, eds., *Ancient Civilization and Trade* (Albuquerque: University of New Mexico Press, 1975), pp. 341–68.

10 Karl Polanyi, *The Livelihood of Man* (New York: Academic Press, 1977).

11 One such study, with references to others, is Morris Silver, "Karl Polanyi and Markets in the Ancient Middle East: The Challenge of the Evidence," *Journal of Economic History*, Vol. XLIII, No. 4 (December 1983), pp. 795–829.

12 The challenge to the "modernizers," who had emphasized the significant role of markets in ancient Greece, can be found in M. I. Finley, "Classical Greece," in *Second International Conference of Economic History, Aix en Provence, 1962* (Paris: Mouton, 1965), pp. 12–35; Finley, *The Ancient Economy* (Berkeley: University of California Press, 1973); and Keith Hopkins, "Introduction," in Peter Garnsey, Keith Hopkins, and C. R. Whittaker, eds., *Trade in the Ancient Economy* (Berkeley: University of California Press, 1983), pp. ix–xxv. A recent contribution on a related topic is James M. Redfield, "The Development of the Market in Archaic Greece" (unpublished paper, University of Chicago, 1984).

13 M. Rostovtzeff, *The Social and Economic History of the Roman Empire* (Oxford: Clarendon Press, 1926), Chapter 5; Finley, *The Ancient Economy*, Chapters 1–2. For recent contributions to this debate, see John H. D'Arms, *Commerce and Social Standing in Ancient Rome* (Cambridge, Mass.: Harvard University Press, 1981), and H. W. Pleket, "Urban Elites and Business in the Greek Part of the Roman Empire," in Garnsey, Hopkins, and Whittaker, eds., *Trade in the Ancient Economy*, pp. 131–44.

14 For a discussion of Marx's views and opposing arguments, see Alan Macfarlane, *The Origins of English Individualism* (Cambridge: Cambridge University Press, 1979).

15 Davies, *Royal African Company*, pp. 63–4.

16 George Frederick Zook, *The Company of Royal Adventurers Trading into Africa* (Lancaster, Pa.: New Era Printing Company, 1919), pp. 18, 42.

17 Davies, *Royal African Company*, p. 156.

18 *Ibid.*, p. 65. David Brion Davis has pointed out that, although Locke has been more famous and influential for his celebration of human liberty, he was also the last major political philosopher to seek justifications for enslaving foreign captives; *Slavery and Human Progress* (Oxford: Oxford University Press, 1984), pp. 107–8.

19 On the competitiveness of the transatlantic trade in indentured servants, and the economic rationality of outcomes, see David W. Galenson, *White Servitude in Colonial America: An Economic Analysis* (Cambridge: Cambridge University Press, 1981), Chapter 7; and Farley Grubb, "Immigration and Servitude in the Colony and Commonwealth of Pennsylvania: A Quantitative and Economic Analysis" (unpublished Ph.D. dissertation, University of Chicago, 1984), Chapters 10–11.

Appendix A

1 These books are cataloged as Treasury 70/936–959. On the history and contents of the records of the Royal African Company in general, see Hilary Jenkinson, "The

Records of the English African Companies," *Transactions of the Royal Historical Society,* Third Series, Vol. VI (1912), pp. 185–220. For a brief overview of the records, see K. G. Davies, *The Royal African Company* (London: Longmans, 1957), Appendix VII, pp. 374–5.

2 The records of the sales in the invoice account books are fair copies of the original individual sale records sent to London by factors in the West Indies. The original records, which do not survive, appear also to have included an oath signed by the factors. Although the company did not transcribe the oaths in its fair copies in the account books, that it did take them seriously can be seen from this rebuke sent to a factor in Barbados in 1687:

The oath made to that accott. of sales as alsoe to that of the sales of the Lucitania Negroes doth not asnweare the ends proposed to you Mr. Skutt for you onely say it is a Just & true Accott. of the Sales whereas you should sware that you have in the Sale of the Negroes by the shipp ＿＿＿＿ used your utmost Skill & endeavours in the Disposall of them to the most Advantage of the Royall African Compa. of England & that the above Accott. is a just & True accott. of the Disposall of each of them both as to the Debtors for them & the vallue for wch. they were sold which words you are to observe for the ffuter;

    PRO T70/57, ff. 14–14v, Royal African Company to Edwyn Stede and Benjamin Skutt at Barbados; London, October 25, 1687.

3 Richard S. Dunn, *Sugar and Slaves: The Rise of the Planter Class in the English West Indies, 1624–1713* (Chapel Hill: University of North Carolina Press, 1972), pp. 81–2. The seventh transaction in the sale shown in Figure A.2 was a sale to William Whaley, the subject of J. Harry Bennett's "William Whaley, Planter of Seventeenth-Century Jamaica," *Agricultural History,* Vol. XL, No. 2 (April 1966), pp. 113–23.

4 The account books also contain the records of a total of 4,831 slaves delivered to the West Indies and Virginia during 1712–25, bringing the total sample analyzed in this book to 74,416.

5 On cargoes sold by prearranged contracts rather than by public sale, see Davies, *Royal African Company,* pp. 294–5.

Appendix B

1 The volume is held in the Public Record Office, London, as Treasury 70/1225. A subheading below the title of the volume indentifies it as "No. 2," but any other volume or volumes in the series appear to have been damaged or lost.

2 This was presumably the ship's "registered tonnage." On its interpretation, see Christopher J. French, "Eighteenth-Century Shipping Tonnage Measurements," *Journal of Economic History,* Vol. XXXIII, No. 2 (June 1973), pp. 434–43.

3 One of the ships that lost a captain in the passage to America was the *Cape Coast Frigate* (entry 7 in Table B.1), which spent nearly five months sailing from Cape Coast Castle to Barbados. The other ships whose captains died during the Middle Passage were entries 2, 36, and 37; the captain of entry 28 died before his ship's arrival in Africa, and the captains of entries 3 and 15 died in Africa.

4 On crew mortality in the slave trade, see Philip D. Curtin, *The Atlantic Slave Trade: A Census* (Madison: University of Wisconsin Press, 1969), pp. 282–4; Johannes

Postma, "Mortality in the Dutch Slave Trade, 1675–1795," in Henry A. Gemery and Jan S. Hogendorn, *The Uncommon Market: Essays in the Economic History of the Atlantic Slave Trade* (New York: Academic Press, 1979), pp. 259–60; and Herbert S. Klein and Stanley L. Engerman, "A Note on Mortality in the French Slave Trade in the Eighteenth Century," in *ibid.*, pp. 266–7.

Appendix C

1 Stephan Thernstrom, *The Other Bostonians: Poverty and Progress in the American Metropolis, 1880–1970* (Cambridge, Mass.: Harvard University Press, 1973), pp. 269–70.
2 Bureau of the Census, *Heads of Families at the First Census of the United States Taken in the Year 1790: South Carolina* (Washington, D.C.: U.S. Government Printing Office, 1908), pp. 103–50.
3 A large proportion of the earliest settlers in South Carolina came to the colony from Barbados, and the continuing close economic connections between the two led a historian of South Carolina to refer to it in the early decades of its establishment as "the colony of a colony"; Peter H. Wood, *Black Majority: Negroes in Colonial South Carolina from 1670 through the Stono Rebellion* (New York: W. W. Norton, 1975), Chapter 1.
4 John J. McCusker, Jr., "The Rum Trade and the Balance of Payments of the Thirteen Continental Colonies, 1650–1775" (unpublished Ph.D. dissertation, University of Pittsburgh, 1970), p. 699.
5 Robert V. Wells, *The Population of the British Colonies in America Before 1776: A Survey of Census Data* (Princeton, N.J.: Princeton University Press, 1975), p. 246.

Selected bibliography

The following lists contain a limited selection of published works that have influenced my interpretation of the early transatlantic slave trade and its role in the history of West Africa and colonial English America. Although this listing is not exhaustive, the works cited here are good starting places for the study of the subjects indicated.

The demographic and economic history of precolonial Africa are currently very active fields of research. The following list includes some key studies of African demography, African systems of slavery, and the internal African slave trade that are of particular relevance to the economic and demographic aspects of the early transatlantic slave trade treated in this book.

Austen, Ralph, "The Trans-Saharan Slave Trade: A Tentative Census," in Henry A. Gemery and Jan S. Hogendorn, eds., *The Uncommon Market: Essays in the Economic History of the Atlantic Slave Trade* (New York: Academic Press, 1979), pp. 23–76.

Cooper, Frederick, *Plantation Slavery on the East Coast of Africa* (New Haven, Conn.: Yale University Press, 1977).

"The Problem of Slavery in African Studies," *Journal of African History*, Vol. 20, No. 1 (1979), pp. 103–25.

Curtin, Philip, D., *Economic Change in Precolonial Africa: Senegambia in the Era of the Slave Trade*, 2 vols. (Madison: University of Wisconsin Press, 1975).

"The Abolition of the Slave Trade from Senegambia," in David Eltis and James Walvin, eds., *The Abolition of the Atlantic Slave Trade: Origins and Effects in Europe, Africa, and the Americas* (Madison: University of Wisconsin Press, 1981), pp. 83–97.

Daaku, Kwame Yeboa, *Trade and Politics on the Gold Coast, 1600–1720: A Study of the African Reaction to European Trade* (Oxford: Clarendon Press, 1970).

Fage, J. D., *A History of West Africa* (Cambridge: Cambridge University Press, 1969).

"Slavery and the Slave Trade in the Context of West African History," *Journal of African History*, Vol. 10, No. 3 (1969), pp. 393–404.

Harms, Robert W., *River of Wealth, River of Sorrow: The Central Zaire Basin in the*

Selected bibliography

Era of the Slave and Ivory Trade (New Haven, Conn.: Yale University Press, 1981).

Hopkins, A. G., *An Economic History of West Africa* (New York: Columbia University Press, 1973).

Kea, Ray A., *Settlements, Trade, and Polities in the Seventeenth-Century Gold Coast* (Baltimore: Johns Hopkins University Press, 1982).

Lovejoy, Paul, *Transformations in Slavery: A History of Slavery in Africa* (Cambridge: Cambridge University Press, 1983).

"Indigenous African Slavery," in Michael Craton, ed., *Roots and Branches: Current Directions in Slave Studies* (Toronto: Pergamon Press, 1979), pp. 19–61. (See also the commentaries on this paper that follow, by Igor Kopytoff and Frederick Cooper; *ibid.*, pp. 62–83.)

Manning, Patrick, "The Enslavement of Africans: A Demographic Model," *Canadian Journal of African Studies*, Vol. 15, No. 3 (1981), pp. 499–526. [See also the two comments on this paper by John C. Caldwell and J. E. Inikori and the response by Manning in *ibid.*, Vol. 16, No. 1 (1982), pp. 127–39.]

Slavery, Colonialism, and Economic Growth in Dahomey, 1640–1960 (Cambridge: Cambridge University Press, 1982).

"Contours of Slavery and Social Change in Africa," *American Historical Review*, Vol. 88, No. 4 (October 1983), pp. 835–57.

Miers, Suzanne, and Igor Kopytoff, eds., *Slavery in Africa: Historical and Anthropological Perspectives* (Madison: University of Wisconsin Press, 1977).

Patterson, Orlando, *Slavery and Social Death: A Comparative Study* (Cambridge, Mass.: Harvard University Press, 1982).

Polanyi, Karl, *Dahomey and the Slave Trade: An Analysis of an Archaic Society* (Seattle: University of Washington Press, 1966).

Robertson, Claire C., and Martin A. Klein, eds., *Women and Slavery in Africa* (Madison: University of Wisconsin Press, 1983).

Rodney, Walter, *A History of the Upper Guinea Coast, 1545–1800* (Oxford: Oxford University Press, 1970).

Tambo, David C., "The Sokoto Caliphate Slave Trade in the Nineteenth Century," *International Journal of African Historical Studies*, Vol. 9, No. 2 (1976), pp. 187–217.

Thornton, John, "The Slave Trade in Eighteenth Century Angola: Effects on Demographic Structures," *Canadian Journal of African Studies*, Vol. 14, No. 3 (1980), pp. 417–27.

Watson, James L., ed., *Asian and African Systems of Slavery* (Oxford: Basil Blackwell, 1980).

Although the Atlantic slave trade has long been of interest to historians, since the publication of Philip Curtin's study in 1969 the Middle Passage has become the subject of intensive study by quantitative historians. The following list includes a few older, classic works on the early slave trade as well as a selection drawn from the many recent studies.

Bean, Richard, *The British Trans-Atlantic Slave Trade, 1650–1775* (New York: Arno Press, 1975).

Cohn, Raymond A., and Richard A. Jensen, "The Determinants of Slave Mortality Rates on the Middle Passage," *Explorations in Economic History*, Vol. 19, No. 3 (July 1982), pp. 269–82.

Craton, Michael, *Sinews of Empire: A Short History of British Slavery* (Garden City, N.Y.: Anchor Press/Doubleday, 1974).

Curtin, Philip D., *The Atlantic Slave Trade: A Census* (Madison: University of Wisconsin Press, 1969).

"Epidemiology and the Slave Trade," *Political Science Quarterly*, Vol. LXXXIII, No. 2 (June 1968), pp. 190–216.

Davies, K. G., *The Royal African Company* (London: Longmans, 1957).

Davis, Ralph, *The Rise of the English Shipping Industry in the Seventeenth and Eighteenth Centuries* (London: Macmillan, 1962).

Donnan, Elizabeth, *Documents Illustrative of the History of the Slave Trade to America*, 4 vols. (Washington, D.C.: Carnegie Institution, 1930–5).

Engerman, Stanley L., and Eugene D. Genovese, eds., *Race and Slavery in the Western Hemisphere: Quantitative Studies* (Princeton, N.J.: Princeton University Press, 1975).

Gemery, Henry A., and Jan S. Hogendorn, "The Atlantic Slave Trade: A Tentative Economic Model," *Journal of African History*, Vol. 15, No. 2 (1974), pp. 223–46.

Gemery, Henry A., and Jan S. Hogendorn, eds., *The Uncommon Market: Essays in the Economic History of the Atlantic Slave Trade* (New York: Academic Press, 1979).

Klein, Herbert S., *The Middle Passage: Comparative Studies of the Atlantic Slave Trade* (Princeton, N.J.: Princeton University Press, 1978).

Lovejoy, Paul E., "The Volume of the Atlantic Slave Trade: A Synthesis," *Journal of African History*, Vol. 23, No. 4 (1982), pp. 473–501.

Mannix, Daniel P., and Malcolm Cowley, *Black Cargoes: A History of the Atlantic Slave Trade, 1518–1865* (New York: Viking Press, 1962).

Miller, Joseph, "Mortality in the Atlantic Slave Trade: Statistical Evidence on Causality," *Journal of Interdisciplinary History*, Vol. XI, No. 3 (Winter 1981), pp. 385–423. [See also the comment on this paper by Raymond L. Cohn and Richard A. Jensen and the reply by Miller in *ibid.*, Vol. XIII, No. 2 (Autumn 1982), pp. 317–36.]

Palmer, Colin, *Human Cargoes: The British Slave Trade to Spanish America, 1700–1739* (Urbana: University of Illinois Press, 1981).

Postma, Johannes, "The Dimension of the Dutch Slave Trade from Western Africa," *Journal of African History*, Vol. 13, No. 2 (1972), pp. 237–48.

Rawley, James A., *The Transatlantic Slave Trade: A History* (New York: W. W. Norton, 1981).

Sheridan, Richard B., "Africa and the Caribbean in the Atlantic Slave Trade," *American Historical Review*, Vol. 77, No. 1 (February 1972), pp. 15–35.

Stein, Robert Louis, *The French Slave Trade in the Eighteenth Century: An Old Regime Business* (Madison: University of Wisconsin Press, 1979).

Thomas, Robert Paul, and Richard Nelson Bean, "The Fishers of Men: The Profits of the Slave Trade," *Journal of Economic History*, Vol. XXXIV, No. 4 (December 1974), pp. 885–914.

Selected bibliography

Thornton, A. P., "The Organization of the Slave Trade in the English West Indies, 1660–1685," *William and Mary Quarterly*, Third Series, Vol. XII, No. 3 (July 1955), pp. 399–409.

Zook, George Frederick, *The Company of Royal Adventurers Trading Into Africa* (Lancaster, Pa.: New Era Printing Company, 1919).

The dramatic story of the early English experience in the West Indies has recently been brought forcefully to the attention of social and economic historians by the work of Carl and Roberta Bridenbaugh, Richard Dunn, Richard Sheridan, and others. The following list of works on West Indian history includes a few particularly valuable contemporary accounts of the seventeenth-century development of the sugar islands as well as some major studies of the region's early colonial period written by twentieth-century historians.

Batie, Robert Carlyle, "Why Sugar? Economic Cycles and the Changing of Staples in the English and French Antilles, 1624–1654," *Journal of Caribbean History*, Vol. 8 (November 1976), pp. 1–41.

Beckles, Hilary, "The Economic Origins of Black Slavery in the British West Indies, 1640–1680: A Tentative Analysis of the Barbados Model," *Journal of Caribbean History*, Vol. 16 (1982), pp. 36–56.

Beer, George Louis, *The Origins of the British Colonial System, 1578–1660* (New York: Macmillan, 1908).

The Old Colonial System, 1660–1754 (New York: Macmillan, 1913).

Bennett, J. Harry, *Bondsmen and Bishops: Slavery and Apprenticeship in the Codrington Plantations of Barbados, 1710–1838* (Berkeley: University of California Press, 1958).

"Cary Helyar, Merchant and Planter of Seventeenth-Century Jamaica," *William and Mary Quarterly*, Third Series, Vol. XXI, No. 1 (January 1964), pp. 53–76.

"William Whaley, Planter of Seventeenth-Century Jamaica," *Agricultural History*, Vol. XL, No. 2 (April 1966), pp. 113–23.

Bridenbaugh, Carl, and Roberta Bridenbaugh, *No Peace Beyond the Line: The English in the Caribbean, 1624–1690* (New York: Oxford University Press, 1972).

Chandler, Alfred D., "The Expansion of Barbados," *Journal of the Barbados Museum and Historical Society*, Vol. XIII, Nos. 3–4 (1945–6), pp. 106–36.

Craton, Michael, *Searching for the Invisible Man: Slaves and Plantation Life in Jamaica* (Cambridge, Mass.: Harvard University Press, 1978).

Craton, Michael, and James Walvin, *A Jamaican Plantation: The History of Worthy Park, 1670–1970* (Toronto: University of Toronto Press, 1970).

Davies, K. G., *The North Atlantic World in the Seventeenth Century* (Minneapolis: University of Minnesota Press, 1974).

Deerr, Noel, *The History of Sugar*, 2 vols. (London: Chapman and Hall, 1949–50).

Dunn, Richard S., *Sugar and Slaves: The Rise of the Planter Class in the English West Indies, 1624–1713* (Chapel Hill: University of North Carolina Press, 1972).

Edel, Matthew, "The Brazilian Sugar Cycle of the Seventeenth Century and the Rise of the West Indian Competition," *Caribbean Studies*, Vol. 9, No. 1 (April 1969), pp. 24–44.

Fraginals, Manuel Moreno, Herbert S. Klein, and Stanley L. Engerman, "The Level and Structure of Slave Prices on Cuban Plantations in the Mid-Nineteenth Century: Some Comparative Perspectives," *American Historical Review*, Vol. 88, No. 5 (December 1983), pp. 1201–18.

Handler, Jerome S., and Frederick W. Lange, *Plantation Slavery in Barbados* (Cambridge, Mass.: Harvard University Press, 1978).

Harlow, Vincent T., *A History of Barbados, 1625–1685* (Oxford: Clarendon Press, 1926).

Higham, C. S. S., *The Development of the Leeward Islands Under the Restoration, 1660–1688* (Cambridge: Cambridge University Press, 1921).

Innes, F. C., "The Pre-Sugar Era of European Settlement in Barbados," *Journal of Caribbean History*, Vol. 1 (November 1970), pp. 1–22.

Jeaffreson, John Cordy, ed., *A Young Squire of the Seventeenth Century, From the Papers (A.D. 1676–1686) of Christopher Jeaffreson* (London: Hurst and Blackett, 1878).

Kiple, Kenneth F., *The Caribbean Slave: A Biological History* (Cambridge: Cambridge University Press, 1984).

Ligon, Richard, *A True & Exact History of the Island of Barbados* (London: Humphrey Moseley, 1657).

Pares, Richard, *A West-India Fortune* (London: Longmans, Green and Co., 1950). *Merchants and Planters*, Economic History Review Supplement No. 4 (Cambridge: Cambridge University Press, 1960).

Pitman, Frank W., *The Development of the British West Indies, 1700–1763* (New Haven, Conn.: Yale University Press, 1917).

Puckrein, Gary A., *Little England: Plantation Society and Anglo-Barbadian Politics, 1627–1700* (New York: New York University Press, 1984).

Ragatz, Lowell, J., *The Fall of the Planter Class in the British Caribbean, 1763–1833* (New Haven, Conn.: Century, 1928).

Sheppard, Jill, *The "Redlegs" of Barbados* (Millwood, N.Y.: KTO Press, 1977).

Sheridan, Richard B., *Sugar and Slavery: An Economic History of the British West Indies, 1623–1775* (Barbados: Caribbean Universities Press, 1974).

Thomas, Dalby, *An Historical Account of the Rise and Growth of the West-India Collonies, and of the Great Advantages They Are to England, in Respect to Trade* (London: Jo. Hindmarsh, 1690).

Ward, J. R., "The Profitability of Sugar Planting in the British West Indies, 1650–1834," *Economic History Review*, Second Series, Vol. XXXI, No. 2 (May 1978), pp. 197–213.

Williams, Eric, *From Columbus to Castro: The History of the Caribbean, 1492–1969* (London: Deutsch, 1970).

Williamson, James A., *The Caribbee Islands Under the Proprietary Patents* (London: Oxford University Press, 1926).

Slavery was introduced at different times into the different regions of colonial English America, and although it came to play a central role in the labor markets of some of these areas, it remained of only minor importance in others. The following list provides references to works that contribute to an assessment of the significance of slavery in the regions of the British North

221

Selected bibliography

American mainland, as well as to some efforts by economists and historians to provide an analytical basis for understanding the differing importance of slavery over time and space in the labor markets of colonial English America.

Bean, Richard N., and Robert P. Thomas, "The Adoption of Slave Labor in British America," in Henry A. Gemery and Jan S. Hogendorn, eds., *The Uncommon Market: Essays in the Economic History of the Atlantic Slave Trade* (New York: Academic Press, 1979), pp. 377–98.

Bruce, Philip Alexander, *Economic History of Virginia in the Seventeenth Century*, 2 vols. (New York: Macmillan, 1895).

Clemens, Paul G. E., *The Atlantic Economy and Colonial Maryland's Eastern Shore: From Tobacco to Grain* (Ithaca, N.Y.: Cornell University Press, 1980).

Craven, Wesley Frank, *White, Red, and Black: The Seventeenth-Century Virginian* (Charlottesville: University Press of Virginia, 1971).

Davis, David Brion, *Slavery and Human Progress* (New York: Oxford University Press, 1984).

Domar, Evsey D., "The Causes of Slavery and Serfdom: A Hypothesis," *Journal of Economic History*, Vol. XXX, No. 1 (March 1970), pp. 13–32.

Dunn, Richard S., "Servants and Slaves: The Recruitment and Employment of Labor," in Jack P. Greene and J. R. Pole, eds., *Colonial British America: Essays in the New History of the Early Modern Era* (Baltimore: Johns Hopkins University Press, 1984), pp. 157–94.

Earle, Carville V., *The Evolution of a Tidewater Settlement System: All Hallow's Parish, Maryland, 1650–1783* (Chicago: University of Chicago Department of Geography, 1975).

Fogel, Robert William, and Stanley L. Engerman, *Time on the Cross: The Economics of American Negro Slavery*, 2 vols. (Boston: Little, Brown, 1974).

Galenson, David W., *White Servitude in Colonial America: An Economic Analysis* (Cambridge: Cambridge University Press, 1981).

"The Rise and Fall of Indentured Servitude in the Americas: An Economic Analysis," *Journal of Economic History*, Vol. XLIV, No. 1 (March 1984), pp. 1–26.

Galenson, David W., and Russell R. Menard, "Approaches to the Analysis of Economic Growth in Colonial British America," *Historical Methods*, Vol. 13 (Winter 1980), pp. 3–18.

Gray, Lewis Cecil, *History of Agriculture in the Southern United States to 1860*, 2 vols. (Gloucester, Mass.: reprinted by Peter Smith, 1958).

Greene, Lorenzo Johnston, *The Negro in Colonial New England* (New York: Columbia University Press, 1942).

Handlin, Oscar and Mary F., "Origins of the Southern Labor System," *William and Mary Quarterly*, Third Series, Vol. VII (1950), pp. 199–222.

Higginbotham, A. Leon, Jr., *In the Matter of Color: Race and the American Legal Process, the Colonial Period* (Oxford: Oxford University Press, 1978).

Jones, Alice Hanson, *Wealth of a Nation to Be: The American Colonies on the Eve of the Revolution* (New York: Columbia University Press, 1980).

Jordan, Winthrop D., *White Over Black: American Attitudes Towards the Negro, 1550–1812* (Chapel Hill: University of North Carolina Press, 1968).

Littlefield, Daniel C., *Rice and Slaves: Ethnicity and the Slave Trade in Colonial South Carolina* (Baton Rouge: Louisiana State University Press, 1981).

Main, Gloria L., *Tobacco Colony: Life in Early Maryland, 1650–1720* (Princeton, N.J.: Princeton University Press, 1982).

Menard, Russell, "From Servants to Slaves: The Transformation of the Chesapeake Labor System," *Southern Studies*, Vol. XVI, No. 4 (Winter 1977), pp. 355–90.

Morgan, Edmund S., *American Slavery, American Freedom: The Ordeal of Colonial Virginia* (New York: W. W. Norton, 1975).

Morris, Richard B., *Government and Labor in Early America* (New York: Columbia University Press, 1946).

Mullin, Gerald W., *Flight and Rebellion: Slave Resistance in Eighteenth-Century Virginia* (London: Oxford University Press, 1972).

Phillips, Ulrich B., *American Negro Slavery* (New York: D. Appleton, 1918).

Life and Labor in the Old South (Boston: Little, Brown, 1929).

Robinson, Donald, *Slavery in the Structure of American Politics, 1765–1820* (New York: Harcourt Brace Jovanovich, 1971).

Rutman, Darrett B., and Anita H. Rutman, *A Place in Time: Middlesex County, Virginia, 1650–1750* (New York: W. W. Norton, 1984), 2 vols.

Smith, Abbot Emerson, *Colonists in Bondage: White Servitude and Convict Labor in America, 1607–1776* (Chapel Hill: University of North Carolina Press, 1947).

Williams, Eric, *Capitalism and Slavery* (Chapel Hill: University of North Carolina Press, 1944).

Wood, Peter H., *Black Majority: Negroes in Colonial South Carolina from 1670 through the Stono Rebellion* (New York: W. W. Norton, 1975).

Index

abolitionists, 37
absentee plantation owners, 120, 133, 145; employees of, 138–40, 141–2
Accra, 24
Africa: capture of slaves in, 37–8; slave market in, 93, 97–8, 105–10, 114
African place of origin (slaves), 39, 46–8, 51; see also West Africa
age composition (slaves), 25, 143, 204n7; in cargo selection, 112, 113, 114; economic analysis of, 97–105; and prices, 61–4, 69; variation in, 93–7
agents (Royal African Company), 15–16, 18, 19, 20, 36–7, 38–9, 68, 143, 149, 200n32; Barbados, 72, 80, 83, 84, 86, 88, 110–11, 113; complaints by, 113, 204n7; Nevis, 86; as purchasers of slaves in Africa, 97; salary structure, 27, 36, 144, 201n38; and sales format, 83–4, 85–7, 88–9; sales records, 73, 77–80, 117–18, 120; and size of cargo, 42–3; and slave sales, 81–2; supervision of, 144 [see also employees (Royal African Company), supervision of]
agents of planters, 91
Angola, 23, 204n10
Anomabu, 24, 180n71
anthropology, 151
Antigua, 2, 16, 43, 119
Arab market for slaves, 105, 108–9
Ardra, 23
Assyrian economy, 152
Atcherly, Edward, 120
Atkins, Sir Jonathan, 89
auctions (slave), 1, 71, 81, 144, 197n6; mean prices, 56t, 57t, 59t, 60t; Royal African Company, 82–5, 87

Babylonian economy, 152
Baillie, George, 199n23
Bank of England, 213n7

Barbados, 16, 18, 25, 80, 81, 85, 200n32; age composition of slaves, 93; censuses, 121, 133–4; economy, 8; indentured servants, 9, 10; laws about debt collection, 28; persistence in, 121–42; persistence measurement, 167–8, 169–70, 171; plantation owners, plantations, 12–13, 88; population turnover among estate owners and managers, 115–42; property census, 12, 89, 121; settlement of, 2; size of slave cargoes, 29, 30, 33–7, 51; slave market, 119–21; slave prices, 53–70, 91; slave sales, 72–3, 83, 89–91, 157; slavery in, 7, 9–10, 13, 14; sugar industry, 6, 7, 9–10; trade with England, 3, 4, 5
Barton, Capt., 110
Bean, Richard, 177n52, 194n22
Beeston, William, 159
Beverly, Mass., 135, 136, 137
Bevin, Robert, 157
black population: West Indies, 2–3, 11–12, 64–5
Blake, Peter, 72, 80–1
boys (slaves): market share, 93, 101, 104, 105, 110, 114; prices, 54, 58, 59, 64, 73, 99
Brazil, 6
Bridgetown, Barbados, 139, 200n25
Bulkey, William, 122
Buttram, Capt., 67
buyers; see planters
Bybrook Plantation, Jamaica, 120–1

Calvert, Charles, 196n27
Calvert, George, 1st Baron Baltimore, 196n27
Cape Coast, 46, 112
Cape Coast Castle (fort), 24, 43, 48, 180n71, 183n22
Cape Coast Frigate (ship), 185n35, 215n3
capitalism: origins of, 1; role of slavery in, xi

Index

captains of ships, 41–3; dishonesty of, 16, 26–7; mortality rate, 166, 215n3; payment in slaves, 15–16, 22, 27, 53; as purchasers of slaves in Africa, 97; and seasonality, 35, 37; skill and judgment of, 48–50, 51; slave sales by, 88

cargo selection, 25, 47, 97, 143, 144; and demographic composition of slave trade, 110–14; time in, 190n56

Caribbean (region), 1; see also West Indies (English)

cash flow (Royal African Company), 16, 22

castle-trade (factory-trade), 23–6, 97, 148

censuses, 115, 118, 129, 167, 171; Angola, 204n10; Barbados, 121, 133–4

chance: in mortality rate, 51

Charles II, king of England, 13, 14, 19, 148, 149, 150, 154

charterparty; see hire contracts ("charterparties")

Chesapeake Bay colonies: slavery in, 68; trade with England, 4, 5

children (slaves): market share, 93, 101–2, 103, 104, 110, 112, 114, 143; mortality rates, 203n5; prices, 98, 109

coffee, 6

colonial America: competitive enterprise in, 145; planters in, 12; slave trade and, 153–5; slavery in, xi, xii, 14–15, 53; trade with England, 3, 4, 5, 6t; white servitude in, 9

commissions: agents, 36, 201n38; ships' captains, 24, 42–3, 53, 88

commodities, 91; and market records, 118; slaves as, 87

communications, 21; lack of rapid, 148

Company of Royal Adventurers Trading into Africa, 2, 13–14, 28, 66, 196n27, 154

competition: between agents and captains, 22, 88; in slave trade, 14–21, 25, 97, 98, 146–7, 149, 150, 151, 153, 154–5

competitive markets, xi, 151–3; beginning of, 1–2; rational economic behavior in, 143, 145, 154–5

concubines, 109

confiscation, 152

contracts, 203n3; indentured servants, 212n30 (see also indentures); slave shipment on, 195n27

Corbin, Gavin, 86

costs (Royal African Company), 51, 52, 150; imposed by charter, 148–9; of West African settlements, 19, 24, 148–9, 150

costs of transportation (slave trade), 69, 143; and cargo selection, 111; and price of slaves, 97, 98, 99, 102, 103, 104, 110, 114; see also freight charges

cotton, 8

courts, colonial, 18

credit financing (slave trade), 1, 35, 54, 82, 149, 202n38, 208n5; problems caused by, 84

Cromwell, Oliver, 174n17

Cunningham, William: "Perversion of Economic History, The," 151

Curti, Merle, 115

Curtin, Philip, 106, 109

custom: effect on economic outcomes, 151, 152

Danish slave trade, 39

Davies, K. G., 16–17, 19, 20, 21, 23, 24, 26, 30–1, 54, 102, 147, 150, 162, 177n55, 178n59, 179n68, 192n10, 195n25, 203n3, 208n5, 213n4, 213n7; *Royal African Company, The,* xii

Davis, David Brion, 214n18

Davis, Ralph, 32

debt, planter, 16, 22, 28, 149, 150, 157

default risk, 84, 201n38

demand (for slaves), 69, 87, 105–6, 152

demographic characteristics (slaves), 84–5, 93–114; and order of purchases, 71–92; selection of cargoes and, 110–14

destination: and size of slave cargoes, 29–30

diplomacy, 21

disease(s), 21, 25, 35, 47, 81, 144; concealment of, 85, 86–7, 91; food supply and, 186n39; and mortality, 44–5, 50–1, 85; resistance to, 40; West Indies, 140

distance, 21

Drax, Henry, 139–40

Drax, James, 139

Dunn, Richard, 88, 135, 174n18, 175n34, 212n27, 212n39

Dutch slave trade, 13, 14, 39, 146–7

Dutch West India Company, 13

dysentery, 51

East India Company, 14, 213n7

Economic Journal, 151

economic opportunity: mobility and, 115

economic theory, 1; applicability of, to history, 150–3

economics of production: and order of slave purchases, 87–8

economies of scale, 12, 45, 52

economy (West Indies): effect of sugar on, 7–13; importance of slaves in, 69

employees (Royal African Company), 19, 24, 25–6; mortality rates, 179n68; performance of, 28, 150; selection of slave cargo by, 110–11, 113; supervision of, 22, 25, 27–8, 144, 148

226

Index

Macfarlane, Alan, 153
Madagascar, 14
malaria, 140
Malin, James, 115
managers (plantation), 133, 139; population turnover, 115–42
market behavior: early modern, xi, 150–1; slave trade, xii
market characteristics: and measurement of persistence, 116–17
market economies, 153
market for slaves, 105–6; Barbados, Jamaica, 118–21; closely connected, competitive, 143 (*see also* competitive markets); internal African, 93, 97–8, 105–10, 114; order of purchase in, 91
market observations: estimating geographic persistence from, 115–42
market participants: names of, 116, 118–19, 120–5, 134
market position (slave trade): Royal African Company, 15–17, 18
market records: population at risk to appear in, 118, 119–21, 129–30; in study of persistence, 116, 117–18
marketing strategies, 51
marketplaces (slave), 200n25
markets: early, 152
Marshall, Alfred, xi, 1; *Principles of Economics*, 151
Mary (ship), 43
Maryland: slavery in, 12, 67, 68; trade with England, 4
Marx, Karl, xi, 152–3
men (slaves), 106; market share, 104–5, 114; prices, 54, 58, 59, 62–4, 66, 69, 73, 74–81, 98–101, 202n38
Menard, Russell, 67, 196n29
mercantilism: Adam Smith's attack on, 145–50
merchants, 152
Mesopotamia, 152
Middle Passage, 15, 29; demographic composition of slave population in, 97–105; mortality in, 37–52 (*see also* mortality)
migration (free): mortality in, 39; study of, 115–16
Miller, Joseph, 184n26, 186n40
mobility: significance of, 115–16
Modyford, Sir Thomas, 28, 158
monoculture, 7, 153
monopoly(ies), 152; effects of, 145–6
monopoly power of Royal African Company charter, 14–21, 24, 67, 82, 146–7, 149, 202n2; value of, 19–21, 25
Montserrat, 2, 119
morality: in/of slave trade, 154

Morgan, Sir Henry, 89, 158
mortality: causes of, 39–51; children, 203n5; disease and, 44–5, 50–1, 85; of English in West Indies, 137, 140, 141; in persistence measurement, 136; probability of, 97, 98; of Royal African Company employees in Africa, 179n68; seasonality and, 35, 39, 45–7, 51; of ships' captains, 166, 215n3; of slaves awaiting shipment, 25, 148; of slaves in passage, 22, 37–52, 81, 104, 144, 163–6, 190n56

Nevis, 2, 16, 80, 86, 119, 121; age composition of slaves, 93
New England towns: persistence in, 135–7, 141
Newburyport, Mass.: migration study, 115
North America: large-scale slavery in, 67, 70; *see also* colonial America
numbers of slaves owned: by purchasers of slaves, 121, 134–5, 141, 144

outmigration, 136, 137–8, 141, 144
overseers, 121

Palmer, Colin, 203n3
Parliament (England), 20–1, 24, 82; debates over abolition of slave trade, 37, 42; House of Commons, 14; subsidy of Royal African Company, 148
payment for slaves, 27; *see also* credit financing
payment in slaves, 15–16, 22, 27, 53
persistence; *see* geographic persistence
physical characteristics (slaves): in cargo selection, 112–13
plantation economy (West Indies): population turnover and, 137–42
plantation management, 138–40, 141–2, 144
plantation owners, wealthy, 12–13; *see also* absentee plantation owners
plantations, large (West Indies), 12; *see also* sugar plantations
planters, 12; failure to pay debts, 83; and health of slaves, 85–7; labor force, 9–10, 11; political power of, 12–13, 18, 19, 28, 82, 149; rational economic behavior of, 143–5; tobacco, 10; *see also* credit financing; debt, planter; market participants; wealth of planters
Polanyi, Karl, 152
political factors: in Royal African Company forts, 148–9; in slave trade, 24–5; *see also* planters, political power of
political prisoners, felons: sentenced to West Indies, 174n17
political turmoil: Jamaica, 140–1

Index

LaVergne, TN USA
23 July 2010
190550LV00003B/34/A